Olympic Media

Inside the biggest show on television

Andrew C. Billings

Routledge
Taylor & Francis Group

LONDON AND NEW YORK

First published 2008
by Routledge
2 Park Square, Milton Park, Abingdon, Oxon, OX14 4RN

Simultaneously published in the USA and Canada
by Routledge
270 Madison Avenue, New York, NY 10016

Routledge is an imprint of the Taylor & Francis Group, an informa business

© 2008 Andrew C. Billings

Typeset in Goudy by
GreenGate Publishing Services, Tonbridge, Kent

Printed and bound in Great Britain by
TJ International Ltd, Padstow, Cornwall

British Library Cataloguing in Publication Data
A catalogue record for this book is available from the British Library

Library of Congress Cataloging in Publication Data
Billings, Andrew C.
Olympic media : inside the biggest show on television / Andrew C. Billings.
p. cm.
Includes bibliographical references and index.
ISBN 978-0-415-77251-8 (softcover) -- ISBN 978-0-415-77250-1 (hardcover) --
ISBN 978-0-203-93335-0 (ebook) 1. Television broadcasting of sports--United
States. 2. Olympics. 3. National Broadcasting Company, inc. 4. Sports--Social
aspects. I. Title.
GV742.3.B55 2007
796.48--dc22
2007027037

ISBN-10: 0–415–77250–8 (hbk)
ISBN-10: 0–415–77251–6 (pbk)
ISBN-10: 0–203–93335–4 (ebk)

ISBN-13: 978–0–415–77250–1 (hbk)
ISBN-13: 978–0–415–77251–8 (pbk)
ISBN-13: 978–0–203–93335–0 (ebk)

For Angela, with love

Contents

Illustrations

Figures

Tables

Series editors' foreword

The social and political significance of the Olympic Games has been a major preoccupation for many scholars in Sport Studies. Equally, the cultural impact of media sport – most especially televised sport – has been subject to analysis in numerous critical texts. Yet surprisingly few texts have engaged in a systematic and detailed way with the actual production processes of television coverage of the Olympic Games.

In writing *Olympic Media: Inside the Biggest Show on Television*, Andrew Billings has recognised the huge influence of the Olympic telecast and by taking a creative approach, he has produced a highly original text that tells an 'insider' story of its production. Moreover, he has done so by looking specifically at America's NBC telecast which is by far the most influential Olympic network in the world, having paid $894 million for the US rights to the 2008 Beijing Games and whose Chairman of Sports and Olympics, Dick Ebersol, negotiated for live prime-time events for American audiences. As a result, the final of the 400-meter individual swimming medley in Beijing will take place just a little after 10 a.m. – 'an ungodly hour for an Olympic swimming final, but a perfect time for NBC: 7 p.m. in Los Angeles, 8 p.m. in Denver, 9 p.m. in Chicago and 10 p.m. in New York'. This decision will disadvantage European viewers – it will be 3 a.m. in London and 6 a.m. in Moscow.

Gaining access to key protagonists in these decision-making processes is extremely difficult, especially for critical scholars. So it is a real coup for this *Routledge Critical Studies in Sport* series that Andrew Billings was able to interview Dick Ebersol himself and also NBC's primetime anchor, Bob Costas, as well as other key NBC professionals. The result is that you will be able to read about their very personal opinions on Olympic sport, and about their eventful and challenging roles as producers and sportscasters. Readers will gain a unique insight into how and why decisions are made about what the viewers see and the language accompanying the television images.

Another original feature of the book is the content analysis of data that were meticulously collected over a period of ten years, concerning the depictions of nationality, ethnicity and gender in Olympic telecasts. The two very different research approaches complement one another, and together tell a fascinating story of the actual workings and hidden effects of a major television sports extravaganza that most viewers in America take for granted. With its innovative research approach, Andrew Billings' book will undoubtedly make an important contribution to the study of sport and the media, and sets the scene for further investigation and analysis of the processes of production and the cultural and social impact of sport on television.

Jennifer Hargreaves (University of Brighton)
Ian McDonald (University of Brighton)

Preface

February 22, 1980

LAGRANGE, INDIANA (USA)—I am seven years old, riding home from the local K-Mart with my father when we witness something odd occurring in a roadside clearing. Three cars are parked; all appear to be in working order. A group of eight disparate people seem to be celebrating. My father dismisses them as "high on something" and we continue home.

A few hours later, we are watching the Lake Placid Winter Olympics on tape delay. The United States ice hockey team is playing the Soviet Union in the semifinals of the medal round. Gradually, we see the events unfold and the improbable 4–3 US victory becomes reality. We wonder about those eight people along the side of the road. Had they known? Maybe they were "high", but without chemical inducements. Later, I read in the newspapers about the sporting phenomenon that had occurred that evening when total strangers were celebrating a victory in a sport that did not have a widespread following in the country—people of different racial, economic, and social backgrounds bonding over the commonality of being proud Americans. The Olympic hockey victory fused a country together at a time when we desperately needed it amidst the Cold War and economic stresses of the era. Who knows—maybe the people on the side of the road did not even know a hockey game was being played. I like to think otherwise.

When I am speaking about sports media at communication conferences or in classes, invariably I am asked the question, "Why do sports matter?" Perhaps that February day in 1980 can tell us more than we know. Sports media matter because they are the way most of us consume sports. Only a few thousand Americans witnessed the actual US/USSR hockey game in person, but millions shared the moment on tape delay several hours later. Even the moniker we assign to the game, the "Miracle on Ice", comes from ABC announcer Al Michaels. The sportscaster's call, "Do you believe in miracles?" is now part of American cultural memory, as evidenced by the hit 2004 film about the event, *Miracle*.

Indeed, sports bond societies and cultures in ways that nothing else can. Much has been said about the immense audience for the finale of NBC's popular sitcom, *Friends*, but more people still tuned in to watch Nancy Kerrigan and

Tonya Harding skate their short programs in the 1994 Winter Olympics.[1] Sports have the power to transcend red state/blue state, white collar/blue collar, and white skin/dark skin. And nothing compels more casual sports fans to watch than the Olympics. Media scholars Susan Eastman, Greg Newton, and Lindsay Pack (1996) coined the term "megasports" to describe events that transcend everyday sport and become a part of the national Zeitgeist, such as the Super Bowl, the Indianapolis 500, or golf's Masters tournament.

Yet none of these events have the potential to turn a casual fan into an avid one the way an Olympics can. When people with no real interest in sports are suddenly tuning in and arguing over whether a diver got fully vertical or if a skater properly landed a quad, something special is going on. Olympic events cause people to pause and experience collective moments—maybe even to stop alongside the road in order to celebrate. Indelible sporting images become part and parcel of the global landscape as well, whether it is the "Black Power" protest of 1968 or Australian Cathy Freeman lofting the Olympic torch in front of her home country in 2000.[2]

Along with this ability to shape cultural memory arises the potential for media representation of sport to evolve into perceived "truth". Sportscasters, particularly at an Olympics when most fans are only casually familiar with the majority of the events and athletes, are assigned inordinate power to produce and create Olympic stories. As they chronicle history, questions arise about how they are negotiating the portrayal of athletes representing different identity groups—specifically, "How do they depict athletes of different nationalities, genders, and ethnicities?" and "What is the impact of a megasporting event wielding disparate renderings of athletes and countries?" Sports are consumed by the masses and, as the saying from another popular cultural phenomenon, *Spiderman*, articulates, "With great power comes great responsibility".

That is why sports matter. That is why I am writing this book.

---

1 Tonya Harding was allegedly involved in a plot to harm her US figure skating teammate, Nancy Kerrigan, that resulted in an injury to Kerrigan which almost kept her from competing in the 1994 Winter Olympics.
2 Cathy Freeman was widely regarded as a symbol of national unity in the 2000 Summer Games, waving both the Aboriginal flag and the Australian flag after winning the 400-meter race.

Acknowledgments

No book is ever a solo effort and the team that aided this project offered diverse skills, insights, and opportunities. First and foremost, I have to thank Routledge for providing me with the opportunity to write my first scholarly book. Ian McDonald and, particularly, Jennifer Hargreaves offered valuable insight to the editing process that has resulted in a dramatically improved final product. Jennifer truly devoted considerable time to improving the manuscript, and her different disciplinary perspective has unquestionably enhanced my scholarship. I thank both of them for their mentorship throughout this process.

Second, this book incorporates a decade of studies that I co-authored with some truly great people. Dr. Susan Eastman has been a valued co-author, advisor, and friend; James Angelini has contributed some amazingly meticulous analysis, and the tremendous work on Olympic content analyses by the following students aided this project immensely: Amanda Booher, Meredith Gammon, Chelsea Brown, James Crout, Kristen McKenna, Bethany Rice, Elise Timanus, Jonathan Zeigler, Connelly-Anne Bartle, Lauren Hoffman, Laura McLeod, and Warrick McZeke. In this professional realm, I also wish to thank my department chair, Dr. Kate Hawkins, who has wholeheartedly supported this effort from its initial conception, and Dr. Bryan Denham, whose counsel as a colleague in sports communication at Clemson University has always benefited my work.

NBC producers and sportscasters deserve an incalculable amount of gratitude as they welcomed the project with a great deal of candor and earnestness. In particular, I must thank NBC Universal President of Sports and Olympics, Dick Ebersol; producers David Neal and Molly Solomon; Editorial Director and Lead Writer, Joe Gesue; and NBC Torino Olympic sportscasters Tom Hammond and Jim Lampley. However, the primary force in allowing me to conduct these interviews was Bob Costas, who embraced my idea for the book despite having only met me face-to-face on one occasion. Bob took the time to not only be interviewed, but made the necessary connections to ensure that the critical people in the NBC Olympic storytelling process would be willing to speak with me and, for that, I am truly grateful.

I was also able to secure four additional interviews with sportscasters who did not work on the 2006 Torino telecast but who have worked intimately in and with the Olympics in many ways. A special thank you goes out to these four former

Olympians, Peter Vidmar, John Naber, Ann Meyers Drysdale, and Donna deVarona, the first woman sportscaster on major American network TV. I also am grateful to my friend, Scott Helmkamp, who provided me with the connection to Peter, who then led me to John, who led me to Ann, who led me to Donna. Sometimes the smallest gestures can yield great dividends.

Finally, I truly do not know how to thank my family enough for their support of this project and their patience with me when I often was overwhelmed. My sons, Nathan and Noah, are a source of immense pride in my life along with my mother, Connie, and sisters, Laura and Mary. Though my father passed away quite a while ago, I thank him for introducing me to sport, showing me how to love playing and watching the competition. And then, of course, there is my wife, Angela, who made this book happen by providing me more love, support, and inspiration that I often feel I deserve.

1 Investigating the biggest show on television

The Olympics are an epic event, so can anything be overstated?
(Bob Costas, 2006)

Olympic telecasts render the biggest of stories on the grandest of stages. The inception of the first live telecast was at the 1936 Summer Olympic Games in Berlin. More than two dozen viewing halls were built in Berlin so the German people could watch the broadcasts. The picture quality was poor, but the link between television and the Olympic Games was established. From that time, the Olympics have been imbued with ultra-competitive nationalism. The Nazis, already exploiting "the new technologies of the mass media in spreading their propaganda domestically", used the Games as a stage for their own political purposes (Beamish and Ritchie, 2006, p. 34). However, what has been remembered through history is that Black American Jesse Owens won four gold medals in front of the citizens of Nazi Germany, challenging Adolf Hitler's aspiration to showcase Aryan dominance.

Twelve years later, London was the stage for the first post-World War II Games, when Fanny Blankers-Koen (dubbed the "Flying Dutch Housewife" and "Mother of two") won four gold medals, becoming a lasting symbol of radical athletic femininity. By 1952, the Olympics had entered the Cold War era, the United States and the Soviet Union became superpower antagonists, and media narratives were created in America and other countries in the West about the notion of communist "professional" athletes disadvantaging amateur athletes from democratic countries (O'Riordan, 2007).

The first international telecasts of Olympic competition took place at the 1956 Winter Games in Cortina, Italy. They were for viewers in only eight countries in Europe, but it was the *start* of the global spread of the Olympic telecast, bringing images of Olympic athletes into local communities and homes across the world. The first Olympic television rights were sold for the 1960 Rome Summer Olympics, which also marked South Africa's last participation in the Games until 1992. It was at these Olympics, as well, that barefooted Ethiopian marathon runner Abebe Bikila[1] became the first Black African to win gold in any Games.

The 1968 Mexico City Games brought another significant racial image, as Americans Tommie Smith and John Carlos protested against racial inequality in their home country while also celebrating Black achievement in a demonstration of "Black Power" on the medal stand.[2] From that time, the Olympics became a world stage of protest against political and social injustices. Another protest that had taken place ten days before the Mexico Games—in opposition to their huge extravagance—resulted in the Tlatelolco massacre of hundreds of students by security forces. The Western media in America and Europe systematically downplayed the tragedy to generate idealized depictions of Olympism throughout the Games.

In 1972, the lasting images of the Munich Olympics should have been 17-year-old Soviet gymnast Olga Korbut inspiring millions of future gymnasts and US swimmer Mark Spitz's incredible seven gold medals, yet the images conveyed by the television monitors of Arab terrorists in ski masks stalking the balcony of the Israeli quarters in the Olympic village, followed by the deaths of 11 Israeli Olympians and one German police officer, together with the words of the late President of the IOC (International Olympic Committee), Avery Brundage— "The Games must go on"—produced resounding memories for the viewers that have lasted through history.

The 1976 Innsbruck Winter Olympics were the last Games at which the title Republic of China was used for the island of Taiwan, as a result of the hostilities between Taiwanese separatists and mainland China (People's Republic of China). The future title adopted by Taiwan for Olympic competition was Chinese Taipei. The separatist struggle was still ongoing at the time of the publication of this book in 2008 and separatists were preparing protests for the 2008 Beijing Olympics.

The 1976 Montreal Summer Olympics spearheaded the "Age of Olympic boycotts" when more than 40 nations withdrew their teams from the Olympics following the IOC's refusal to ban New Zealand from the Games after their violation of the international sports ban on apartheid South Africa. The 1980s brought a decade of further boycotts, including the US-led boycott, with 50 other countries, of the 1980 Moscow Olympics in protest against the Soviet invasion of Afghanistan (with an associated loss of worldwide television exposure) and the counter boycott by the Soviet Union, East Germany, and a dozen

---

1 Ethiopian runner Abebe Bikila ran barefoot, noting after the race that "I wanted the world to know that my country, Ethiopia, has always won with determination and heroism".
2 After winning medals in the 200-meters in the 1968 Mexico City Summer Olympics, Smith and Carlos received their medals in atypical fashion to bring attention to pressing Black issues, including wearing no shoes but black socks (to recognize Black poverty), a scarf around Smith's neck (to recognize Black pride), and beads around Carlos's neck (to recognize Black lynchings). In addition, each wore a Black glove and raised their arm during the playing of the Star-Spangled Banner, the US national anthem (Hartmann, 1996, 2003).

other countries of the 1984 Los Angeles Games (with no loss of television revenue). The East–West athletic cold war was at its height, and was reflected in all forms of media discourse and representation.

The 1980s brought tremendous achievements as well, including the 1980 "Miracle on Ice", when an American ice hockey team of young college players took down the "mighty Red Machine" from the USSR, depicted by *Sports Illustrated*[3] as "the single most indelible moment in all of US sports history ... that sent an entire nation into a frenzy" (*Sports Illustrated*, 2000). The People's Republic of China competed for the first time at the 1980 Winter Olympics in Lake Placid in the US, which marked an increased concern in the Western media about state-controlled drug abuse under Communism. In 1984, Nawal El Moutawakel from Morocco made history when she became the first woman from the African continent to win a gold medal and simultaneously the first Arab woman and the first Muslim woman to win gold.

The Seoul Summer Games of 1988 featured a militarized culture with antigovernment protests by students, thousands of the urban poor, and leftist intellectuals denouncing the Games for promoting a sports circus for the "haves" at the expense of the "have nots". Yet the predominant media discourse was about "The Friendly Games" with representations of colorful costumes and flying doves at the Opening Ceremony. Also at the Seoul Games, Ben Johnson, the "World's Fastest Man", was stripped of his Olympic 100-meters gold medal and world title for testing positive for banned drug use. Not surprisingly, the media debate about drug-taking in sport reached a new peak and was reflected in NBC's telecast. NBC (National Broadcasting Company) was the television network that had won the rights to televise the 1988 Summer Olympics for the American public viewership. In the next two decades, NBC evolved to be known as the "Olympic network", securing multiple Olympic television bids at once and building a group of producers and sportscasters with tremendous Olympic experience. (An empirical study of NBC's telecasts over a period of ten years—with a particular focus on the Torino Winter Olympics in 2006—provides the major focus of this book.)

The 1990s heralded the first Olympics after the fall of Communism and the reunification of Germany (the 1992 Winter Games in Albertville, France), and the last entry of a team from the Soviet Union (the Unified Team). The decade also offered advents in the ways in which viewers consumed the Games, with NBC offering a Triplecast so that people could pay for hundreds of additional hours of the 1992 Barcelona Summer Olympics. This decade also gave rise to professional Olympic athletes, allowing the American basketball "Dream Team", who resoundingly won a gold medal, to enter for the first time. Participating nations continued to expand in number, with Cuba and South Africa being welcomed back into the Olympic fold, further increasing the ethnic diversity of the

---

3   *Sports Illustrated* is a long-running popular American sports magazine with a weekly readership of 23 million people.

athletes. The Summer and Winter Olympics began alternating in even-numbered years beginning in 1994. The fear of terrorists targeting the Olympic Games became a reality in 1996 in Atlanta in the USA when a pipe bomb exploded in the Centennial Olympic Park, killing a woman and injuring over one hundred people.

The new millennium brought the 2000 Summer Olympics to Sydney, Australia—described by International Olympic Committee President, Juan Antonio Samaranch, as the "best Olympics ever". The Games had an epic quality, with 10,651 athletes from 199 countries competing in 300 events covered by 16,033 media professionals and with hugely spectacular opening and closing ceremonies. But the most memorable image of the Games for millions of viewers across the world was sprinter Cathy Freeman running the race of her life to win the 400-meter Olympic gold medal in an all-in-one Nike Swift Suit that encased her whole body from head to toe. But while Cathy Freeman symbolized Aboriginal pride and multicultural Australianness, outside the stadium Aboriginal activists were protesting about the human rights abuses against their peoples. Their protest was downplayed by the Australian and international media and the sense of a "ruptured nation of difference and inequalities" was in most cases ignored (Hargreaves, 2000, p. 125).

Personalities, politics, and problems have continued to be part of the Olympic equation. For example, Nina Suratger carried the flag for Afghanistan at the Opening Ceremony of the Athens Olympics in 2004, bringing to the attention of the viewing audience that it was the first time Afghani women had competed in the history of the Olympics, in common with other Muslim women from countries in the Gulf States. A major focus of this book was an investigation of data gathered from the 2006 Torino Winter Olympics. North Korea and South Korea marched together under the Unification Flag for the first time at these Games. The continuing fear of terrorism was the reason for the greatly increased security measures that were put in place for the Torino Games and in his opening address the IOC President, Jacques Rogge, said, "Our world today is in need of peace and brotherhood, the values of the Olympic Games ... May these Games be held in peace in the true spirit of the Olympic Truce".

The first Summer Olympics after the publication of this book will be in Beijing, in the People's Republic of China. Despite the fact that, in March 2004, China amended its constitution to read, "The State respects and protects human rights", there is evidence to the contrary. But it is specifically the position of media professionals that will most immediately affect reports of the Games. Sophie Richardson, deputy Asia director at *Human Rights Watch*, reports that:

> The Chinese government is already failing to deliver on its pledge to fully lift restrictions for foreign journalists ahead of the Beijing Games ... arbitrary restrictions on press freedoms undermine the new regulations, and raise questions about the government's commitment to implement them in the first place.
>
> (*Human Rights News*, 2007; *Human Rights Overview*, 2006)

NBC prepares for its telecast seven years in advance of every Olympic Games. Dick Ebersol, chairman of NBC Universal Sports and Olympics, lobbied successfully for some of the Games' premier events to be scheduled so that American audiences can see them live on primetime television (Thompson, 2007). Given that NBC Universal paid $894 million for the US television rights for the Beijing Olympics, the IOC was heavily criticized for caving in to commercial pressure (Thompson, 2007). Ebersol also revealed details about NBC's coverage of the Beijing Olympics, referring to its "first-ever wireless coverage with streams of highlights—and access to live streaming of 24 sports—1,200-plus hours in all". He went on to say, "NBC will offer 'full rewind of key events' and daily highlights of every sport" (Pearce, 2007). NBC has produced a website video in preparation for the Beijing Games which focuses expressly on top American athletes—in motion, competing, winning medals—preparing for China with the hope of maintaining "America's position as one of sports' certified powers". Michael Phelps, the winner of six gold medals in Athens 2004, said, "When I get in the water, I know what I have to do, and I know what I want to do ... I want to swim faster". The commentary goes on, "He goes to China with the possibility of becoming the greatest Olympic champion of all time". Beijing is represented as "the most populous nation on earth ... a place of wondrous scale where men once made structures that stretch towards infinity ... a country in fast forward as a global superpower has become the most fascinating headline of this new century". The Beijing Olympics is depicted as "The TV event of the decade [that] is coming to NBC August 8, 2008" (NBC Sports, 2007).

That the Olympic Games are unique in their ability to bring together thousands of competitors and officials from the majority of the countries in the world, and to put on a showcase of unmatched athletic triumphs as well as catastrophes has been evident from Olympic telecasts since 1948. Where else could one witness a Jamaican bobsledding team, a women's hockey team from Russia, a South Korean ski jumper, and women competing in the dangerous event of skeleton melded into one telecast? The Olympics provide a unique opportunity for the viewer to be teleported to a new country and to witness people from nations and cultures across the world bonded over a common Olympic dream. But, as Bianco (2006b) asserts, "The Olympics are more than just games". Referring to NBC's telecast of the Torino Winter Olympics in 2006, he continues, "And that will be particularly true in China, which is less familiar to many of us than Italy and far more politically charged. We'll expect a broader picture" (Bianco, 2006b). The examples above also reveal that the Olympics reflect links between the social, political, and economic influences on sport, embodying both homogeneity and difference within individual nation states, and friendship and hostility between different nation states, juxtaposing the Olympic ideal with the reality of winning at all costs. Mixed together with coverage of the actual competitions, these are the ingredients of thrilling histories and breathtaking stories of emotion, drama, and spectacle.

Not surprisingly, therefore, the Olympics have tremendous appeal, and thousands of people travel enormous distances from faraway places to watch them live. But millions (indeed, often billions) who cannot travel to the Olympic events nevertheless, as we have seen, witness them through the eye of the most ubiquitous of all modern media: television. It is estimated that in Beijing there will be a worldwide television audience of as many as eight billion people (IOC Marketing Fact File, 2006). Maurice Roche (2004, p. 167) claims that "Mega-events such as the Olympic Games undoubtedly qualify as examples of 'media-events'" which, he goes on to explain, "go beyond news and entertainment, and also can be said to 'make history'". There is credence to the belief that history is written by the winners, but in relation to the Olympics "it is also written by those with the television rights" (Billings *et al.*, in press, n. p.).

Since 1988, the American network exclusively "writing" the history of the Summer Olympics has been NBC; beginning in 2002, NBC has chronicled the history of the Winter Games as well. NBC is the biggest and most powerful Olympic network in the world[4] and has won the rights to televise the grandest of all megasporting events (Eastman *et al.*, 1996). The outcome is NBC's Olympic telecast. The specific aims of this book have been to investigate the production processes and influences of this hugely powerful cultural and economic phenomenon. I have done so by investigating: (1) the roles and attitudes to those roles of NBC's Olympic producers and telecasters; (2) the attitudes to and the effects on viewers of the telecast; and (3) the significance of the telecast discourses associated in particular with nationalism, gender, and ethnicity.

Some excellent academic books have been written on the Olympics (e.g. Bass, 2002; Beamish and Ritchie, 2006; Espy, 1979; Larson and Park, 1993; Lenskyj, 2000, 2002; Moragas Spa, Rivenburgh *et al.*, 1995; Pound, 2004; Puijk, 1997; Schaffer and Smith, 2000; Senn, 1999; Toohey and Veal, 2000), and thousands of journalists have scrutinized the manner in which the Olympic telecast is conveyed. Without question, there is no shortage of opinions about the strengths and weaknesses of the modern Olympic telecast, yet what *this* book provides, which is not present in the present literature, is a closer look inside the Olympic telecast. Interviews with the key NBC producers (including Dick Ebersol) and sportscasters inform the investigation in new, intriguing ways. Although the interviews took place in the months following the 2006 Torino Winter Olympics, the questions—and subsequent interviewee responses—incorporate NBC's collective institutional memory since Dick Ebersol began overseeing the Olympic telecast in 1988.

Content analysis and media surveys have been combined to form a more complete picture as to how Olympic reports move from NBC Sports to the television screen and then to the at-home viewer. This book (a) uncovers what NBC

---

4 NBC Universal includes much more than just the titular network, NBC, including channels such as USA, MSNBC, CNBC, Bravo, and Telemundo, allowing it to significantly permeate both free and pay cable network viewerships.

claims or hopes they are achieving within their Olympic telecast, then (b) analyzes the actual broadcast to see if these aims are achieved, and finally (c) comments on biases or differences in the coverage that relate to societal perceptions of identity (see Morris, 2006).

Establishing Olympic television dominance

Most television executives will postulate that more has changed in their industry during the past ten years than in the entire history of the medium. Cable offerings provide hundreds of counter-programming options to mainstream free-network telecasts; on-demand television, Internet re-airings, and digital video recorders allow viewers to consume their favorite programs at virtually all hours of the day; and increased media options and formats supply elevated competition for networks struggling to avoid ratings erosion. Viewers watch more television per day than ever before (Ayres, 2006), yet do so in starkly different ways. Few standards of television viewing have remained static over the past several decades. Many might question the initial premise of Olympic media dominance, particularly when no single Olympic telecast was the number one show of the week in the United States during the 2006 Torino Olympics (that distinction belonged to *American Idol*[5]), and after the lackluster ratings when many critics were quick to announce the death of the Olympic telecast (UPI Report, 2006). But despite its detractors, the Olympic telecast remains the only telecast that can capture not just a national but a global Zeitgeist for weeks on end.

It is encouraging to report that the discussion of the sports media has progressed significantly over the past few decades. In his book, *Fields in Vision,* Garry Whannel (1992) needed to first justify the study of sports media at all, arguing that "television sport is by any standards a component of popular culture and to understand it better is to understand more about the culture in which we live" (p. 2). Now, with US television sometimes offering several dozen sports telecasts in the same time period, and the enormous international appeal of megasport events such as the Soccer (Football) World Cup and the Wimbledon tennis championships, that argument appears to be irrefutable. But the Olympics are consistently considered to be the most superlative of all sport competitions. Whannel (1984) argued over two decades ago that the Olympics are the "ultimate media festival" (p. 121); more recently, Hiestand (2006b) maintained that "with the Olympics, TV has more power to shape viewer perceptions than with any other sports event" (p. 2C). Indeed, the Olympics are the only television behemoth that can make all other mass media slow to a near halt for weeks on end.

---

5 *American Idol* is the US version of international singing "star search" shows that can be found in many countries, including *Pop Idol* in the U.K. and *Canadian Idol* in Canada.

To consider the immensity of the insight and influence stemming from an Olympic telecast, four factors will be articulated and extrapolated upon: (1) media saturation, (2) political influence, (3) network prestige, and—most closely related to the crux of this book—(4) viewer attitudes about sport-portrayed identity and diversity.

Olympic viewership: the saturation factor

When considering the prospective impact of the Olympic telecast, the initial significance can first be measured in terms of the number of people (in the United States and globally) who watch the Games—a saturation variable. Estimates abound as to the total number of viewers in the world who watch each Olympics, but whether one employs the conservative estimates of between 700 million and one billion viewers (Moragas Spa *et al.*, 1995) or the larger approximations that quintuple that number (3.5 billion in 1996; Gordon and Sibson, 1998), one witnesses that the Olympics saturate the globe over the course of 17 or so continuous days of athletic competition. Research indicates that the only areas of the world where less than 90 percent of all citizens watch substantial portions of the Olympics are in developing countries where access to television is limited (Rowe, 2003; Sweeney and Associates, 1992).

Specifically regarding viewing figures for the NBC telecast in the United States, over 203 million Americans watched the 2004 Athens Summer Olympics at some point (Stewart, 2004) with even the lesser-hyped Winter Games of Torino being watched by over 168 million American viewers (Ryan, 2006). Compare these numbers to the grandest of all US megasporting events: the Super Bowl, which drew a still very healthy 90 million watchers (Stewart, 2006), and one begins to comprehend the magnitude of the Olympic reach. American viewers watch NBC's Olympic coverage en masse and at unprecedentedly high levels when bearing in mind that a top-rated US primetime program like *Grey's Anatomy* typically garners a viewership of 20–22 million (*USA Today*, 2007).

Additionally, other telecasts (such as the Super Bowl telecast) offer extremely high ratings, but only do so for one programming segment. In the United States, a full season of a network program is 22 episodes, meaning that, for instance, the 2006 Torino Games (televised on NBC[6] for 65 primetime hours) offers the equivalent program ratings of three highly rated one-hour programs for an entire year. One could sum an entire year of first-run episodes for both *CSI* (America's top-rated drama in the spring of 2007) and *Two and a Half Men* (America's top-rated situation comedy in the spring of 2007) and still only amass 33 hours, little more than half of the Olympic primetime telecast. Clearly, NBC oversees a colossal media undertaking when airing an Olympics. NBC's 2006 Torino telecast, often maligned for failing to yield the ratings of the 2002 Salt Lake City Winter Games,

---

6   Along with ABC, CBS, and FOX, NBC is one of the "Big Four" US major non-cable networks.

still dominated over three-quarters of the primetime hours and nearly doubled the average rating of the second-place American network, Fox. The only real ratings competition for many Olympic nights (particularly the Summer Olympics) was to determine if viewing figures for NBC's Olympic coverage would surpass those of the other five major free networks (CBS, ABC, Fox, UPN, and WB) *combined.*

The primetime coverage of any Olympics is now just a mere fraction of the overall coverage available for viewer consumption. In 1960, CBS aired 15 hours of Winter and 20 hours of Summer Olympic coverage (Moreland, 2006). In 2004, NBC aired more than 1,200 hours over six different networks (Moreland, 2006). In 2006, the Winter Olympics (with fewer events, participants, and less viewer interest than a Summer Games) nonetheless were shown for 418 hours on these same networks (Cox, 2006). Since the Triplecast[7] for NBC's 1992 Barcelona coverage, in which NBC asked viewers to pay an additional fee of $95–170 to view more live and secondary events, primary networks have utilized sister networks (e.g. CBS with TNT or NBC with Bravo) to air more Olympic content and, subsequently, more hours (Weiner, 2006). The results have been quite positive economically (see Gratton and Solberg, 2007), as these partnered networks—usually mired in much lower ratings—are happy to show, say, curling, and, by doing so, double their viewership. In late 2006, NBC even announced a new proposal for more media saturation by planning to offer over 1,000 hours of streaming video on the Internet during the 2008 Summer Beijing Olympics (Christie, 2006).

The Olympic telecast represents one of the few remaining opportunities for men and women, both young and old, to watch the same television program together in an otherwise fragmented world of media consumption (Anderson, 2006). Even the less all-encompassing Winter Olympic coverage draws both men and women viewers, aged 25–54, in record numbers. Young viewers watch snowboarding, older viewers flock to curling and skiing; men watch hockey, women embrace figure skating. One consequence of the media saturation is that the Olympic telecast is the only megasporting event that gains more female viewers than male viewers. Former Olympic producer Rick Gentile notes that growing numbers of women viewers were first noticed two decades ago, in 1988, and goes on to state that:

> It is well known that when you schedule and plan an Olympic Games, the audience is going to be as much as 65 [percent women]. It's heavily watched by women, principally for figure skating, and that influences the way events are covered, by featurizing coverage. It's not traditional hard-core sports coverage.
> (Hiskey, 2006, p. 1A)

---

7 The Triplecast was largely regarded as a failure in 1992 as far fewer Americans purchased the additional hours of coverage than NBC had anticipated, yet is still regarded as a "tipping point" for expanded coverage, as NBC found additional ways to promote the Olympic telecast and increase advertising revenues through its cable networks.

As a result, wide demographics are gained with personality-driven formats, including profiles that allow the viewer to get to know more about the athlete, something that research has shown compels the woman viewer to watch. The converse assumption is that men will watch regardless of production packaging, as they represent the heavy consumers of all other televised sport. Since gaining the majority of the Olympic contracts in 1988, NBC responded to this demographic-seeking opportunity by creating a telecast that has highlighted sports that establish greater women viewership (i.e. figure skating and gymnastics) to the detriment of sports that entertain more men viewers (i.e. boxing and hockey). The end result is a more personalized telecast that creates Olympic personalities in a post-Cold War era in which a purported "villain" is no longer determined by the nation he or she represents (Gorrell, 2006).

Furthermore, the Olympic telecast captivates all of these demographics for weeks and, in the case of the Winter Olympics of 2006, does so in the midst of one of three "sweeps" months (February, along with November and May) when ratings are used to determine commercial rates for advertisers. Past practice has dictated that the other networks surrender to the Olympic telecast by airing repeat episodes of their popular shows; the 2006 Games varied from this practice as most networks offered at least a modicum of their highest-rated programs opposite the Olympics. The success of this strategy was mixed. Some programs, such as *American Idol*, proved remarkably elastic in their appeal opposite Olympic programming; most others failed to yield their customary ratings. The outcome offered some spheres in which the Olympics were not the number one option of a time slot, but where the Olympics ultimately dwarfed the overall ratings of any other network. The Games still hold the power (Senn, 1999) to make the world stand still and watch ... every day for over two weeks.

Broadening the scope: the political factor

The international scope of the Games includes host countries, governments, and societies about which most Olympic viewers only have a passing understanding. Consequently, the telecast is a culturally broadening experience for millions of people in the United States (and potentially billions abroad). Witness the hosts of the Winter and Summer Olympic Games over the past 20 years: Calgary, Seoul, Albertville, Barcelona, Lillehammer, Atlanta, Nagano, Sydney, Salt Lake City, Athens, Torino, and, in 2008, Beijing. One must also take into account that NBC's athlete profiles bring stories from scores of countries in the world, such as Argentina, Bahrain, Czech Republic, China, Ethiopia, Iceland, India, Japan, Kenya, Kuwait, Monaco, New Zealand, Slovenia, Ukraine, and literally two hundred more into the living rooms of millions of Americans, many of whom cannot even locate these places on a map, much less formulate attitudes about them. The Olympics—by their very nature—exude a global perspective by routinely introducing mass audiences to cultures that they have never witnessed before.

As a direct result of its international scope, the Olympics also direct attention to many different types of governments with many different types of politics. As we have seen, hosting an Olympic Games often highlights political turmoil, and social discrimination and unrest, sometimes augmenting hostilities within and between nations, lending credence to George Orwell's contention that international sport is "war minus the shooting" (Orwell, 1992 [1945]). The Olympic telecast can open up dialogue about differences between cultures and governments throughout the world, but can also bring to the surface "the ugly underbelly of nationalism—xenophobia and its twin sister, racism" (*Racism needs a penalty flag in Germany*, 2006, p. B6). The Olympic telecast has the potential to provide a glimpse into political relationships in a way no other sports airing can achieve (Schaffer and Smith, 2000).

Branding the Olympics: the prestige factor

The manifest prestige of the Olympics has led to NBC's clear desire to be inextricably linked to the event. The five interlocking Olympic rings have become part of the network symbol, or "bug" that brands NBC.[8] However, this partnership between the host network and the Olympics has proven costly—especially recently. The Olympics have been (and continue to be) consumed by mass audiences in many ways, via the radio, newspapers, television, or more recently, the Internet. However, they have become most closely paired with television. With CBS securing the first television purchased rights to the Squaw Valley Winter Games for $50,000 in 1960, the price that networks have been willing to disburse to be the home of the Olympics has exponentially swelled. Television rights were elevated in 1980, when NBC acquired the rights to the Summer Olympics in Moscow for a then-record $87 million. Despite the fact that NBC suffered when President Ronald Reagan announced a US boycott of the Moscow Games in 1980, networks remained eager to obtain this crown jewel of the sports media and the rights for the 1984 Los Angeles Summer Games were sold to ABC, almost tripling to $225 million. In our current decade, NBC purchased the rights to the 2000–2008 Games for $3.5 billion collectively, and then announced an extension for 2010 and 2012 for an additional $2.2 billion.

So why does NBC pay such extravagant rights fees? The most obvious answer is that the Olympic image is something with which networks are thrilled to associate. NBC gladly pays the rights fees for the Olympics in order to acquire what is widely acknowledged to be the summit of all network sports programming. NBC gained the rights to telecast National Football League (NFL) games beginning in 2006, but for an extended period of time the network did not air any of the major American sports (basketball, football, or baseball). Nevertheless, mainly because of the Olympics, they have remained a sporting media empire.

---

8   A "bug" is a network symbol/logo that can be found in the lower corner of the screen on many US channels, immediately informing the viewer as to what network they are watching.

Coaches and athletes regard the Olympics as the pinnacle of their lives as well. Despite living in a new era in which elite sports are characterized by commercialism and greed, most Olympic athletes remain fixated on an Olympic gold medal as their crowning achievement. College basketball legend Bob Knight won three NCAA titles at Indiana University, but still reverently speaks of winning the 1984 Olympic gold medal for the United States in Los Angeles as his greatest achievement. Countless athletes who fail to medal at an Olympics work tirelessly (and often in obscurity) to return for another chance at Olympic glory four years later. The gold-medal fixation and the cult of the sports star (Martin and Miller, 1999) have become the constant components of the Olympic telecast that drive its production processes. Their combination generates the drama and tension of sports events that, in turn, attract viewers. But most importantly, NBC continues to yield a profit from the Olympics, something that rarely happens with contemporary inside-America sports network contracts. For example, Fox secured the rights to televise NFL fixtures primarily in order to gain recognition as a viable fourth major US network (which they did), but they lost several hundred million dollars in the process. Meanwhile, the Olympics continue to provide advertising revenue—in 2006, the rate was $700,000 for a 30-second spot (Howard, 2006)—while NBC gains the prestige of being the Olympic host while remaining financially in the black.

Finally, the Olympics aid the promotion of a host network's primetime programming. NBC telecasts the Olympics and other major sporting events in order to attract the largest possible viewing public from the most diverse demographic groups, so as, in turn, to attract advertisers. Healthy demographics will subsequently be exposed to hundreds of promotions for NBC's primetime shows (Billings *et al.*, 1998; Newton *et al.*, in press). The power of these promotions is inestimable. For instance, the 2004 Summer Olympics in Athens, Greece, took place in August; NBC believed so strongly in the ability of the Olympics to jump-start its fall season that chief executive Jeff Zucker began new fall programming a month early to take full advantage of the promotional power of the Olympic telecast. The result? Studies have indicated that the Olympics can increase the ratings of established primetime programs and build excitement for a host network's new programs (Eastman and Billings, 2004). While scholars have found that external factors can influence ratings depending on (a) whether the Games are held in the US, (b) when the Games are scheduled on the programming calendar, and (c) whether results of events were already aired on news programs before NBC showed taped events at night, more programs have proven to gain ratings than lose them (Billings *et al.*, 1998; Eastman and Billings, 2004).

Negotiating identity: the diversity factor

The diversity that is inherent within the Olympic Games also allows for the examination of nationalistic, gender, and ethnic portrayals within the Olympic telecast. For instance, few viewers watch women's sports regularly, but the Games obviously provide a grand opportunity to witness women's sport. The Olympic telecast possesses immense power in this regard.

Social identity theorists (Nakayama and Martin, 1999; Tajfel, 1972; Tajfel and Turner, 1986) have integrally linked the media framing techniques to concepts of identity, often noting that media frames (Goffman, 1974) enact societal discussion of issues such as nationality and ethnicity. Social identity theory additionally posits that communication processes contribute to, and serve as, the differentiation processes for the development of group norms in the development of self and group identities (Hogg and Reid, 2006). Given the role that cultivation (Gerbner, 1998; Potter, 1986) can play in shaping the terms of the debate, a negotiation of identity cognitively and sometimes orally and behaviorally often occurs. Thus, the wide number of women's events offered (and televised) in the Olympics provides an opportunity for the discussion of the advancement (or lack thereof) of women's athletics. Similarly, the success of a Black speed skater or a Middle Eastern sprinter affords the prospect of a discussion about different ethnicities, cultures, and countries.

In sum, the Olympic telecast depicts men and women, from various ethnic backgrounds and with different country affiliations, the opportunity to compete on the same world stage and, in the process, yields an appropriate occasion for the discussion (and, hence, negotiation) of identity.

The Olympic telecast: bumps along the road

Although the Olympic telecast is an incredible juggernaut of mass media power and influence, it has not been trouble-free. Complaints continually abound that coverage of the Games is nearly always put on tape and pre-produced as a veritable highlight wheel of Olympic achievement. The primetime telecast is just 16 percent of all the Olympic coverage shown on all the networks of NBC, but viewers presume it is the *most important* 16 percent to watch, given that the primetime telecast rating dwarfs any other Olympic rating for any other part of the day (Hiestand, 2006a). The NBC telecast informs viewers in a highly edited, packaged format, even when the Games are on Olympic soil. For example, both the following events were shown on tape even though they took place in New York and Georgia respectively: the 1980 US men's Olympic ice hockey team semifinal win against the USSR—known as the "Miracle on Ice"; and the 1996 US women's gymnastic Olympic gold medal win, when, following an injury on her first vault, the gymnast Kerri Strug courageously landed her second vault perfectly.

Given the powerful television draw of the Olympic Games, sports and communication scholars ask fundamental questions about who and/or what gets shown, who and/or what does *not* reach the airwaves, and how the Olympians and their stories are depicted in terms of their nationality, gender, and ethnicity (Billings and Angelini, 2007; Billings and Eastman, 2002, 2003; Daddario and Wigley, 2007). For instance, the primetime telecast is perceived to be the most prominent and most salient form of Olympic broadcasting, with a significant bias towards the coverage of American nationals. American viewers quickly learn that if they are exposed to a wrestling match or another "secondary" sport, it will almost always be because an American has done well in that event and NBC has therefore elected to show a tape not necessarily of "the best of the best", but of "the best of the Americans". Programmatically, the Olympic telecast is said to serve a dual purpose: to secure high ratings while telling Olympic stories in their most accurate and/or authentic form. The unstable balance between these purposes is discussed throughout the book. An important question arises about whether issues of identity influence this duality and, if so, whether it is nationality and/or gender and/or ethnicity that influences NBC's choices.

The significance of sports on television

Few areas of scholarship permeate so many disciplines in the way that sport scholarship does. From communication to kinesiology, sociology to marketing, management to psychology, the connections underscore how sport resides in the lifeblood of modern society. In 1997, Boyd argued that "sports and the discourses that surround them, have become one of the master narratives of twentieth-century culture" (Boyd, 1997, p. ix), which was symbolized in the United States by the production of a special sports calendar with sports "holidays" from January's Super Bowl to college basketball's March Madness to baseball's World Series in the fall. As we advance through the twenty-first century, the grand narrative of sport continues.

Billions of people play sports, but billions also consume them. Bellamy (2006) postulates that "sports have evolved from a business that had a series of highly beneficial relationships with the media business to one of the central components of the increasingly global media entertainment industry" (p. 75). In fact, most Americans watch sports (and discuss them) more than they play them (Rawlins, 1993). With mass consumption comes the potential influence on viewers, placing a great onus on sportscasters concerning the content and orientation of their coverage. Radar (1984) contends that "television has had a large impact on the ethos of sports; on the motives and behavior of athletes, owners, and spectators; and on the organization and management of sports" (p. 3). Television shapes the actual sport events through the commentary and production values that can magnify or diminish athletic achievements, commanding authority over not just what events get shown, but what viewers think about the televised event. As Wenner (1989) explains:

> The fan at home is aided and abetted in interpreting the contest by the television camera, which focuses on action deemed important. Announcers add to this focus, as their commentary reinforces and heightens the significance of the contest and its players.
>
> (p. 15)

Networks feel massive pressure to deliver the most compelling sportscasts possible because of the tremendous size of audiences and overwhelming dollar figures devoted to televised sport (Pound, 2004). The result is an uneasy alliance between megasporting events like the Olympics and the television networks that win bidding wars to air them (Lenskyj, 2000). Casting the widest demographic net becomes the ultimate objective so that the network can garner exceedingly high advertising rates (Howard, 2006) and colossal ratings. The commentary is a vital feature of the telecast's money-making process, making the link between telecaster and audience, and incorporating storytelling and dramatic narratives that capture the imagination. The idea that good commentary balances realism with entertainment (Whannel, 1992) has shifted discernibly over the years, in particular in relation to broadcasts of the Olympics which are mediated increasingly through discourses of high emotion—excitement, suspense, and danger, for example.

NBC's theme for the Opening Ceremony of the 2006 Torino Games was "Tonight, the world comes to hear stories", leading *New York Times* sportswriter Mike Lupica to dub the Olympics the "world's most spectacular reality series" (Lupica, 2006). Dramatic narratives are employed for "re-presenting and reconstructing sports reality" (Vande Berg and Trujillo, 1989, p. 205). Larry Novenstern, whose Deutsch Inc. advertising agency bought significant Olympic time for the Athens Games in 2004, conceded that "this is not sports, it is storytelling" (Martzke, 2004, p. 7F), while Crepeau (1996) argued in his radio broadcast that the Olympics are "an excellent storyline—better even than a soap opera".

Critiques of the Torino Games mirrored the contention that storytelling trumps sports achievement. *USA Today* columnist Robert Bianco (2006a) aggregated these thoughts most concisely when arguing that "The network [NBC] sees the Olympics less as sports than as spectacle, at least in prime time ... [It is] an athletic variety show" (p. 1D). Arguing that the Olympics are synonymous with no other sporting telecast, he goes on to note that "This is not Monday Night Football. The game is not the thing" (p. 1D).

Indeed, these critics claim the Olympic telecast is being conveyed less like the world's greatest megasporting event and more like a pre-packaged reality show, replete with well-cast heroes to cheer for and villains to root against, partly because of the nationality, gender, or ethnicity with which they identify.

Sport media scholarship and research methods

Debates about how communication phenomena (Turow, 1990) can best be scrutinized continue to pervade modern academe, specifically in the study of media sport. During the research for this book, a mixed-method model with different methodological underpinnings was used to collect data and analyze the multiple messages and social constructions embedded within the telecasts (Ingham *et al.*, 1999; Ingham and Donnelly, 1990). Some scholars (including myself) have taken quantitative empirical approaches to studying aspects of sport media that are readily measurable, including surveys of athlete attitudes and analysis of sports texts. One particular focus has involved the measurement of differences between various identity groups in megasporting events (e.g. Foley, 1990). Critics contend that such work could compartmentalize different identity groups into manufactured identification variables. Thus, Tiger Woods and Vijay Singh both become "Black" golfers even though the former labels his ethnicity as Cablinasian (Eagan, 2001), a mixture of his Caucasian, Black, Indian, and Asian backgrounds (Nordlinger, 2001), while the latter is Fijian—a very different ethnic and cultural background from Woods. The research for this book illuminates these often myopic distinctions utilized by media gatekeepers—for example, six Olympic telecasts were amalgamated in order to generate a large amount of data about different broad identity classifications, specifically nationalism, men and women, Black and White. Using content analytic methods, significant differences were uncovered which were investigated further using other methods, specifically surveys and interviews (see below).

Contrasting qualitative approaches arise from critical and/or cultural perspectives (see Gramsci, 1971). Hall (1971) argued that television's primary goal is creating everyday life as artistic communication within specific historical and cultural contexts. With this in mind, understanding media sport would entail taking account of (for example) institutional, technical, political, economic, and ideological practices that are prevalent in television and in sport. The more sport becomes a part of a nation's fabric, the more it also is critical to the understanding of hegemony, subsequently defined as "a process of experience, negotiation, and struggle by individuals in real-life situations, rather than one in which subordinate groups are simply duped by dominant ideologies" (Hargreaves and McDonald, 2000, p. 50). This conception of "struggle" is critical to the understanding of a cultural studies approach, most notably the contention that nothing is ever in a fixed state, but rather there is a "constant battlefield" (Hall, 1981, p. 233) with humans negotiating both meaning and identity repeatedly and persistently. In sum, "whereas cultural practices, such as sport, are produced from specific social and historic contexts, they are also actively engaged in the ongoing constitution of the conditions out of which they emerge" (Sullivan, 2002, p. 115).

Gruneau (1983) argues that sport is a classic example of the hegemonic struggle. Indeed, cultural scholarship provides for conflicting views of tradition, power, class, and identity with these issues frequently being negotiated not only on the field of play but also within mass media. Sport at its highest level represents "modernity and rational progressivism" as viewers increasingly turn to it to understand various forms of identity (Whannel, 1992, p. 182). Thus, political and social realities are performed within athletics, often with a dominant cultural worldview being reinforced or, in some cases, empowered through processes of negotiation (Critcher, 1986).

Understanding the athletic experience through a critical lens (when both playing and watching sport) takes account of relations of power with regard to constructions of nation, gender, and ethnicity. McDonald (2006) argues that power has been reconceived in sports scholarship in three manners: (1) through the application of hegemony theory to sport and the sport media, (2) through the expansion of hegemony theory to include relations of gender and race within the sport and the media, and (3) through the promotion of "contextual cultural studies" of sport (p. 501). More specifically, Hargreaves (1982) views cultural studies as a means for understanding dominance and subordination in sport, specifically querying standards and practices in terms of who makes the decisions, who is affected by the decisions, and how deliberation (or a lack thereof) enacts decisions that tend to inordinately benefit one group over another.

One of the research methods that has been favored by critical theorists is interviewing—a method used very effectively for this book in order to determine the opinions and values of the producers and sportscasters working for the NBC Olympic telecast. I wanted to understand the thoughts and feelings of the very people who were constructing the stories that were presented to the viewers and to allow them the leeway to speak freely about the procedures they put in place and the reasons for them. The result is an interpretive approach to the interview data in which my goal was to let their words come alive and then determine whether their opinions provided valuable heuristics for the enhanced understanding of media sport.

The power of the media: storytelling in megasports

Niche markets can be found in taped sports outlets (like US-based ESPN[9] Classic[10] television), yet the majority of sports television is offered in live broadcasting form, offering the viewer a greater sense of authenticity as they consume events in a more "naturalistic" mode (see Hall, 1975). Even if people in America's Eastern time zone fall asleep at work the next morning because the athletic contest went on well past the midnight hour, it is the most popular way to watch sport on television. When a live broadcast is impractical and impossible—which often happens with the Olympic telecast because of extreme time differences—many viewers voice distress at having to watch the story in less-than-live (or, as dubbed in the Olympics, "plausibly live") form. Events such as the Olympics become pre-packaged events mega-designed for streamlined and effective storytelling at the expense of the naturalistic, "in the moment" feel that sports on television can uniquely provide. The most common complaint with the Torino Games was the taped coverage in an information age in which most viewers knew results before the primetime telecast, which resulted in the feeling that NBC was attempting to dupe them into believing the Olympics were still being shown in naturalistic form.

With the ability to construct a taped sport telecast comes the opportunity to select the storyline that best exemplifies the aim of the telecast. Ritual theorists

---

9 ESPN is the Entertainment and Sports Programming Network, launched in 1979 and especially known in the United States for overwhelming offerings of myriad sports on over a dozen different television channels.

10 ESPN Classic offers repeat viewings of sporting events, often allowing a viewer to witness games and other competitions decades after they have occurred.

claim that such forms of communication represent a "symbolic process whereby reality is produced, maintained, repaired, and transformed" (Carey, 1989, p. 177). Such assertions dovetail with the work of Stuart Hall (1975, 1984, 1992), who argues that mass communication becomes one of the main ways in which non-fictional storylines are targeted for societal consumption. Sportscasters are the visible presenters of these narratives, but, ultimately, the narratives are conceived, crafted, and subsequently generated through sports media producers, researchers, and other gatekeepers, each bending macro-narratives in a fashion that is expedient for the media outlet and also easily consumed by the sports fan watching at home.

These storylines also provide expedient ways to identify and analyze social constructions and social issues. Whannel (1992) describes "binary tensions" that are common to sports telecasts, as follows:

1   Uncertainty vs. predictability
2   Amateurism vs. professionalism
3   Sportsmanship vs. victory
4   Nationalism vs. individualism
5   Tradition vs. modernity
6   Patriarchy vs. feminism

Employing a cultural studies approach, Whannel identifies how these issues are rendered within a sportscast. One can easily witness how issues of national and gender identity play critical roles within Whannel's stated tensions. Wenner (2006) later identifies the following "Super Themes" prevalent in media sport, providing a fuller scheme for analysis of events, such as the Olympics. Unlike Whannel, he includes race and ethnicity as one of his themes:

1   Pop and hip-hop
2   Sex and gender
3   Race and ethnicity
4   Young and old
5   Celebrity and hero
6   Mass and fragments
7   Technology and activity
8   National and global
9   Super and ordinary
10 Frame and game
11 Selling and distraction
12 Control and denial
13 Deviance and distaste

The 2006 story of Black American Olympic gold-medal-winning speed skater Shani Davis can be scrutinized using many of Whannel's and Wenner's categories simultaneously. Davis was a highly controversial figure and also the first

Black male to win a gold medal in a Winter Olympic Games. His story can be examined through the lenses of "race and ethnicity", "celebrity and hero", and other super themes such as "deviance and distaste", "super and ordinary" and, given that he was an American on NBC, "national and global", is central to the understanding of his story.

Putting the book together

This project constructs an analysis of the Olympic telecasts within a ten-year time period (1996–2006). Much of the analysis, as already indicated, relates to the content analyses of the telecasts, providing specific evidence of long-term trends and changes. The quantitative data was augmented by interviews which were less prescriptive and allowed for more intense interrogation of the telecast processes, adding color and polemic. When I interviewed and audiotaped producers and sportscasters from NBC Sports, I stressed that the goal was not to play the role of a sensation-seeking journalist who often can exploit comments from celebrities in the sports media world to justify pre-held notions. Instead, the aim was to draw upon insights from people inside the industry in a way that fuses their practical experiences with scholarly analysis—to let their words "breathe" and then to "test" them empirically and comment on them critically. Media professionals bring a tremendous dedication and sense of duty to the Olympic telecast because of its role as the most pivotal and influential sports product in US network television as well as the function the telecast serves in the conveyance of historical occurrences. NBC's Olympic production enacts, literally, a seven-year process. What happens in that time period is meticulous, exhaustive, and rigorous. However, the NBC professionals admit that there is an ebb and flow, and they continually tweak the telecast in attempts to find a balance between "dutiful" storytelling and Nielsen ratings.[11] The content analyses in this book also give assessments of the roles of nationalism, gender, and ethnicity in this process.

Bryant *et al.* (1977) found that 73 percent of all commentary was describing the action in factual terms but that 27 percent of all sports commentary was dramatic, or interpretive, in nature. This study of the Olympic Games is especially interested in what happens within that 27 percent of the dialogue, the words that shape the frameworks of the discussion and connect the dots, so to speak, between the actions at a sporting event and the representation and interpretation of the actions at a sporting event. It is within this 27 percent that issues of identity can be colored and swayed. It is within this 27 percent that dominant societal impressions of cultural issues can emerge and can be changed. With 168 million Americans watching some portion of the Torino Games (Ryan, 2006), that, indeed, signifies a great deal of influence.

11 Nielsen ratings are the dominant method employed to determine the number of viewers who watch any American television program.

Chapter overviews

In Chapters 2 and 3, my main focus is the 2006 Torino Winter Olympic telecast, and the interviews that were conducted with NBC producers and sportscasters respectively. The interviews occurred in the months immediately following the Torino Games. However, the work of these media professionals during previous Summer and Winter Games often informs their responses, as I asked questions that even harkened back to the Olympic telecasts of the early and mid 1990s. In Chapter 2, you will hear from the Olympic producers that jointly bring the biggest show on television to millions of households. Four interviews are highlighted within the chapter; most notably I had a rare opportunity to discuss Olympic production with the President of NBC Universal Sports and Olympics, Dick Ebersol. In addition, the Executive Producer of the primetime Olympic telecast, David Neal, the Coordinating Producer of NBC's vast Olympic cable outlets, Molly Solomon, and the Editorial Director and Lead Writer for the Olympic telecast, Joe Gesue, imparted valuable insights. These four individuals were queried on a variety of subjects regarding Olympic production, storytelling, and the issues of nationality, gender, and ethnicity that permeate the process.

For Chapter 3, seven sportscasters were interviewed along similar lines, with the focus moving from production (exposure) aspects to the shaping and molding of an individual story. These interviewees were asked questions about their split-second instincts in telling a story and whether issues of identity overtly or covertly colored the story in a given manner. I was able to incorporate insights from interviews with anchors Bob Costas, NBC primetime anchor for the Olympic Games, and Jim Lampley, NBC weekend and late-night anchor for the Olympic Games. In addition, I interviewed on-site reporters and sportscasters, including Tom Hammond, NBC sportscaster for figure skating (Winter) and gymnastics (Summer), Donna DeVarona, first woman sportscaster and former Olympic swimming sportscaster, John Naber, gold-medal-winning Olympian and former swimming sportscaster, Ann Meyers Drysdale, medal-winning Olympian and Olympic basketball sportscaster, and Peter Vidmar, medal-winning Olympian and former gymnastics sportscaster. As a result of interviewing the key people involved in the commentary process of NBC's Olympic telecast, Chapter 3 provides very personal and detailed comments about the preparation and enactment of developing storylines and chronicling history within the unfolding process.

Chapters 4, 5, and 6 collectively form the transition from applied interview data to content analyses about the manner in which nationality (Chapter 4), gender (Chapter 5), and ethnicity (Chapter 6) have actually been conveyed in Olympic telecasts of the past ten years (duly noting that the 1998 Nagano Winter Games were not televised by NBC, but by CBS). Material was extracted from a mountain of Olympic data that was collected during this longitudinal study, much of which I completed along with Indiana University's Susan Eastman and James Angelini (e.g. Billings and Angelini, 2007; Billings and Eastman, 2002, 2003; Eastman and Billings, 1999). Production influences were largely measured through the calculation of raw clock-time (the number of hours, minutes, and seconds devoted to each gender in each sport) but also within characterizations of pre-produced profiles and promotions. Each descriptor ascribed to an athlete was classified within an Olympic taxonomy for sportscaster commentary, with comments largely dealing with explanations for athletic success/failure and external variables dealing with the depiction of personality and physicality. In sum, these three chapters collectively answer questions as to whether the NBC producer and sportscaster aims of even-handedly treating issues of nationality, gender, and ethnicity are borne out by the content analytic data gathered within the primetime telecasts.

Chapter 7 offers yet another transition to a third form of methodological measurement: survey data. In essence, this chapter reports what light and heavy Olympic viewers believed they saw within the 2006 Torino telecast—a media effect variable, so to speak. A total of 300 people were asked about their attitudes regarding the 2006 Winter Olympic Games. I queried these people as to what they thought they learned from watching the Olympics and compared it to what actually occurred. For instance, would respondents indicate that the US won more than the 11 percent of the medals they actually did win in the 2006 Games? If so, is there a correlation between increased viewership and over- and/or under-estimations? By asking these Olympic watchers questions about nationality, gender, and ethnicity as they witnessed it within 17 consecutive nights of Olympic telecasts, I was able to determine whether and in what ways the viewers were influenced by the telecast.

Finally, Chapter 8 serves as a synthesis chapter, melding notions and concepts gained from interviews, content analyses of the on-air content, and viewer responses. The chapter postulates upon the ebb and flow of modern sports television, asking questions about whether production choices influence content and viewer attitudes, or whether issues such as viewer desires drive primary production choices. No easy answers are evident, yet the chapter takes the amalgamation of data reported in the research and attempts to makes sense of it holistically. Directions for future research are postulated as well.

In sum, this book takes the three critical components (NBC gatekeepers, the actual on-air product, and the viewer him or herself) to form a composite understanding of the Olympic telecast from its inception to the effects on the chronicling of history that often reverberate years after the extinguishing of the Olympic torch.

2 Meet the "framers"

The Olympic producers

Television sports production involves a wide range of processes of visual and narrative representation—choices regarding the images, language, camera positioning, and story line are required to translate 'what happened' into a program that is 'good television'.

(Gruneau, 1989, p. 135)

Media framing (Goffman, 1974) has been integral to the discussion of sports media influence for decades. While sportscasters obviously have the ability to determine storylines and shape narratives (most notably when overseeing a live sporting event), the producers determine what events (and subparts of main events) will be shown. Frames, then, are "conceptual tools which media and individuals rely on to convey, interpret, and evaluate information" (Neuman *et al.*, 1992, p. 60). Many studies (see Dayan and Katz, 1992; Halbert and Latimer, 1994; MacNeill, 1996) have illustrated how television's narratives shape the viewers' interpretations of sporting events and many interrelated issues of identity.

The use of media frames is unambiguously essential to the comprehension of Olympic television production and the nuances therein, as the primetime telecast shapes and edits sporting event content to streamline the best spectacles and stories, even when the Olympics are held in television-friendly time zones for viewers in the United States (such as Atlanta in 1996 and Salt Lake City in 2002). As a result, Olympic frames hold the power to enlighten an audience as to what is (or is not) important, with the most basic of these frames being exposure (the sporting events and athletes worthy of the spotlight in the coveted primetime broadcast). As Entman (1993) explains,

to frame is to select some aspects of a perceived reality and make them more salient in a communicating text, in such a way as to promote a particular problem definition, causal interpretation, moral evaluation, and/or treatment recommendation for the item described.

(p. 52)

That is, in a nutshell, what sports producers execute.

In an Olympic telecast, NBC production professionals make overt choices about what to show (selection), what to show a lot (emphasis), and what to avoid (exclusion) within a given telecast (Gitlin, 1980). For example, NBC's Olympic primetime telecast offers sports like swimming and skiing in a moderate amount, shows virtually every competitive minute of gymnastics and figure skating, and excludes events like boxing and hockey that have not proven to impart the wide demographic net that producers hope the Olympics will cast. Indeed, one of the main goals of Olympic production over the past two decades is to build demographic pluralities in all age groups for both men and women. For instance, *American Idol* is a program that does particularly well with younger demographics, but not nearly as well with older demographics; at its peak, *The West Wing* was a program that yielded ratings that were solid, but more enviable than most would think because the program drew highly educated, high-income viewers that were particularly appealing to advertisers; *Dancing with the Stars* is quite popular with women, but not nearly as accepted among men. In contrast, the Olympic telecasts attempt (and often succeed) in garnering appealing ratings for all Americans— young and old, male and female, educated and uneducated, affluent and impoverished. The most prominent development in this achievement has been the production decisions about what events to show. Producer decisions are based on the findings of NBC's ratings experts who utilize vast amounts of data to determine which events will create the "perfect storm" effect to which all demographic groups will tune in. One of the NBC producers' aims is to maintain the largest, most diverse audience in contemporary American television.

In addition to producing high ratings, producers are required simultaneously to fashion a telecast that frames the fullest and most complete "Olympic experience" they deem to be attainable—a task that is controversial and constantly moving. Producing an Olympic Games is no small task. In fact, many would argue it is the biggest job within the biggest show on television. Torino offered seven different cities for athletic competition (Torino, Bardonecchia, Cesana, Pinerolo, Pragelato, Sauze d'Oulx, and Sestriere) and three separate Olympic villages (Torino, Bardonecchia, and Sestriere) with all of the action being produced and edited in one of the 31 different NBC editing rooms. With a grand total of 2,767 NBC employees, the Olympic telecast represents a confluence of media production options. To control this veritable maelstrom of variables (along with over a million spectators), sports directors and producers function as auteurs who aid in enacting a sport as a dynamic spectacle (Morris and Nydahl, 1985). The fine line a producer must manage is in giving audiences what they desire—entertainment, spectacle, drama—without providing an overly biased depiction of the Games. As executive producer David Neal said before the Torino telecast, "We are here to document the Olympics; we're not here to be cheerleaders" (McCarthy, 2006, p. 3D). But avoiding partiality is difficult, particularly when covering an event that has been coined as a "postmodern culture of excess" (Real, 1996, p. 20).

It was with this dilemma in mind that I posited questions to several key Olympic producers with an immense amount of experience. First and foremost was Dick Ebersol, the President of NBC Universal Sports and Olympics. Ebersol is largely regarded as the biggest name in sports production, once described as the most powerful man in all of sports by *Sporting News* magazine (Kinsley, 1996). Ebersol is the protégé of legendary ABC Sports executive Roone Arledge, and his vast résumé includes decades of work in megasports (e.g. the Olympics, Major League Baseball World Series, National Basketball Association Finals, horse racing's Triple Crown, and the Super Bowl) and beyond (e.g. *Saturday Night Live* and the *Today* show). While primarily an organizational leader, Ebersol also labels his role within the Olympics as Executive Producer. The Olympic Games is the one event in which he remains thoroughly involved throughout the production process at NBC Sports.

Telephone interviews were also conducted with Executive Producer David Neal, who produces the primetime telecast, and Coordinating Producer Molly Solomon, who oversees the cable telecasts, and email correspondence took place with Joe Gesue, Editorial Director and Lead Writer for the Olympic Games. These four people imparted valuable insights into how the NBC Olympic telecast materializes over a seven-year period.

Olympian preparation: seven years to the Opening Ceremonies

NBC Sports initiates work seven years in advance of any Olympic telecast (shortly after a city receives a bid), meaning that, for instance, the 2006 Torino Games commenced pre-production before the turn of the millennium. The interviewees were quick to point out that throughout that seven-year process, they relied primarily on Dick Ebersol's leadership and trusted him unequivocally. As David Neal explains:

> DN: He's the ideal boss because he's a producer at heart. He clearly sets the tone, and is always on point, leading us to where we're supposed to go. He is a supportive boss who then says, "All right, let's go execute the plan".

Coordinating producer Molly Solomon believes the foundational aspects of the telecast are interpersonal relationships with preestablished Olympic agencies such as the Olympic Organizing Committee. She verbalizes, as follows, the necessary rapport a network like NBC must retain with the International Olympic Committee:

> MS: The first step [for me] is getting a competition schedule. It's like putting together a really big puzzle. It's fascinating to make sure you

> have strong nights every single night. We have to make sure we've got strong sports every night, but the process gets continually refined for the scheduling. Two and a half to three years out we get a really good look at the competition schedule, and then we can start to look at our shows and how many hours we'll be on the air.

The term "strong night" needs unpacking. NBC producers realize that they have a fairly set number of "big ticket" or "big draw" events; the aim is to spread them out in a manner that garners the greatest audience for the greatest duration. For instance, the strongest night for any modern NBC Winter Olympic telecast has been the women's figure-skating finals. Six skaters compete in the final group, each only skating for a total of four minutes. Yet, NBC can easily stretch out this drama over the course of several hours (particularly in tape delay). By doing so, people watch other sports interspersed with the high profile figure skating, producing a "strong night". The goal, then, for people like Solomon is to undercover a "hook" or a story that will make viewers watch each telecast.

Solomon clarified that the more intricate Olympic planning usually occurs almost immediately following a preceding Games, so that an Olympics gains daily attention from the chief producers for two years.

> MS: For example, for Torino, we got home from Athens on September 1st, 2004, and really we dug in starting October 1st, 2004. This is not to say we haven't laid the plans for all this, but we're really focusing solely on Torino as of that October. Then we're actually getting to the point where you want to be over there surveying, seeing the venues as they're built, seeing the weather during game time. By then, we've got a pretty good skeleton plan.

Ebersol concurrently enacts the dual roles of leader and producer within the Olympics and this is a choice unique to the entirety of the remaining sports programming that NBC airs on a weekly basis. He explains that his production tasks largely begin 18 months before the Olympics are staged:

> DE: The Olympics are the only thing I actually feel I produce myself. I have some of the greatest producers and directors in sports television, but this is the one project where [I oversee] every format laid out over a period of eighteen months before the Games right up until the day

before the Games. In Australia (Sydney, 2000) for example, I probably had 16 or 17 different formats over that 18 months of stories developing which I do as much for the exercise, so that everyone will know how I want a story to flow, how I want a night to flow, right down to what speeches are going to be done at the Opening Ceremony.

Neal and Solomon both indicated that casting the on-air talent for anchor and sportscasting roles actually occurs quite late in the process, approximately one year before the Games begin. Producers have already had six years to construct what they feel is a good "skeleton plan" for the Games and only then do they place the people who will enact the storytelling process into the massive Olympic mechanism. Solomon contended that giving on-air talent a year's notice is still a substantial amount of time for a sportscaster to become proficient in their knowledge regarding all of the athletes and storylines in the events they will be reporting. Neal spoke of the impracticalities of executing the process any other way.

DN: We have a relatively small core group of senior production—about six of us—who work on the Olympics year in and year out. We're well over 90 percent freelance when we go to an Olympics because no sports division has the luxury of carrying large numbers of staff anymore.

Meanwhile, another feature of NBC's Olympic preparation is the diligent toiling required to determine those stories that are worthy of clock-time and the manner in which these stories should be rendered. While the Olympic producers may be determining what events should generally be offered in each time slot, Editorial Director Joe Gesue and his research team are industriously ascertaining the specific athletes and storylines to fit these broad Olympic frames. As Gesue indicates:

JG: Leading up to the Olympics, I manage a team of researchers who travel around the world interviewing athletes and coaches and officials to learn their stories and help prepare our production team for the Games. We work hand in hand with the Olympic Profiles department, which produces the athlete stories that appear in our coverage.

A wholly different degree of focus and rigor is employed a month prior to the Olympics as Dick Ebersol travels to the site and enters what he designates as his "Olympic cocoon" in which the Olympic telecast becomes his single focus despite the massive sports organization he continues to oversee. He describes below a very detailed process that he has refined over time and now wholeheartedly endorses.

DE: I like to go with no more than seven or eight of the key production people four weeks before in a more relaxed atmosphere. For the first two weeks, I try to spend six or eight hours discussing a major sport—our final plans, how we're going to do it, and review in detail the formats for how we plan to allot the time. Then the really big exercise, which usually lasts three very long days—about 14 hours a day in the Summer Games—the key production people will go through every day, first the network primetime, then the network daytime, then network late night, then each one of the cables, and how we plan minute by minute, to do every one of those. Obviously, we know there's going to be change, but I find that an exercise like this—really intense, nobody around, no phone calls, no other business allowed—builds into your brain all of the possibilities. With the flood of information and change that comes when the Olympics actually unfold, you'd be up a creek if you didn't know all the possibilities of what you could change, if you were planning on six segments and the story you thought was going to happen crashes. It's the post-producing part of the Olympics where you're going to make it up somewhere else in the show. Then I try almost every night to put us all in a social setting, and the dinner becomes a mix of fun and further discussion. Basically, from dawn to dusk and beyond, they're immersed in it. Most of them love it. In many ways, it's the most intimate, productive, creative time that we ever have in our own professional lives. You just don't ever have that kind of luxury for an event that's going to happen in one day or two days. It's only the Olympics.

In many ways, Ebersol is compelling other key contributors to endorse his notion of what the Olympic telecast should entail and, by doing so, enter into an "Olympic cocoon" as well:

DE: I take all of the key people, remove them from anything else they're going to do, and put them in this setting for a month. Nobody's really done anything like this, but I believe in it deeply.

It is quite clear that while NBC's 2,767 people have many chiefs within various departments, all critical decisions flow through one person: Dick Ebersol. This process seems to work well for all involved, as even the main producers realize what a wealth of information Ebersol brings to the process. The organizational structure might work in quite different ways if Ebersol were not as clearly established as the preeminent pioneer of modern sports television. Given his stature and diligent nature, Ebersol is able to influence the process quite overtly. As he admits, he is a producer at heart and this is his opportunity to get away from the business aspects of being president of a sports empire and to enact explicit production choices to generate what he feels the Olympic telecast should be in terms of tone and content.

Connections between production and on-air talent (e.g. anchors, on-site reporters, and announcers) are often handled through pre-production seminars, primarily managed by David Neal. Neal declined to provide any of the materials used in the seminar because he felt that restricting them to internal use ensures that colleagues are confident that the process is confidential. He argued that confidentiality is crucial as the NBC seminars are essentially for discussing decision-making strengths and weaknesses, offering a playbook on how incidents have previously unfolded and how the telecast can be enhanced in the future. Neal did, however, pinpoint some of the conventional frameworks and themes of the seminars, noting that it is imperative for sportscasters to comprehend how an Olympics differs from the other sporting events that the on-air talent is used to covering regularly:

> DN: A lot of what we do is the philosophy of storytelling ... comparing work from the past. We remind everyone at the beginning that you check your ego at the door and don't take offense if some work of yours of the past is shown as an example of how not to do it. It's the basic building blocks of storytelling—how you personalize the athletes. It's how you explain sports which are, for the most part, far from the mainstream, and give members of the audience an easy way to identify what's going on to hopefully establish a personal interest.

Neal's noting that these sports are predominantly "far from the mainstream" is important for understanding the potential effect of a telecast during which the producers and sportscasters have the opportunity to provide millions of viewers with an initial glance at sports that they may never have seen before. Because of this, viewer attitudes about athletes and events are likely to be less engrained going into the telecast than when consuming, say, baseball's World Series or professional American football's Super Bowl. Production and storytelling choices wield the potential for shaping a first impression of people from different nations and backgrounds.

The seven years of pre-production are used to create a broadcast skeleton framework—an extrapolation of possibilities of what could happen in the hope of properly anticipating the changes that must be expediently enacted over the course of the actual 17-day broadcast, what Solomon refers to as the "fun part". Without question, aspects of framing are performed within these processes, yet, as with any non-fictional telecast, NBC Sports will not know what storylines can be brought to bear until the Games begin. What NBC forecasts to happen can be quite different from the events that unfold. In 2006, NBC presumed that the Torino coverage would be constructed to focus on the expected successes of athletes such as Michelle Kwan and her quest to attain a much-anticipated gold medal in women's figure skating, and colorful US downhill skier Bode Miller, who won two medals in the 2002 Salt Lake City Games and who later admitted that he enjoyed skiing while drunk and that winning medals was not a chief concern to him. However, NBC's storylines dramatically shifted when Kwan withdrew from the Games, citing a nagging injury, and Miller failed to win a medal in any of his five events. Such examples highlight the "moving target" nature of NBC's preparation; no matter how much time is devoted to managing the numerous possibilities, the staff must be prepared to "call an audible"[1] in their production plan when necessary.

On the same page? Coordinating almost 3,000 people

For Torino, NBC assembled one of the largest on-site crews in the annals of sports television with nearly 3,000 employees covering the various Italian venues. One of the most critical concerns for such a large sports department (particularly when the overwhelming majority are employed by NBC exclusively for the Olympics and arrive from working in demonstrably different types of sports media environments and with divergent expectations) is to ensure that everyone appreciates the overall objectives of the NBC broadcast. Solomon spoke about the need to get everyone "on the same page":

> MS: It's getting the information out ... simplistic stuff like what graphics we're using, but also getting the group together and promoting an identity as NBC. It's reminding them that we don't want to be the bull in the china shop. We want to be good neighbors, good international guests, because we don't put up with any of that "Oh, I'm NBC, let me go to the front of the security line". There's an on-air philosophy; a way of doing things—reminding them about storytelling and personalizing international athletes, because that's very important to get the audience emotionally invested in the product.

---

1 A term often used in American football in which a designed play is abandoned because of a change in situation.

Concerning the potential for overlap of roles that could generate a "too many chiefs and not enough Indians" dilemma, Ebersol clarifies how he serves as the organizational leader with lead producers and anchors:

> DE: While we're on the air, whatever Bob (Costas)[2] is doing live to tie together the other taped Olympics, or whatever he's doing live to pull together the other live Olympics—the person talking in his ear is David Neal, but David's getting every direction we're going to go from me. I wish I could produce 52 weeks a year rather than be an executive. You can't really do that and run an organization, so the only time I do really do that anymore is the Olympics.

In sum, Ebersol works hard to construct an organizational identity and then imparts his vision upon the rest of his NBC Olympic counterparts. Micro-managing would be impossible with the number of Olympic hours aired daily, but Ebersol ensures that the most crucial aspects (particularly the Opening Ceremonies, but also the primetime telecast, which represents 85 percent of the aggregate Olympic viewing audience over the course of any single day) of the telecast correspond with his overarching vision. Ebersol confided that the Opening Ceremony is the most severe test of a sports producer, but that it is integral to the rendering of the Olympic experience, so he works even longer hours to ensure the television product is of high quality:

> DE: As a producer, the most difficult part of every Olympics is the Opening Ceremony. It's only four hours, but it's always fraught with peril because there are parts of it that simply aren't going to work and you have to make the determination—if it's an overseas Games—how much you're going to edit out of it. We never sleep the night after the Opening Ceremonies because we're still fine-tuning until the show goes off the air.

Ebersol's comment draws attention to the often vast differences between standard, structured production practices and the real-life applications of procedures that are informed by experience and acquired history (Hall, 1972). Whannel (1992) maintains that "It is important to hold open the distinction between what formally happens (i.e. according to the structure) and what actually happens" (p. 25). Dick Ebersol enacts this distinction in maintaining that producers

2 Costas hosted all 17 nights of the Torino primetime telecast, fulfilling the "anchor" role.

do not merely determine where to place the cameras and document history; instead, producers collectively work on the *best manner* in which to present this "authentic" event. Ebersol possesses a very high degree of credibility to do this from his decades in sports media and his experiences in producing highly regarded Olympic telecasts.

Molly Solomon spoke about the different types of role that the main Olympic producers assume over the course of the Games, with responsibilities changing depending on whether the Games are in the pre- or post-production period and the time slot (and network) in which the events are being aired.

> MS: I would say my role is somewhat different [than producing the prime-time telecast] because the hours are greater, so you have an opportunity to put on more. It depends on if you're talking about Winter or Summer. In the Winter, there's not a huge diversity of events that weren't on in the primetime shows; a little bit of cross-country [skiing] may air in primetime, but mostly biathlon, hockey, and curling ended up either on the networks' morning, afternoon, or cable shows. It goes back to that timing issue; in the morning there's biathlon and there are cross-country races. Those deserved to play out in a bigger bulk of time, and we had the weekends to do that.

Production is also inherently tied to the editorial department, as producers are largely accountable for anticipating what events will be shown, but people such as Joe Gesue provide the focus—who should be shown and how the stories should be told. The manner in which storytelling takes place is based predominantly on sacred trusts between producers, editors, and writers. Solomon explains:

> MS: Joe Gesue heads up our Olympic researcher group. They comb the web, go to all these events, and actually find the best stories. They critically analyze and give us cheat sheets about what the best stories are, and what people are going to be interested in. Once you have those tools, you can create a show. Guys with helmets on going down a mountain 80 miles an hour—you've got to know something about them to make it compelling.

Nonetheless, the most crucial personnel to coordinate within the NBC Olympic mechanism remain the sportscasters and, particularly, the anchors. Dick Ebersol inexorably has an overall vision and possesses the power to ask for a second take in any taped situation, but must be able to trust the people who reside behind the anchor desk providing a primary face for the Olympics (especially given the fact that on-site reporters are normally heard but not seen). Ebersol has chosen anchors (Bob Costas and Jim Lampley) who are not merely well recognized by US viewers, but who are also regarded as intellectuals within the industry—people who possess the ability to bind sports with political, cultural, and social issues of a host or competing country. Ebersol was asked about the criteria employed when determining anchor roles and replied as follows:

> DE: Bob [Costas] has hosted so many Games and does a fantastic job while Jim [Lampley] has a treasure trove of Olympic information the likes of which nobody else working today has. In Jim's favor, over the last 20 years he probably knows more about the Olympic sports than anybody working. Jim McKay certainly held that banner through Calgary, but ABC hasn't had the rights and Jim [McKay] is sort of in semi-retirement right now.

Solomon principally works with Lampley and terms him "the smartest man I know", which one must presume aids the producer/anchor relationship tremendously. Speaking of this bond with Lampley, Solomon illuminates how crucial this dimension is in coordinating the essential pieces of the Olympic telecast.

> MS: It's a very personal relationship. You can read each other's minds. You've been through so many of these experiences before, and you can see the pitfalls.

Casting the rest of the production and reporter roles is important to the process as well, and David Neal and Molly Solomon both reported that a major benefit of securing multiple Olympic bids is the consistency of people who have worked multiple Olympics (Solomon refers to them as the "varsity team").

> MS: It's like muscle memory—they understand what we're looking for. They also can produce classy and journalistically strong shows. More and more we bring freelancers in, because we balloon from a unit of 50 to 60 people, to three thousand. You have to have these freelancers who have worked four or five Olympics for us, and it's not a retraining process—they know what we want, and we depend on them. You hope that you've picked up some people who do a good job and who know their sports, but you also want to pick out people who are contemporary to their sport as well.

The notion of "muscle memory" is an interesting one to interrogate, as it gets to the core of having an "Olympic-style telecast". NBC Sports is constantly looking for ways to improve and innovate within the Olympic telecast (Neal notes that complacency is their biggest enemy), yet, when hiring personnel to work on the Games, experience is a critical factor. Many people are returning to an Olympics working from an expectancy baseline of how things were produced and conveyed in the previous Olympics, meaning differences over the years are more likely to be subtle and still within the overall rubric of NBC's Olympic vision (as largely envisioned by Dick Ebersol).

David Neal was explicitly asked whether diversity in the telecast was central to determining who should be working as on-site reporters. Neal argued that critics who believe the telecast favors White male Americans largely because of a lack of diversity among their sportscasters are "wholly inaccurate" and that recent more diverse casting choices, such as Black female Carol Lewis working the bobsledding venue, was incidental. He claimed that:

> DN: In complete candor, we are looking for the best broadcasters, and Carol's an excellent broadcaster. She's done outstanding work for us on track and field for many years. She approached me because she had had some experience as an athlete with the women's bobsledding team. She so enjoyed the Olympic experience, and it was her idea. But goal number one is still to find the best broadcasters because the Olympics are such a difficult undertaking, that you want your very best people there.

Without question, coordinating a staff of thousands is arduous for chief producers and management. Still, they report that what makes the job easier is that they largely have their pick of who they desire to work with on the Olympic project (because even rival sports networks are agreeable to releasing their sportscasters as a result of the prestige and visibility the Olympics provides). Sportscasters in particular will undoubtedly continue to bring their own style and manner of telling the Olympic story, but Dick Ebersol and other lead producers feel they at least achieve NBC's primary ambition: to establish a common tone and style for conveying the Olympic experience.

Natural selection: what events make it to the airwaves?

Construction of media frames (Goffman, 1974) refers to Olympic clock-time and dialogues regarding the determination of which events and athletes are worthy of airtime, specifically within the primetime telecast. Furthermore, the process of agenda-setting (McCombs and Shaw, 1972) injects insights that aid an understanding of the exposure variable (See Gitlin, 1980). Agenda-setting theory posits the idea that mass media outlets such as television cannot tell us explicitly *what* to think, but can be marvelously effective at outlining what a viewer *should* think about. For instance, if a television news channel were to insert a "national debt clock" as a bug in the corner of the screen, the news network would not be arguing overtly one or another side of the debate over the ballooning US deficit, but the network would be making the story particularly salient, leading many viewers to consider the topic seriously. Within the Olympics, similar cues exist, such as a quick, three-second insert that informs the viewer that in 17 minutes, US short-track speed skater Apolo Anton Ohno will compete, cuing the audience that this is a "must-see" moment. Given that NBC has set the agenda in this way for years (e.g. Thursday night programming is literally dubbed "Must See TV"), it is clear that NBC is cognizant of how to alert viewers to seminal programming.

A handful of sports dominate NBC's primetime Olympic coverage. For the Summer Olympics, swimming, gymnastics, track and field, and diving routinely encompass 85 percent of the entire primetime telecast (Billings, 2007) and the Winter Games, offering a third of the possible sport outlets, focuses (albeit to a lesser extent) on figure skating and skiing. David Neal explains how the Olympic telecast is meticulously crafted:

> DN: It's based on an awful lot of audience research. You can run through minute-by-minute ratings and effectively look at a line graph that tells you what has traction and stickiness with the audience, and conversely, what doesn't hold an audience. In many ways, it ends up being a roadmap for us because that and the various focus groups—where you can actually listen to the voices of our viewers—tell us what they like and what they don't like. That combines with hopefully a good intuitive sense of what's compelling drama and what isn't. You put all that together and out of that comes your daily programming plan.

Agenda-setting principles have rapidly expanded over the course of past decades, evolving into a series of characteristics that media can use to augment the salience of a subject (McCombs, 1992). Arguing for the convergence of the mostly quantitative agenda-setting scholarship with the mostly qualitative framing studies, McCombs and Ghanem (2001) claim that both investigative procedures suggest a common focus (Chyi and McCombs, 2004; Wanta and Ghanem, 2006). The most prominent characteristic of Olympic programming agenda-setting is the focus on women viewers, which is starkly unique compared to any other sporting telecast. Women now constitute 55 percent of all Olympic viewers, but this trend has been very steady for decades. Dick Ebersol reported that seeking out the woman viewer is not a function of an agenda-setting shift that was enacted when NBC secured multiple Olympic contracts:

DE: It's not something that NBC is totally responsible for. It started back in Munich, I'm guessing. That's when the Olympics began to evolve much more into the gymnastics/swimming model. Track was still really important, but you saw richer stories and it didn't matter whether they were American or international.

Neal concurred that women viewers have always been incredibly loyal to the Olympic product and that NBC's objective was always to secure as many demographic groups as possible, once more a result of closely scrutinized audience research:

DN: With a property this important—you're talking about 17 nights of primetime television—you have to be exacting about your programming choices and philosophies. Certainly we pay rapt attention to the composition of our audience and, therefore, to the elements of each Olympics which will, logically, be most appealing to the composition of our audience. And you're right: it's the only sporting event where the audience is more than half women. We pay very close attention to that.

One area of clock-time that was influenced by gendered demographics was the exclusion of boxing, which was last aired in primetime in 1988. Ebersol postulated that sometimes a person in his position has to react to his instincts and then consult viewer data to determine whether those instincts have validity. He intuited that boxing was not drawing a wide demographic, and takes responsibility for the programming shift.

Regarding the elimination of boxing from primetime coverage, Ebersol stated:

DE: That's 100 percent something that I came to when I took the job in '89. I had a very strong feeling during the Seoul Games (in 1988), that every time they went to boxing in primetime, they drove the women away. As soon as I got the job in the spring of '89, I gave that whole exercise to someone to study. They found that during the course of the Seoul games, when they went to boxing, they would lose as much as two-thirds of the female adult audience in a matter of minutes. That told me that I had to find a different way.

The result, according to both Solomon and Ebersol, was a severe programming shift moving boxing to one of NBC's Olympic cable outlets. Solomon explained:

"We found a place for it. That's where we're very lucky to have cable", while Ebersol contended that boxing aficionados could find expanded coverage on cable that was targeted for the avid boxing fan, rather than packaged for the masses. He noted that "they could go someplace and immerse themselves in it for three hours in a stretch".

Another example of a programming shift was the institution of a stand-alone daily program about the Olympics, *Olympic Ice*, which discussed previous Olympic figure skating rather than showing new coverage of it. Calling the show her "baby", Molly Solomon said the idea took years to develop and could only be done in the Winter Games for figure skating because, she explained, fans of the sport "are incredibly loyal to a fault. You can talk figure skating forever". Solomon discussed how the show evolved and why it was necessary:

> MS: Dick actually came up with the idea of doing a show initially called "Torino Tonight", and it was more of a preview show of the day. I thought there was an opportunity, when he said "I want you to concentrate on figure skating". I went away from there thinking that I needed to convince him to do all figure skating, because it has enough storylines ... the soap opera, the drama, the tragedy, the costumes. We had never done a show which didn't have competition that was dedicated to a single sport, so it was a whole different ball game for us. It got critical acclaim because there was an honesty to it, a candor, an openness. It was like watching reality TV because it wasn't a polished show. It was a talk show with a sense of humor, a fresh, new kind of look at the Olympics.

Indeed, *Olympic Ice* provides another example of the persuasive function of agenda-setting (Sutherland and Galloway, 1981). Sometimes the agenda is influenced by outside forces—most notably viewer desires—making agenda-setting into more of an agenda-building archetype wherein viewers and media gatekeepers exhibit reciprocal influence on each other (Lang and Lang, 1983). Neal argued that NBC does not try or is not able to exert the type of influence on the programming schedule that many would presume they could, stating that, "If we only had a quarter of the influence people like to think we have!" He spoke specifically about clock-time issues regarding gender equity:

> DN: The Olympics, by their very nature, have a high level of gender equity, so it's not a daily consideration one way or the other. We're really driven by the competition schedule and the events that we believe the American audience will be most keenly interested in. It's a natural

> progression, not the product of sitting in some boardroom in midtown Manhattan and making a profound decision one way or the other. I can't portray it as the result of some grand decision-making process.

In the end, agenda-setting and/or agenda-building in the Olympics succumbs to the ultimate agenda-setters: the participating athletes. Sometimes this unfolds quite beneficially for NBC, such as in 1996 when nearly every heavily promoted US athlete won gold, from track star Michael Johnson to the "Magnificent Seven" women's gymnastics team. Other times, such as in Torino, the best laid plans are quickly scrapped, as the promoted athletes (e.g. Bode Miller) faltered while other Americans (e.g. alpine skier Ted Ligety) became surprise gold medalists. Neal spoke about the degree of luck any Olympic agenda must receive to garner high ratings and to allow the program to run as anticipated:

> DN: It's just the odds; sometimes things follow form, sometimes they don't. If you went back and looked at any of the major publications the week before the Opening Ceremony, Bode Miller was on the cover of *Time*, *Newsweek*, and *Sports Illustrated*, so it's not just NBC that was expecting him to do well. Nor was Michelle Kwan being overlooked by publications. It didn't follow the form that the prognosticators in the Olympic world thought it would. That's just the way things break sometimes.

Crafting the plotline: storytelling

Even with nearly thousands of people on the NBC's Olympic team, it is a yeoman's task to decipher which should become the preeminent narratives within the primetime telecast, particularly when some of the most compelling stories involve athletes with little to no chance of winning an Olympic medal. Media framing applies not only to the exposure (i.e. clock-time) of certain athletes and sports, but also to the manner in which the rhetoric (both audio and visual) unfolds. David Neal argues that his editorial team does a solid job of identifying key stories, but that the network invariably relies heavily on sources outside of NBC Sports:

> DN: We certainly pay an awful lot of attention to the media going in. You want to have your finger on the pulse and understand who the athletes are—which ones are capturing the public attention—so it'd be

> foolish not to pay attention to that. But we're so focused on covering the Games in the way that we think is best, that at that point, you stop paying nearly as much attention to what other outlets are doing because our plate is very full doing what we're doing.

Molly Solomon explains that producers are often not involved at the inception of the storytelling process; rather, the editorial team (led by Joe Gesue) aids in consolidating a proposed agenda that producers can consult and discern whether to follow:

> MS: Joe will put up a booklet of the best stories in the Games and what days if, for instance, we want to start building a sprinter who's going to be there throughout the second week of the Games. The Winter is harder because people tend to compete on one or two nights and that's it. But they'll have them handicapped saying, "You know, (speed skater) Joey Cheek might be somebody, he's into these humanitarian causes; he's a smart kid; he won a medal in Salt Lake. We should do something on him". Then we decide if and when we would like to profile this person because you also don't want to look like you're just doing profiles of people who win medals or the audience will catch on.

In essence, the agent of the agenda-setting process is the editorial team, whose critical job is not only determining which stories need to be conveyed, but also resolving a heuristic for grading the stories into different echelons—stories that must be told, stories that should be told, and stories that could be told if time and circumstances permit.

Gesue explains:

> JG: My team makes recommendations about which athletes to profile, which is reviewed by the senior production and management team. We base our decisions on a number of factors, including how compelling and unique the story is, and how often or prominent the athlete will be in our coverage. To serve the viewers, it makes sense to go in depth with athletes they likely will see often. Of course, there are exceptions as some stories are so compelling we will tell them regardless of the sport or the athlete's medal chances.

Several storytelling devices are utilized within the Olympic broadcast, the most prominent of which are pre-produced profiles, which used to be called "up close and personals", but now Dick Ebersol refers to simply as "stories". NBC has recently revised how they perform this storytelling practice, providing fewer pre-packaged stories and allowing on-site reporters more opportunity to tell stories as an event unfolds. As Ebersol explains:

> DE: I don't want to see more than four [pre-produced profiles per night]. They're all so much shorter now. They used to be on average just under three minutes; now they average about two. Because there are fewer of them, we still want as much storytelling, so we've now gone through the exercise of telling the announcers which are the featured stories of that night. They then have to figure out an encapsulated way of telling the stories that we would have otherwise put in features of the past.

The primary aim of this programming shift, claims Neal, is to provide a more consistent, streamlined, and immediate type of broadcast.

> DN: There's no question that, beginning with Salt Lake City [2002], we've moved towards more competition-driven programming. You don't want to stop the show unless you're going to leave it for a very good reason, so what we've done since Salt Lake is to put the onus for the vast majority of the storytelling on our broadcast talent. We want them to weave the stories of the athletes into their commentary, rather than making a specific stoppage in the show to change locations for a pre-produced story. We did a fair number of traditional profiles in both Athens and Torino, but we're much more judicious about when we put them into the programming mix.

Nonetheless, Neal contends that NBC began receiving media criticism in 2006 for not profiling more athletes in pre-produced formats for Torino, arguing that NBC's coverage had strayed too far from traditional storytelling models. On this conundrum, Neal concedes that no matter how the Olympics are formatted, "You're never going to come up with the single formula that pleases everyone".

Given the reduction of pre-produced "stories", the question becomes the manner in which the stories that do make the air are told. Gesue offers his guiding principles:

JG: Since most of our pieces tend to be shorter, we do not approach a profile like we have to tell the athlete's whole life story. The profiles are meant to focus on one aspect of the athlete's life—one compelling hook—personal and/or competitive that will help viewers remember who they are, and help them care more about the results in sports they rarely see outside of the Olympics. Our venue broadcasters supplement the storytelling as part of the competition coverage.

Dick Ebersol knows the biggest criticism NBC's coverage has received dwells upon how many critics feel NBC manufactures conflict and prepares stories that overstate the challenges athletes have to surmount in order to compete in the Olympics. This seemed particularly apt in the 1996 Atlanta Games, when seemingly every US athlete had overcome major barriers to become a champion. Dick Ebersol has tried to reduce hyperbole about athletes, but regrets once joking that "We've downgraded asthma—it's no longer a fatal disease", because he knows asthma can be very serious for some people. To him, the issue now involves the determination of which stories are genuinely inspirational and which could be assessed as contrived hyperbole. Nonetheless, Ebersol claims that there are amazing stories of accomplishment in the Games and that NBC will not shy away from them for fear of being adjudicated as sensationalistic:

DE: The vast majority of the audience comes to the Olympics to hear stories of people overcoming obstacles. The people who come for sports are the same people who will go to any sporting event. The Olympics earn a premium of loyalty from the viewer and a premium of support from the advertisers because they have had special appeal to a much larger audience. The '96 Games had a lot of athletes who'd been through really serious diseases. In that one Olympics, I think there was a three or four night stretch where we probably had a total of seven or eight of [these types of stories], but the Olympics *is* about overcoming obstacles. People who are following the Olympics see these athletes as having gone the extra mile at not an inconsiderable amount of sacrifice.

David Neal claims that the focus on sacrifice is dictated from Ebersol to the rest of the Olympic team and that these stories are usually among the most compelling, concurring that the Olympics are on such a grand stage that one has to underscore the huge dedication that being an Olympic athlete necessitates. Neal notes that it is important to remember that:

DN: For one Bode Miller who has the million dollar endorsement deals and the entourages, you've got hundreds and hundreds of athletes who aren't that far removed from having mom and dad take them to swim practice at 5 a.m. before school.

Storytelling also incorporates aspects of modern culture that permeate the Olympics at many levels. For example, issues of identity percolate within the telecast, as do political and social constructions within and between various competing nations. Calling the Olympics a "global celebration for sports", Gesue maintained that the goal is to "educate just a little while we entertain". Ebersol concurred, but notes that it is not NBC's aspiration to manufacture hard-news stories within the Games, believing that if people yearn for these types of stories, NBC offers other formats such as the *Today* show that more readily assembles these connections. Still, there are times that Ebersol believes non-sports issues must be addressed:

DE: I feel that we should touch a lot [of the social and cultural aspects] but we're basically there to document the stories of those particular Games. If we can give you a little bit of the culture of the people of that country, then I think we've really performed well. The politics only enter into it if there's a particular issue with those Games. You never really know. We lived under the overhang of terrorist images of what could have involved the Athens Games. It never happened, so we talked about all of that stuff the night of the Opening Ceremony, and in our daytime programming when we first came on the air the next morning, but we never went back to it again, because it all proved to be an empty threat.

Arguing that there needs to be a "proper mix" of the sporting, the political, the cultural, and the social, David Neal asserts that there needs to be a sense of place within the coverage, but that these sorts of "outside of the box" stories often unfold within the 17 days of coverage:

DN: You can't—and shouldn't—treat the Olympics as if it was just happening in a nondescript playing field in a city to be named later. It needs to reflect the part of the world that it's taking place in and the culture of the host nation. At the same time, we have to remember that the primary reason our viewers are tuning in is for the action on the field, the stories of the athletes that make them care about the results. It's a moving target; what is right on night one—when we're doing the Opening Ceremony—is most likely not going to be right for night three when we're two days into competition. It's an ever-changing landscape that we have to adapt to. You still have to keep saying to yourself, "All right, that worked yesterday; is it going to work today, or do we need to adjust?" One size fits all does not apply to the Olympics.

Flexible storytelling incorporates conceptions of nationalism. Molly Solomon professes that if NBC is successful in allowing the US audience to become familiar with international athletes, their histories and cultural differences will be an inherent part of the process:

MS: I'm still in the camp where you go into the Games actually excited by having to personalize and tell the US audience about all these other great athletes from other countries. When I grew to love the Olympics in the seventies and eighties, the Cold War was at its height, and it was the USA versus the USSR. Now I think the burden is on us to tell stories to make you want to watch. Why are you tuning in to watch a snowboarder from Finland? Why should you stay tuned for the next three hours?

Together with the need to internationalize and familiarize the audience with athletes of different identities is the requirement to not thrust a story onto the air simply because NBC planned to show it or in order to balance the coverage in some way. As Joe Gesue maintains:

JG: There are typically a handful of profiles that are shot but never air. This happens if an athlete completely fizzles and doesn't make air or if other storylines or circumstances lead to changes in our coverage. We will follow the ongoing and constantly changing storylines rather than force in a story if the relevance has changed.

In other words, storytelling is another part of the biggest show on television in which the best laid plans could be abandoned because the non-fictional plotline fails to fit into NBC's skeleton plan. This ongoing, adaptable process is foundational to any other subsets of storytelling, such as the identity issues focusing on nationalism, gender, and ethnicity (See Chapters 4, 5, and 6). The process of story construction begins seven years prior to an Olympic Games, but, as Gesue notes, all the best laid plans can be abandoned minutes before airtime, depending on the athletic performances and overarching storylines that develop within any Olympic Games.

Producing identity: influences of nationality, gender, and ethnicity

The criticism most often levied at NBC is that the coverage is overly nationalistic, providing the US audience with what they want to see in preference to conveying a more global experience. However, there seems to be no clear consensus over what fair and equitable treatment of international athletes would be. For instance, Joe Gesue feels there is a good balance in terms of nationalism because there is roughly the same number of profiles of US athletes as there are profiles about all other athletes combined. However, one could counter that the US (which tends to win 11–13 percent of the overall medals in a given Olympic Games) should not receive as much as half of all pre-produced profiles. Ebersol believes that NBC does quite well in terms of nationalistic equilibrium when applying the measure of any other Olympic telecast in the world:

> DE: I've had this conversation many times with broadcasters from other parts of the world. They're always amazed that media in the United States criticizes us for being too nationalistic. They feel just the opposite. They think we have the most diversity, because they literally will put a camera on one of their swimmers who's not going to finish any better than fifth. We would never do that in a million years. Our only issue is that, because of the strength of the American team, we're in every event. Most countries don't make finals in most of these sports, let alone all of them—which pretty much we do. We'd be nuts if we weren't there to document every American story that we possibly could, but at the same time, we have no hesitation whatsoever about building a whole night around a foreign athlete trying to do something they've never done before.

David Neal's beliefs coincide with those held by Ebersol, as he claims all other home broadcasts place considerably more emphasis on their own athletes, which he claims is fine, as "each broadcaster presumably knows their market and their audience better than someone from outside the country does". He provides some examples of the international narratives that he feels NBC highlighted in similar prominence to any US athletic story, arguing that these stories are among his favorites to render:

DN: Ideally, what you want to do is present the unscripted drama of the Olympics. It's not specifically geared towards American athletes. I've done seven Olympic Games, and two of my most memorable moments didn't have a thing to do with American athletes. One was Cathy Freeman winning the 400-meters in front of her home crowd in Sydney. After four years of carrying the weight of expectation of a gold medal around on her shoulders, she went out and did it with an entire country behind her. Then four years after that, in Athens, an unlikely winner, Fani Halkia, was the 400-meter hurdles gold medalist. She was someone who only a few years before that had been a broadcaster, had stopped competitive running, and all of a sudden decided to train for the Olympics. Maybe boosted by that vociferous Greek crowd behind her, she won an unlikely gold medal. To watch those moments transpire and then watch those athletes stand on the gold medal podium and hear their anthem played and hear the fans behind them singing the anthem in unison—those moments are as dramatic and memorable as any and they had nothing to do with an American athlete.

Once again, though, problems with overt nationalism concern more than merely the amount of time devoted to the athletes of each country; these matters are also pertinent within the dialogue of the NBC sportscasters. Ebersol concedes that he will regulate the approaches of his sportscasters in order to avoid coverage that is perceived as jingoistic patriotism at best, xenophobia at worst:

DE: As an announcer, you really risked going home if you ever fell into [nationalistic biases]. None of the pros who've done the gymnastics, swimming, diving, or track and field for us have ever fallen into that, but in some of the lesser sports, where you're dealing with people who may have spent their entire lifetime working on that [US] team before they retired, you might hear a "we" or an "us" that slips through. They'll not have a very pleasant conversation with somebody after that. We're the only people in the world who absolutely forbid it. We roll tapes with the talent, remind them of errors, and then we also show them how it's done right.

The use of personal pronouns ascribed to American athletes is what Molly Solomon dubs a violation of NBC's "cardinal rule". It is drummed into the cognitive psyche of sportscasters that they should avoid using preferential language for US athletes at opening seminars before the Games even begin. There is an agenda-setting (and framing) function to this, but NBC regards the avoidance of such biases as integral to its overall mission.

> MS: We do a montage of on-air clips where people use "us", "we", or "them", and, it's been terrific because over the years, we can't find examples on NBC because we have really gotten the point home to our on-air talent. That's the way it's supposed to be—we're impartial.

Langer (1981) argues that sport creates a personality system even more than a star system, in which athletes are placed in roles that imbue protagonist and antagonist constructions in order to form sporting narratives that capture audiences. This was quite evident in the Olympics during the Cold War, with ready-made adversaries to counter pre-packaged US heroes. Ebersol believes that the fall of the Berlin Wall in 1989 (the same year Ebersol became chief of NBC's Olympic division) was the "biggest seminal change" to the Olympics because it resulted in the "absence of ready-made 'villains'". Consequently, he claims NBC's coverage may receive considerable flak for stories of overcoming obstacles and personal achievement, but this became the primary way of urging the viewing audience to care about who wins in the post-Cold War era:

> DE: It became about the athletes and their dreams. Whether or not we could make you feel empathetic for them—whether they were American or international. It changed the whole complexion of the Games, because it's no longer "us against them". We don't run medal counts anymore. If we see a medal count, it's in the newspaper. But more importantly, there's not any instance in which it's "we're from the Western part of the universe and the world, and we're good, and they're from the other side and they're bad". That all went away.

Solomon asserts that the "sports as war" substitute metaphor was lost after the fall of the Berlin Wall, but that despite the altered tenor of the telecast, the primary truism NBC could rely upon was that US viewers want to see their home country do well. As a result, she acknowledges some increased focus on US athletes because of ratings and the concurrent desire to give viewers what they want to see:

> MS: Let's be honest: Americans do like to watch their countrymen! Back in the eighties, when the Olympics were oh-so-popular, you wanted

> to see the US versus the USSR, whether you wanted to watch the Soviet athletes, you did want to watch the Americans. That's the point of the Olympics [for many US viewers].

She concludes that increased US success in the Winter Games has made some of these issues a "whole different ballgame", but that someone will receive a much vaster landscape of the overall Olympic experience if they watch hours beyond primetime:

> MS: Look at our biathlon coverage and our cross-country coverage where we're not talking about the Americans. The Americans are finishing far back in the pack, but we're showing the entire race, we're personalizing the international stories. Even in figure skating, the Americans weren't the stories in pairs, aside from the throw triple-axle the first night, so, overall, we're showing so much non-American coverage.

Solomon observes that sizeable audiences will stay tuned to see which of two people from continents other than North America will win gold. Nevertheless, US athletes are shown in proportions far greater than their successes might warrant—a phenomenon that is true of any telecast of the Games internationally. Surprisingly, Dick Ebersol believes that NBC's telecast is perhaps the least nationalistically skewed of all Olympic telecasts worldwide. This assertion will be tested in Chapter 4.

Gender can also be portrayed through a network-controlled shaping function in which discourse and images are manipulated to appeal to the broadest Olympic viewership. Media frames (Goffman, 1974) help explain the modes of shaping that could be present within such telecasts, as selection, emphasis, and exclusion purposes (Gitlin, 1980) do not merely apply to clock-time and overall exposure measurements, but to the classifications of dialogue varieties that may or may not be employed by on-air network talent (anchors and reporters). For example, discourse about women's strength is emphasized if mentioned a dozen times over the course of an hour's coverage; likewise, it is excluded if a one-hour duration fails to mention women's strength a single time. Tankard (2001) argues that media framing is much more complex — and thus more influential — than media bias. The frame moves beyond the simple dichotomy of positive versus negative, defining the situation inside media discourse. However, Dick Ebersol contends that issues of gender are less likely to be a function of NBC gatekeeper choices now than they were several decades ago as the success of women Olympians mandates increased coverage and diverse dialogue. He points to the

1996 Atlanta Summer Olympics as a tipping point for US women athletes as this was the first Games in which nearly all of them had grown up with the advantages of Title IX legislation—seminal to the foundation of US women's athletic advancement.[3]

> DE: The 1996 Games, with the performance of all those women's teams—the gymnastics team, the basketball team, the soccer team—allowed any eight, ten, 12-year-old girl in America who had athletic leanings to dream at a higher level than they ever had before. For example, the performances in the '04 Olympics in large part can be drawn right back to those same people—particularly the gymnasts and swimmers—who before might have dreamed of making their high school team, but now saw there was a real chance to be on a world plane. I think the Olympics got into their dreams in the '96 Games and I'd be surprised if it ever changes again.

Molly Solomon argues that US women Olympians now do so well that gender equity is an issue that simply is "happenstance", as NBC's attempts to highlight the stories of all successful American athletes inevitably position women athletes at the forefront of much of their coverage.

> MS: We do great, but it's funny because we never think about it. Gender seems to balance out in the Olympics. Can you think of a sports festival or anything that's created like this? Where women are on equal footing as men? We're lucky to have it, and it has created some of the most popular and most influential athletes in American sports history. The Olympics have given female athletes a platform on which to make an impression on the American people.

Gesue asserts the same is true with the profiles, as he claims virtual equality in terms of the number of men's and women's profiles that are produced and aired. Nonetheless, Ebersol did admit there may be a broader gap between men and women in terms of clock-time in the Winter Games than in the Summer Games.

---

3 Title IX legislation was enacted in 1972 to ensure fair participation opportunities for both men and women at the collegiate level.

DE: I don't think I've thought it through as much with the Winter Games after the fact, but certainly since '96 with the Summer Games there was a turning point where I think the American women's teams and key women athletes became as important as the men's stories. They're really the only reason that we've held on to our superiority in the Summer Games.

Thus, in terms of clock-time, NBC doesn't feel there is considerable difference between the men and women and Joe Gesue claims that storytelling approaches are similar for both genders as well.

JG: I don't think there is a different approach between the way we characterize men athletes and women athletes. Each athlete is characterized according to their own story and all of those stories are different. Whatever is most interesting or compelling or appealing is what we will try to portray.

Referring specifically to the Winter Olympics, Solomon contends that it would be difficult to claim that the genders are treated differently because virtually everything is shown at some point since there are just a dozen events, roughly one-third of what is offered in the Summer Olympics. She explains that:

MS: We put everything on in the Winter Olympics. There's nothing left on the floor; everything's on the table. You would almost think we'd put on even more females because of all the women's figure skating that is on. There's more men's hockey games than for the women, but we put on every single women's hockey game.

However, although the clock-time devoted to each gender may be equal, the stories about male and female athletes may still be gendered (Duncan, 2006; Lorber, 1993). The issue of gender parity is investigated in Chapter 5, taking account of content analysis and the placement of sporting events—for example, whether items are positioned specifically in the primetime sportscast or during a late-night telecast on a cable network, and the nature of the commentary and use of language.

Ethnicity was the one issue that it seemed producers had thought the least about in terms of the balance of their coverage. Dick Ebersol, for instance, admitted that he'd never discussed ethnicity issues with the Olympic telecasters and that my interview with him may have been the first time he has addressed the topic:

> DE: Whatever's about to come out of my mouth will be the first time that I've ever even thought about this. The job just absolutely blinds all of that. I'm going for what I think is the richest story. If the richest story happens to be an African-American, a Malaysian, or an Ethiopian, it's of no issue to me. Some of the richest stories that we've done have been about African people and I've never thought once about whether or not there was an audience for that story. I just assumed if the story was well-told there was an audience because it was about who was the best in the world.

Thus, Ebersol declares, the lack of concentration on ethnicity issues has not been the result of negligence but rather a form of colorblindness in which the richness of the story dictates whether expanded coverage should be devoted to an athlete. Nonetheless, particularly in the Winter Games, non-White winners are so sparse that when, for instance, a Black athlete wins gold (such as Vonetta Flowers in bobsledding in 2002 or Shani Davis in speed skating in 2006), the story inexorably becomes more dynamic, making it more likely to be highlighted in the telecast. David Neal agreed that cases such as Flowers and Davis are "wonderful American stories that I think we told in full detail", but that NBC's coverage can only be as diverse as are the participants in the Games. In the Winter Games, approximately 85 percent of the athletes competing are White, making virtually any non-White winner more anomalous almost by definition. Neal claims that sometimes Black athletes are granted more salience because any "first", be it a world record or an athlete from a specific ethnic background winning an event for the first time, is noteworthy. Solomon indicated that "ethnicity is not critical to storytelling" and Ebersol dissected why the cases of Shani Davis and Vonetta Flowers made for uniquely compelling television:

> DE: In the case of Shani Davis, it was really a remarkable story, considering the single-race nature of that sport (speed skating) and living in the circumstances that he did in Chicago, quite a few miles from the best track in West Allis. It was a phenomenal story. In Vonetta's case, the day she won the gold in the women's bobsled in Salt Lake, it just didn't enter my mind that she was the first. There were only two American teams, and I actually thought the other team was going to win the morning of the event. I just don't think that way.

Joe Gesue reported that profiles of athletes of different ethnicities invariably provide stark contrasts, not in an overt sense that NBC manipulates, but in the cultural and social dynamics that led to their competing in the Olympic Games:

> JG: We make every effort to tell an interesting story about each athlete we profile; each one has a unique story to tell. Of course, the Shani Davis profile was different than the Sasha Cohen profile because their stories are different, and one of the reasons why their stories are different is because of their backgrounds. Capturing athletes in their own environment—as opposed to in their competitive space—is an effective way to make a connection between viewers and athletes. We want to show viewers where these athletes come from, which can help frame who they are. The athletes are extraordinarily talented and dedicated, but the vast majority are regular people with whom viewers can identify.

In sum, NBC producers feel the telecast acknowledges ethnicity when legitimate firsts are achieved and when background stories dictate divergent storytelling devices, but they feel limited in the Winter Games specifically because they would need to manufacture stories about why athletes are not competing in order to allow for more ethnic salience. As Solomon concludes, the overwhelming European influence of the Winter Games is likely to continue, making White athletes perpetually prominent foci of NBC's coverage. She dismisses arguments that there is some sort of bias or racist nature in who competes at a Winter Games, as she feels countries from Africa and South America are more than welcome, but that "there's a paucity because there's a lack of ice" in these arid countries.

Plausibly live?

Post-production is an additional issue distinctive to the Olympic telecast. Nearly all other US sports are shown live, but rarely is the Olympics shown live in primetime, particularly when there are immense time differentials as happened in Sydney or even in Europe. The result is that there is a tendency for the primetime telecast to be aired many hours after the event takes place (although, for instance, the odd hours for some of the cable telecasts allowed 70 percent of the Torino coverage to be shown live). Theoretically, network framing could occur not just before or during the sporting event, but could even happen after the event takes place, creating new storylines and allowing for new voiced discourse to produce an Olympic product that is more appealing. Nonetheless, Neal declares there is no way NBC has the time to exert this type of micromanaged influence:

DN: The nuance that is overlooked by 99 percent of the people who are trying to analyze what we do from the outside looking in is that, in the Olympics, when you're doing hundreds and hundreds of hours of coverage over multiple platforms, you don't have the luxury of sitting around, painstakingly doing some sort of post-production work. Even though the European Olympics certainly present a time-delay situation for us, we cover the events live as they're happening. Al Trautwig's (gymnastics sportscaster) commentary, for example, is live to tape as the events are happening. That's the way we want it, too, because we want the spontaneous reaction of both our play-by-play people and our analysts. We want them to react to things as they see it transpire so it has authenticity when it goes on the air.

NBC seems to universally resist the term "plausibly live" which many sportswriters now use rather than "live to tape", which replaced the concept of "tape delay" to assure the audience that the actual athletic performance is not being reinterpreted for easier viewer consumption or to alleviate errors or misrepresentations that NBC may not want to convey. Solomon says that producing the studio show (with the anchor) is different from producing the actual athletic event (with on-site reporters) because the studio show is where the pieces of the puzzle allow for cohesion of the overall Olympic product. Consequently, the dialogue of the host may change after an event takes place to allow for a better lead to the story or to assemble the telecast in a more unified format (e.g. if a presumed favorite fails to make the finals of an event, the programming may shift). With the actual sporting event, however, Solomon asserts that there is little practical difference between the taped product and what is seen several hours later:

MS: I don't think of it as plausibly live because I think that puts you in a hole. Our sportscasters do their best work when they call the action live. It guarantees that we capture the emotion of the moment and the authenticity of our announcer's reaction as an event happens. Tom Hammond (figure skating and track and field sportscaster) calls the event just as the viewer sees it unfold at home. For me (producing a studio program) it's the same attitude. I'll know that a certain biathlete has won a race, but I'm not going to let that influence myself or my writers in how we lead to the event. Sure, you have a little more time to prepare for the tag because you know how it ends, so maybe you can dig a little deeper for information, but it doesn't change where I put it in the show.

Still, of all the barriers to continued Olympic ratings successes, NBC producers seem to be in agreement that showing taped coverage in primetime is the biggest obstacle to overcome. Solomon notes that "the audience doesn't put up with taped coverage anymore, because they know the answer" and Ebersol and Neal maintain that time-delay issues diminished their favorite Olympic telecast, Sydney in 2000. Neal felt it would be nearly unanimous among the NBC personnel that Sydney was their favorite, but the 15–18-hour time difference (depending on East vs. West Coast) made the Games nearly impossible to convey with a sense of immediacy. Ebersol characterized Sydney as perhaps his most difficult challenge as an organizational manager for this same reason:

> DE: From a leadership standpoint, almost all of us had an incredible love affair with Sydney. We loved doing those Games. But because of the time difference, those Games weren't the enormous ratings that many of us hoped they would be. There was so much of a barrage on the ratings drop in the American media back home, so I had to make all our people know that they're doing the best possible job that they can, and you can't change anything back at home just because they know the results 15 hours in advance.

The problem of airing the Olympics on tape in a world increasingly in touch with immediate information (e.g. Internet, cellular phone updates, or 24-hour cable sports reports) presents a looming test for the NBC team. Many ideas have been proposed, but some appear suicidal to a network (showing all events live could mean airing a high-profile event at 4 a.m.) and even ideas that have some merit (showing some events twice—one live and one taped in primetime) represent incredible risks. For those who would like NBC to virtually reinvent their Olympic telecast, Solomon counters that "You've got a huge product that's worth a lot of money and it's hard to take too many risks at one time".

Conclusions

NBC Sports producers admit that the Olympic coverage is not perfect, conceding that it will never be, largely because of the grand scope and epic nature of the whirlwind event. Still, they all were earnest in their desire to continually develop the Olympic telecast and welcomed interviews such as the ones for this book which examined interlocking issues of identity, storytelling, and framing. Neal claimed that this type of Olympic analysis is "something that is long overdue" because of the misinformation that can become pervasive in the popular press. He considers the large majority of criticism lobbied at NBC's Olympic telecast to be "groundless", but that NBC Sports nonetheless examines worthy critiques because:

DN: Complacency is probably our biggest enemy, and it's always good to hear from people who have paid real attention to it from the outside. That makes us stop collectively and reexamine if there is anything we missed. It's always good to stop and have a little introspection as well.

The production schedule for the Games dictates that producers nearly immediately bound on to the next Olympics after the torch is extinguished at the previous Games. For instance, attempts to interview Ebersol and Neal shortly after the Torino Winter Olympics necessitated waiting for their return from China, where they were already making production decisions about the 2008 Summer Olympics in Beijing, two and a half years prior to their commencement. As a result, producers are afforded little time to scrutinize their work (Solomon argues that producing for the Olympics requires a person to be "like an athlete who's peaking every two years"). Still, Neal looks forward to another chance to improve in 2008, noting their biggest upcoming challenge:

DN: I think we need to do an even more effective job of bringing a sense of place to the broadcast. When we're in Beijing in 2008, we need to capture what it's like to be there. We need to convey a sort of magic carpet ride for our viewers and let them see what it's like to be there in the middle of the capital of China with the athletes of the world there. The atmospherics are a great opportunity; I believe there's a natural curiosity on many Americans' part on China. We need to recognize that and feed that curiosity.

Innovation appears to be at the forefront of many producers' thoughts as they move forward, mostly in terms of technological advancements of the visual depiction of the televised Games, but also with regard to ties to other digital media, notably the Internet. Neal claims that the "natural realities of the business require us to keep looking for ways to be more efficient", but that the ultimate goal is to portray an unscripted and innovative Olympic experience. He places most of the credit for the work that has been done thus far on the shoulders of network pioneer, Dick Ebersol:

DN: It all begins with Dick. He sets the tone for all of us. The Olympics are really more of a remarkable global gathering with sports as its coincidental centerpiece. Dick often talks about how the favorite moment for him at any Olympics comes in the Opening Ceremony of the

Summer Games, where all of the athletes stand on the infield and when the last contingent, which is always the host nation's team, marches in there are some 200 nations gathered as one. That, arguably, is the most important moment of any Olympics, when the youth of the world is gathered there for this peaceful, sports celebration. He reminds us that it's vitally important for us to be true to the competition. To be accurate in our descriptions and pictures.

The nebulous notion of accuracy is mentioned again here. Perhaps that is the grandest goal of all Olympic production: to be viewed as conveying a fair, unbiased, and accurate vision of Olympic achievement. Rowe (2003) notes that "being the Olympic station brings with it a great deal of kudos" because, if handled appropriately, NBC can prove that it "can handle with distinction one of the world's largest media events" (p. 75).

3 Chronicling history

The Olympic sportscasters

> The color man puts the game in its emotional and historical perspective; the play-by-play ... is the discourse of liveness ... a sense of immediacy and virtual reality to the representation of sports on TV.
>
> (Rose and Friedman, 1997, p. 6)

The most visible agents of sports media processes are, unquestionably, the sports-casters. They have the power to shape and frame a story like no other by using vivid and dramatic forms of language (Wenner, 1989). Sports fans (see Real and Mechikoff, 1992) can often imitate their all-time favorite sportscasters whose vocal styles and personalities have become etched within elaborate memories of sport experiences. Viewers in the United States, for example, have certain sporting moments that are indelibly coupled with the language of the sportscaster, such as Kirk Gibson's walk-off home run in the 1988 Major League Baseball World Series when Jack Buck exclaimed, "I don't believe what I just saw!"[1] and Bobby Thompson's "shot heard 'round the world'".[2] Furthermore, "even with the express purpose of providing play-by-play descriptions of moves and skills and results, 'game' announcing provides a goodly portion of dramatic commentary" (Wenner, 1989, p. 30).

Sportscasters of all types have a tendency to create their personas and on-air styles through a process that is influenced by cultural standards and practices. As Whannel (1992) points out, "the development of the practice of commentary, the decisions as to style and types of contributor, [are] all dependent on a set of assumptions and hypotheses as to the nature of the audience of sport" (p. 30). The result is that, particularly within the 27 percent of all coverage that is interpretive

---

1 Gibson was injured and could not have even run to first base, but was able to limp to the plate and win the game for the Los Angeles Dodgers.
2 The New York Giants' Bobby Thompson hit a home run to defeat the Brooklyn Dodgers and win the National League pennant. The phrase particularly pertained to servicemen listening to the game while stationed at the Korean War.

in nature (Bryant *et al.*, 1977), commentary is influenced by the sportscasters' personal identity/background (Hutchby, 2005) and—perhaps more importantly—the desired role of the sportscaster within the mediated sporting event. Interpretive commentary is usually not rendered by the play-by-play sportscaster, but instead is spoken by the "color" commentator, whose job is to place athletic performances within broader contexts in order to enhance the overall understanding of a sport. As Schultz (2005) articulates, the play-by-play sportscaster focuses on the "who and what", whereas the color analyst provides the "how and why" (Schultz, 2005, p. 136).

Three sportscasters who are central to the reporting of NBC's Olympic experience were interviewed specifically regarding the role of storytelling and narrative as they relate to nationality, gender, and ethnicity: (1) Bob Costas, who has served as primetime host (anchor) for the Olympic Games since 1992 in Barcelona; (2) Jim Lampley, who worked his record thirteenth Olympic telecast in Torino as an anchor for afternoon and late-night coverage; and (3) Tom Hammond, who is the sportscaster for two major Olympic events—track and field in the Summer Games and figure skating in the Winter Games. In addition, interviews were conducted with four former US Olympians who have also served as Olympic sportscasters: (1) Donna deVarona, the first US woman sportscaster and gold medalist in swimming; (2) Ann Meyers Drysdale, member of the 1976 silver-medal-winning basketball team and Olympic sportscaster for basketball; (3) John Naber, gold medalist in swimming and Olympic sportscaster in several different sports; and (4) Peter Vidmar, gymnastics multi-medalist and sportscaster. Collectively, the seven sportscaster interviews have provided original insight into the role of the sportscaster within the US Olympic telecast. Several megathemes were present in their comments, including (a) *grandiosity* [arguing that the Olympics is such a large event to produce that problems naturally occur], (b) *progress* [indicating that while problems may remain, the telecast has alleviated many of them], (c) *history* [highlighting a noble sense of chronicling historical events within social, cultural, and political contexts beyond merely documenting sporting achievement], and (d) *equality* [indicating whether the balance of any dichotomous issue, whether it is men/women or heavy drama/lighter moments, is considered by the sportscasters to be appropriate for the occasion].

Preparation for the Olympic telecast

The three NBC sportscasters for the Torino Games were first queried as to how they prepare for the Olympics. The sportscasters agreed that planning is imperative specifically for the Olympics because the event involves thousands of athletes—the large majority of whom are not readily recognized by the general population or even the sportscasters themselves. Bob Costas indicated that his role is to be that of a "generalist" with the goal being to bridge gaps between countries and athletes, making connections that are otherwise not readily made:

BC: You try to become familiar, at least in a general way, with the history of the host city and the host country. Does the country have a president or a prime minister? What are the security arrangements and chain of command? What are the key issues facing the city and nation? What is its significance globally? Are they an ally of the United States? How do people in the country feel about US government and/or US citizens (which are not always exactly the same thing)? What is their Olympic history?

Costas felt that it was imperative for the Olympic anchor/host to know about political, cultural, and social issues within not only the host country, but for any of the countries competing. He could then affix his knowledge of the athletes and sports to these broader issues beyond the immediately observable athletic performances, whether that concerns economic or political issues, personal triumphs or tragedies, judging scandals or performance-enhancing drug allegations:

BC: You basically want to know the 20 or 25 top athletes or stories that are likely to emerge. It's a waste of time and an impossible task for any person to know every bobsledder from every country, or every whitewater rafter. And it's not the job of the primetime host to know that. It's my job to know the two dozen or so particular stories that likely will need to be told.

Indeed, Bob Costas viewed the Opening Ceremonies, in particular, to be an opportunity to frame big stories. For instance, he mentioned drawing some criticism in 2004, when he indicated that Greece was overwhelmingly pro-American, but was not enamored with the current policies of the US government. He felt such a remark was apt given that (a) the Greek team had just entered the stadium, (b) Athens was serving as host of the Olympics, and (c) the United States was a country at war.[3] Others felt he should confine his commentary to sports and the athletes participating in the Games. Costas vehemently disagrees, claiming that there is a "vast mosaic" of issues that should be addressed and that:

---

3   The US-led war in Iraq began in 2003 and was a primary focus of the national landscape during the 2004 Summer Olympics in Athens.

> BC: If it feels like a newscast or C-SPAN,[4] it's gone way too far. But there is a time and place for discussing serious issues outside the traditional boundaries of the sporting venue. The host's job should be to interweave these issues into the Olympic story along with [reports of] the athletic competition.

Jim Lampley spoke of his preparation as something that is "internal and cumulative", given that he has worked on so many Olympic telecasts (dating back to Innsbruck in 1976):

> JL: I have a kind of internal orientation to the process that only comes from depth of experience, so my preparation is probably less intense in some ways than people would suspect. NBC sends out a series of compendiums—research reports, six to seven pages of up-to-date information on all of the sports every couple of weeks for the few months leading up to the Olympics. I read the *Sports Illustrated* Olympic preview issue, and *USA Today's* Olympic preview. Beyond that, I don't try to put too much in my saddle bag.

As Dick Ebersol contends, this minimalist approach serves Lampley well, as his expertise provides him with a sense of history that even the Internet cannot duplicate. As a result, he appears to rely chiefly on his own first-hand accounts. He spoke of his role as anchor in a similar manner to Costas:

> JL: The host's role is to establish an atmosphere; to cue the audience as to the majesty of the event and where it's pitched on the social spectrum. To encourage people to keep blowing from story to story, gathering the whole experience. I go to work with the basic orientation that I need, and try to be curious, eager, and responsive. Tom Hammond's role is quite different given that he is an on-site reporter.

Whereas Costas and Lampley need to possess a breadth of information across all sports, Hammond, in turn, must provide the depth of information that avid fans of a specialized sport demand, especially since the sports he covers (figure skating

---

4 C-SPAN (Cable-Satellite Public Affairs Network) is a television channel exclusively devoted to government and public affairs matters.

and track and field) have mass followings during the Games. As such, his preparation is slightly different:

> TH: You can't kind of "cram", like you would for an exam, days before the Olympics. You have to stay current. You have the US Olympic trials, which gets you pretty much up to speed on the US athletes. Every time there's a figure skating or a track and field event on TV, I'll record it. I read the publications and try to stay current on everything. Then, about a month out, the preparations get more intense with reading all the newspaper clippings NBC provides us. So then you go to work on that, whittling out the important information. By the time we get to the site, we'll sit there with the major athletes—both foreign and US—and get their stories first-hand.

All three primary interviewees spoke of the vital role of the research team, which has evolved from a single person at Jim Lampley's inaugural Olympics in 1976 to a group of 30 three decades later. This cluster of researchers cue the sportscasters as to what stories are likely to transpire and what the "inside story" could potentially entail. Costas indicated that at any given time, three people are in the studio with him to supplement his work with additional information. He is also cautious not to insert himself as a core component too often, frequently opting to be like a ringmaster in an elaborate show:

> BC: There are times when you're basically being a traffic cop. You're getting it from Point A to Point B; you hope to do it smoothly and credibly. But then there are times not only when you do interviews, but there are times when you do commentary. Straight reporting, highlights, traffic copping, commentary, some kind of perspective, hopefully some humor ... it's all part of the job description.

Lampley was amazingly impressed with the product that can be generated at an Olympic Games, claiming that the availability of information and access to dozens of research assistants make his job "the easiest gig known to man". The 30 people who work full-time providing information for anchors and sportscasters represent more than he has experienced in any previous sportscast in his vaunted career. Consequently, Lampley purports that the situation provides such an opportunity for success that "if you can't succeed in that environment, you can't work in our business".

In sum, NBC gives tremendous importance to advance planning for the Olympics so that the preparation for the Olympic sportscasters is more intensive than for any other sporting event (Lampley explicitly concurred by comparing his Olympic work to boxing telecasts). While the producers, Ebersol and Neal, are working on any given sportscast seven years in advance, sportscasters have significantly less time to prepare. NBC therefore utilizes research compendiums and a large group of experts who produce the information necessary to supplement and augment the storytelling process. Costas, Lampley, and Hammond, three of the most visible and recognizable personalities at the NBC telecast, all appreciate that their job is made infinitely easier by the thousands of additional NBC employees at the Games who are present, at least in some small way, to make them look good.

Storytelling

The theme NBC employed for the 2006 Torino Olympic Opening Ceremony was "Tonight, we come to hear stories". I asked each of the sportscasters about the role of storytelling within the telecast, and, in particular, whether storytelling played a markedly dynamic role within the Olympics as opposed to other sporting events. They were also queried about how they would respond to avid sports fans who assert that they do not "come to hear stories" but rather come to watch sports. Hammond replied:

> TH: It's always the fine line that we walk and we don't always successfully do it. Let's use track and field. The people that follow it religiously are going to be offended by all the emphasis on storytelling. They want to just see action because they already know all the stories; they just want to see the action. But our idea is that those people are going to watch no matter what, because whether they're satisfied or not with the way we do it, they're going to want to see it. It's our job to tell the uninitiated—the casual fans—stories of all the different athletes, so they have some reason to care whether they win or lose. There's no sense in watching a race, or any athletic event really, unless you have an interest in who wins and who loses.

Costas finds the Olympics to be quite different from other sportscasts partly because storytelling must be a major thrust of any work that is done within the telecast. He contends that, "It's all the context, the meaning, the mythology, the drama, the history of the Olympics that give it such appeal" and claims that while the primary function of the telecast is to show sporting events, it is also secondarily about "political and social issues existing within and among countries". Hammond was unequivocal and unapologetic about storytelling being a vital part of what he does, implying that there are roles within any story that must be fulfilled to have someone to root for and, conversely, someone to dislike:

TH: It's our job to give the stories, whether they're good stories, bad stories, touching stories, or stories that might make someone angry. We have to create heroes and villains and all of those things by telling the individual stories. Especially in an event like the Olympics, storytelling is important.

Many critics argue that, for better or worse, NBC's Olympic telecast provides a stark contrast to other national broadcasts of the Olympic Games that tend to veer from minimalism to unrepentant nationalism. The sportscasters also view themselves as neutral agents who must inform a largely uninitiated audience about not just the enacted athletic moments, but the cultural, social, historical, political, and personal contexts in which such performances reside. Lampley contrasts the US coverage with the Olympic experience in European television, noting that the American tradition has been "to reach out and touch them. To extend an arm out of the set and touch somebody"—a mode of storytelling that Lampley claims allows NBC's telecast to "documents things from people's inner experiences out".

As for the tone of the Olympics, Costas was well aware of critiques of the NBC telecast as schmaltzy, dramatic, and over-emphasized inspiration but feels he does a sound job of maintaining the balance between hyperbole and genuine emotion. He cites the massive scope of the Olympics as the reason why there is a tendency for people to view it as unadulterated pomp and circumstance:

BC: The Olympics are an epic event, so can anything be overstated? Yes, you can always overplay any hand, and I think it's fair to say that I tend to be less hyperbolic than some people. But they happen only once every four years, the whole thing happens within two and a half weeks, and it's the largest global event there is. So, there is an epic quality about this.

Costas has probably worked for more megasporting events than any other working US sportscaster today, ranging from the World Series to the Super Bowl to the NBA Finals to golf's United States Open. Yet, he classifies the way he works at an Olympics as "quite different", partly because he's previewing and detailing sports that usually are not discussed in Western societies other than every four years when the Olympics occur. As a result, the host must be proficient enough to anticipate questions that the viewing audience might ask and provide information so that viewers are not puzzled by what they are consuming:

> BC: What the hell is curling? Why should we care about it? It seems sort
> of quirky and weird. Race walking—what's that about? Why do peo-
> ple do it? And are there parts of the world—and there are—where
> this is a big deal? Where a top race walker is a big celebrity? There
> are parts of the world where a badminton player is a big deal?
> Absolutely. Say, here's a diver from China. She may be roughly the
> same skill level as the diver from California. But the circumstances
> that produced this person are entirely different. If you don't give peo-
> ple at least some sense of what the path was that brought them here,
> why should they care?

Costas also spoke about the amount of control he has over his on-air dialogue.
Given the immensity of the events, it would be understandable if the host became
a virtual "talking head" who simply reads what has been prepared for him and has
talking points when conducting interviews. However, Costas preserves some sta-
bility between being overwhelmed by the assignment and being able to control
and regulate what he conveys within the primetime telecast. He admits that he
has tremendous help in assembling the stories he tells, but that he understands he
will ultimately be responsible for what he says on air. He says that writers and
researchers and producers help produce formats and spreads but that "every word
I ever say I'm either ad-libbing, I've written myself, or I've edited or rewritten to
some extent". Costas's comments underscore that no matter how many producers
and researchers are present to aid the sportscaster, the praise (if a telecast is
deemed successful) or blame (if it's dubbed a failure) resides chiefly on the shoulders of the on-screen talent. Lampley sums up the gravity of the work of a
sportscaster when he asserts that he has the "ultimate control in the sense that I
do it. I execute it. It comes through my being and I am powerfully disposed".

Portraying nationality

The bias that most critics of the Olympics claim is especially rampant within
NBC's telecast is pro-American sentiment, contending that NBC's telecast
focuses the overwhelming majority of air-time on US athletes and describes US
athletes in markedly different ways from their descriptions of foreign athletes.
Such beliefs can be explained by psychological theory, specifically self-categorization theory (Turner *et al.*, 1987), which postulates that there are times when
people view themselves as individuals and other times when people believe they
are part of a group. Self-categorization theorists contend that perceived group
memberships play integral roles in the formation of self-identity. The fact that
NBC's Olympic story is told predominantly by White American males
(www.nbcolympics.com) could influence the ways in which Whites, Americans,
and male athletes are depicted, providing a sharp contrast to sportscaster discourse about, say, Blacks, females, and non-American athletes.

Questions arise concerning who the sportscasters believe they are representing at the moment when they speak on-air—whether they exhibit biases in favor of athletes with whom they self-identify; whether they are ignorant or prejudiced about people of other nations, genders, or ethnicities, or whether there are moments when they pay less attention to athletes from their own identity group for fear of being perceived as less than objective.

Some of the sportscaster comments intimated that their primary focus was to be a mouthpiece for NBC and to follow its philosophy and directives. For example, the interviewed sportscasters confirmed what the producers had already reported: that one of the biggest faux pas a sportscaster could commit at the Olympics was to use personal pronouns such as "us", "we", or "our" to describe the US team. NBC's on-air talent are specifically told before the Games to avoid such cheerleading (overtly supporting one athlete or team over others) at all costs. The interviewees felt NBC did a fairly solid job at achieving this objective, as Hammond suggests below:

> TH: I did basketball with Al McGuire in Seoul in 1988. He was guilty a couple of times of saying "our" and "their", and was ... reprimanded would be too strong a word, but he was gently reminded. It's a cardinal sin at NBC to say, "Well *our* team did this" or "*our* team did that". It's always the "US" team. Maybe that's just window dressing, but that's the heart of the philosophy: that we're trying to give everybody equal press.

Scholars such as Williams (1994) have argued that sport can, indeed, influence the way cultures are portrayed on a global level. John Naber claimed that while things have changed (i.e. "There used to be someone to root for and someone to root against") and might revert back to an "us vs. them" mindset in 2008 in Beijing (i.e. "I do believe the Chinese have opened the door to allow the Beijing Olympics to be a test of America versus China"), nationalism always trumps specific athletic achievement. Says Naber:

> JN: To be honest with you, nobody has ever known the difference between a hundred-meter backstroke in 55.5, or a hundred-meter backstroke in 54.8. They're not looking at the athletic achievement itself; it's always in relationship to whether or not they win the gold. We all know that Carl Lewis won the long jump, but how far did he jump? Those issues aren't important.

Peter Vidmar agreed, noting that when an athlete competed in the Cold War era, it was "Eastern Bloc versus Western Bloc, [but there] really aren't any arch rivals anymore". Ann Meyers Drysdale explained the role of nationalism in a compare/contrast fashion as well:

> AMD: With communism in the seventies and eighties, it was the concept of the good guy/bad guy. We wore the red, white and blue. Communist countries wore red. I find it interesting that the majority of these other countries are now wearing red, white, and blue!

The reduced emphasis on Cold War political antagonisms has resulted in the increase of storytelling formats, which also allows an opportunity for NBC to convey more stories about foreign athletes. The post-Cold War era has offered NBC the opportunity to utilize its telecast to chronicle history and offer a less jingoistic approach to the Games.

Nonetheless, the stigma that appears to be the most lasting is that NBC's broadcasters are emphatically pro-American. After all, the viewing audience in the US rarely tunes in to "see how the men are doing" or claim that they want to "see if the Caucasian can win the speed skate". However, millions watch to support their national team—in this case, the United States. Jim Lampley contends that the notion of "feeding the beast" does not result in an overly pro-American sportscast.

> JL: Among the people who work in the building, there is absolutely no conscious pro-American bias. If you drink the Kool-Aid, if you buy into the Olympics, as I most certainly do, then one of the things you're buying into is the sheer international quality of it all. I think all of us can get just as enthused about an athlete from Belarus as we can about an athlete from the United States. The biggest hero in Sydney was Cathy Freeman, not just for Australians, but for everybody.

Lampley contended that if there was a group with which the sportscasters self-identified, it was not necessarily the American athletes but rather the athletes and teams—regardless of country—that most aptly exhibited the Olympic spirit. He provides a powerful example to illustrate the assertion that NBC is not unabashedly rooting for the US team:

JL: I'll never forget that night in Australia when, in the men's basketball semifinal, Lithuania had a one-point lead with about 29 seconds to go and seemed to have a shot—they were going to knock off the United States. I happened to be in the broadcast center. It was close to midnight, still probably 115 people in the NBC broadcast center working that night. Everybody had a monitor. I don't care where you were, everybody had the game on. If there were 115 people watching, there were 115 people rooting for Lithuania. I guarantee it. There wasn't a person in the building who didn't want Lithuania to win that game. So the bottom line is, I think we err dramatically towards the other side. But on the other hand, we have audience decisions to make; we have conscious decisions to make about which story is going to attract the largest audience. And, as that process filters through, inevitably you're going to see stars and stripes. That's just intelligent programming.

Lampley separates the clock-time issue—which he concedes favors Americans largely in order to secure high ratings—and sportscaster dialogue, which he claims, if anything, leans away from praising American athletes (likely because of the stigma-consciousness discussed previously). Tom Hammond holds a similar position:

TH: Yes, we're primarily interested in US athletes. Let's say we have to shorten an event, and we'll just show the finish. We're more likely to show it if a US athlete is involved perhaps than a foreign athlete that no one knows, but we try to give everyone the same play on the airways.

John Naber articulates the catch-22 situation that NBC is in with regard to chronicling history while securing high ratings, ardently maintaining that:

JN: You're not trying to cover the event fairly; you're trying to draw viewership into the program. As such, we believe that ratings must be the ultimate end-game because, without them, the Olympic telecast is significantly diminished. If I'm a General Electric stockholder, I don't want Dick Ebersol to be "fair".

He adds that sometimes tremendous stories of non-American athletic achievements fail to appeal to US viewers:

> JN: In 1988, I worked with NBC and Janet Evans and Matt Biandi[5] who were the big superstars of the team. But the top female swimmer of all time was an East German named Kristen Otto, who won six gold medals at those Olympics. I don't think that we gave her nearly the attention that she deserved because she wasn't one of "ours".

Some sportscasters have attempted to remedy nationalistic biases by ensuring that fundamental features of the stories of athletes from across the world are conveyed accurately. Notes Ann Meyers Drysdale:

> AMD: You really have to do your homework. Mike Breen and I worked very hard in the Olympic telecast to ensure that we were saying the names correctly. It sounds simple, but you have to be willing to go down there and ask an athlete how they say their name if you want credibility in covering international sports.

Bob Costas compares the NBC coverage to that of other countries, claiming that NBC is far more balanced than other countries in rendering a full palate of Olympic experiences. When asked explicitly about whether NBC's coverage is unabashedly American, he claimed it was a myth, noting that:

> BC: Sometimes a notion will take hold and it doesn't make any difference what the actual facts may be; it's just an easy notion and people return to it. One of the notions that people have—not without some historical basis—is that American television is xenophobic in its coverage of the Olympics. If that's true, then most every other nation is xenophobic to the tenth power because, if you look at non-American TV, they tend to focus on their own competitors to an even greater extent including sometimes when they have no chance to win. You go to Pakistan, they'll show you badminton all day long because they're good at it. All countries do this to one extent or another.

5   Both Evans and Biandi are highly decorated, gold-medal-winning US swimmers.

Costas also contends that other factors influence how much the "home" (as defined by the network's home rather than the Olympic venue) country is shown within a given telecast. As Dick Ebersol contended in the previous chapter, one of the reasons US athletes are highlighted a significant amount is that they are usually major players in the majority of high-profile Olympic sports. Many Americans are key focal points of other national Olympic broadcasts as well. For example, track and field star Carl Lewis has said that he's more frequently recognized in Europe than in the United States. The American athletes are not the only story but, for many of the major sports such as gymnastics, track and field, and figure skating, they are key components of the storytelling experience. Costas illustrates:

> BC: Let's say in Canada, the impression may be that they concentrate less
>   on Canadian athletes. But, in fairness, while Canadian athletes may do
>   well, a smaller percentage of them do well than American athletes.
>   There's a limit to how many Canadian athletes you can show with a
>   medal around their neck, if they win ten medals and the United States
>   wins 62.

Costas concedes that American athletes sometimes receive more air-time than their successes would seem to warrant, but he also feels this is an aspect of NBC's telecast that has significantly improved over time and that few critics have noticed the shift:

> BC: I'm not saying that it is never true that there's too much emphasis on
>   American athletes; I think it has been true at times in the past. But it
>   has become less true in the last two or three Olympics. A lot of
>   observers have been slow to catch on. If an American wins a gold
>   medal in swimming and they show the medal stand, I always make it a
>   point to talk about the guy from Peru who got the bronze, and the
>   guy from Germany who took the silver. That is a criticism which once
>   was apt, but it's a fair criticism much less often now. Still, people
>   almost repeat it by rote.

One of the criticisms directed toward NBC is that the telecast had tremendous influence in how the 2002 Salt Lake City Winter Olympic pairs figure-skating scandal developed, leading to the awarding of gold medals to both the Russian and the Canadian teams because virtually everyone but the majority of the judges felt the Canadian team should have won the gold. Percolating controversy resulted in many ensuing features on NBC, which some claim led to the investigation of a corrupt French judge, who later admitted to fraudulent behavior that had resulted in the Russian win. Hammond was asked about the role NBC played in the scandal:

> TH: I don't think anyone could help but be influenced by the way we covered it. The emphasis we put on it, all the resources we poured into it, examining it and everything else. Our analysts were so adamant and had to start somewhat of the push for restitution. Then the print media started picking it up, because it was what everyone in the country who watched the broadcast was talking about. They reacted to it as well, and that added more momentum to the push to do something.

I also asked Hammond whether he felt that if these two skaters were not from North America, a second gold medal would not have been awarded—essentially a query arguing whether reversing the nationality of the two pairs of skaters substantially changes the story (and subsequent outrage at the results):

> TH: I don't think that's correct. We go out of our way to be as impartial as we can be. Any kind of injustice—whether it affects US and Canadian athletes or Russian athletes—we try to be as fair as we can be, to tell the real story rather than let the allegiances get in the way. Maybe that's naive, but that's my contention.

A potential test of the reverse-identity group phenomenon could be argued to have become reality two years later in Athens, when US gymnast Paul Hamm won the individual all-around gold medal, only to discover the next day that South Korean gymnast Yang Tae Young received a lower score on the pommel horse than he should have because the judges placed a 9.9 start value on the routine when it should have been a 10.0, a difference that would have given Yang the gold. Hamm ultimately kept the gold medal, as the argument was made that gymnastics is a fluid competition, with gymnasts reacting differently depending on what the scores were at the time. In other words, Yang Tae Young and Paul Hamm's later routines could have changed if the higher pommel horse score had been in place. Still, an argument was made that Yang should be awarded the gold, with Hamm dropping to silver. Others felt the answer was to again have dual gold medalists as was the case in pairs figure skating two years earlier. However, the results remained, with Hamm keeping the gold medal. Would the results have been changed if Hamm had been the one petitioning for the gold? Would NBC have made it a bigger story, injecting more pressure to the situation? Costas admits that more could have been done within the coverage to highlight the controversy:

> BC: When Paul Hamm was awarded the gold and the South Korean probably was screwed a little bit, I think that you can do almost a miniature *Nightline*[6] about that. Not something that belongs on PBS[7] but something that has both television appeal and journalistic content. Many journalistic stories can be presented in a way that is also good television.

Hammond concludes that what sportscasters should strive to achieve is to unearth the best stories to render, whether they are American or international in nature. He believes that if you tell the correct story in the proper way, ratings will naturally follow:

> TH: It's up to us to give the interesting stories of the other athletes so that people are interested in watching them as well—not just the US athletes. It's so important, especially in the Olympics. Just think of all the interesting foreign athletes that people have not heard of. Maybe there's someone that's only interested in watching US athletes, but if you give them a story about foreign athletes, they usually find that that's extremely interesting. They have a reason to watch his race or her race as well.

Hammond noted that if the stories are constructed properly, no one minds if the athlete is from the United States or not:

> TH: If you watched the figure skating, it was difficult not to root for [Russian] Irina Slutskaya[8] after you saw the picture of all the trouble she's had with her health, her mom's health, how devoted she is to her mother, all her frustrations in her skating, coming up just short. It was difficult not to be for her, or to want her to do well, whoever you were. The personal story transcended all else.

6 *Nightline* is a long-running, hard news, late-night network program on the ABC broadcasting network.
7 Public Broadcasting Service, a not-for-profit American network that tends to run significantly more hard news programs than for-profit networks.
8 Slutskaya was a European and World champion figure skater competing in her third Olympics in 2006.

In summary, the sportscasters seem to view nationalism issues as a double-edged sword, admitting that the telecast must inevitably veer toward US athletes more than athletes from other countries, but also firmly maintaining that compared to any other telecast in any other country, NBC's telecast is the least flagrantly biased with regard to nationalism. Examination of airtime content in Chapter 4 throws further light upon the question of potential pro-US biases.

Portraying gender

Without question, the Olympics showcase women athletes in ways that no other sporting events (barring, perhaps, professional tennis) provide. Still, studies have shown (Billings and Eastman, 2002, 2003; Tuggle and Owen, 1999) that women have not been showcased adequately if comparing their relative successes at the Olympics over the past several decades to the clock-time they receive or the number of times they are mentioned, both of which are critical salience appraisals regarding gender. Coakley (2004) highlighted the important role that the media play with regard to gender, claiming that "Seeing women athletes on television and reading about them in newspapers and magazines encourage girls and women to be active as athletes themselves" (p. 244). Messner (1993) adopts a similar tack in asserting, "It is reasonable to speculate that gender is a salient organizing theme in the construction of meanings, especially with respect to the more aggressive and violent aspects of sport" (p. 168). The long history of male power and hegemony (Hargreaves, 1994, 2000) and the significance of gender as an organizing theme in the sports media underpin the following investigation about how each of the NBC sportscasters believes the Olympic telecast portrays gender. Bob Costas was sensitive to the Olympic telecast's standing as a supporter of women's athletics.

> BC: I think we do real well. It speaks well of what people expect of the Olympics and, by extension, from the Olympic network. They hold it to a higher standard, so they expect it to be a platform for both men and women. People don't expect the women's college basketball tournament to get the same amount of coverage as the men's, but they expect some parity in the Olympics. Jackie Joyner-Kersee ought to get just about as much time as Carl Lewis, when they're at their respective peaks. By and large, that's what happens. It's good television.

The notion of "good television" relates to Lampley's contentions about gender in women's sport as well:

> JL: Women athletes certainly get more even exposure at the Olympics than throughout the overall culture of sports television. Does that

happen because there's a preponderance of women in the audience and producers and executives are heavily conscious of that? Or did a preponderance of women in the audience evolve because the Olympics are the kind of event that invite you to look at the women's story taking place on the same playing field, in the same timeframe, shoulder to shoulder with men's athletics?

Hammond echoed this sentiment, suggesting that the network shows more women's sports because ratings dictate it. NBC has found that American audiences enjoy seeing Olympic events regardless of gender—sometimes even showing a preference for women's events (as evidenced by the high ratings NBC attained in 2004 when beach volleyballers Kerri Walsh and Misty May forged their way to a gold medal). Americans particularly like watching their national team win gold and the female members of the US Olympic team have clocked more and more successes in recent Olympics. As a result, women Olympians are more likely to be aired than sportswomen in other events and other telecasts.

Nevertheless, Costas concedes that sometimes women's stories are underplayed, such as with the 1996 gold-medal-winning US women's soccer team. Many of the sportscasters regard 1996 in Atlanta as the tipping point for women's athletics as it was the first Games to have the majority of women athletes who had grown up in the post-Title IX era. As Donna deVarona (widely credited with being the first US woman sportscaster) describes:

DdV: Although there has been an increasing acceptance and appreciation of the talents of women athletes and the Olympic doors have been opened wide, there is still much more to be done. A breakthrough came after the Atlanta Olympics when NBC Sports Chairman Dick Ebersol realized that the Olympic audience was uniquely interested in seeing women athletes. Therefore, in subsequent Olympics, he has given them more coverage. However, it was during the Atlanta Games that NBC failed to cover the sold-out and very popular women's soccer and softball finals. In respect to non-Olympic-year sports coverage of women's sports, the traditional attitude that women's sports does not sell can be evidenced by the scarcity of women's sports coverage.

Hammond claimed that the more women athletes are successful, the more likely gender parity would be naturally attained without any overt change in production or focus. He argued that the hegemonic influences that promote a dominant patriarchy would change if women watch the Olympics in droves and US women continue to win large portions of the country's medals. Hammond sees no reason why NBC's Olympic telecast would not follow by showing more women's events.

> TH: Television is a reactive medium. We give the people more of what they *want* to see than what they *ought* to see. It's not perfect; it's not there yet. But we do give women the closest thing yet to equality with men in terms of coverage.

The on-air commentators that were interviewed were conscious of perceptions of gender inequalities that surround an Olympic telecast and endeavor to make choices that enhance the coverage of women's sport, especially in relation to the historic quantitative differences between male and female coverage (Adams and Tuggle, 2004; Halbert and Latimer, 1994; Higgs and Weiller, 1994). They are also sensitive to the stigmatization (Goffman, 1963; Shih *et al.*, 1999; Pinel, 1999) of women in sport in the past; for example, the way in which female strength, speed, and muscularization have been compared unfavorably with men's achievements in sport or have been associated with butchness or "deviant" (lesbian) sexuality (Caudwell, 1999; Lenskyj, 1994). The sportscasters themselves are undoubtedly deconstructing previously stigmatized versions of sportswomen and constructing positive images of female Olympians in their place. At the same time, however, sportscasters are self-conscious about specific qualitative differences in their treatment of men and women athletes. For example, Tom Hammond offers the following introspective account of the coverage of skating:

> TH: Perhaps we're more dazzled by the grace of a woman, but the jumps are very important for them as well. Maybe it's phrased in a different way in terms of "graceful" or things you wouldn't normally ascribe to a man ... you say "style" in a man or "grace" in a woman, I'm not sure. But I don't make any conscious effort to put more emphasis on the grace and the manner of skating of a woman more than a man.

In this comment, Hammond reveals the duality that any Olympic telecaster must face: being conscious of the criticisms of gendered reporting while avoiding paranoia about uttering words that may be considered to be inappropriate for one gender or another. Gymnast and sportscaster Peter Vidmar claims that sometimes a duality of language about men and women athletes is warranted and other times there is a lack of any sense of the gendered context when there needs to be one. He used his sport, gymnastics, to illustrate the character of the commentary regarding women gymnasts who tend to be teenagers and the perception that if they fail it is more likely to be because of inexperience.

> PV: There's this thought that these are immature little girls. Do they have stuffed animals in their gym bags? Yes. They are young, but that doesn't mean they are inexperienced; many of these girls have competed in major international competitions. You can always say "inexperience", [but] they're all in the same boat, they're all eighteen years old, so you have to look at it from a relative standpoint.

One specific instance in which gender was undoubtedly significant was in the coverage of perhaps the most jarring collapse of the Torino Games—at least for the US team—when American snowboardcrosser, Lindsey Jacobellis, was cruising to a gold medal and made the decision to flaunt her victory with a trick, causing her to crash before the finish line and lose the gold medal. I asked Costas about his interview with her, which had a fairly gentle tone (opening with the simple question "What were you thinking?"). However, when I specifically asked him if he would have been as compassionate if this had been a male snowboarder, he responded that he felt his genteel nature during the interview was more attributable to her youth than her gender:

> BC: I think we got to everything and made all the points that had to be made without drawing blood. I don't think people wanted to see blood in that situation. Still, I recognize that no matter how even-handed we may aspire to be, a large portion of the audience will always see a young woman as more vulnerable than a young man in a comparative situation.

Basketball sportscaster Ann Meyers Drysdale contends that different types of comments arise primarily because of the preponderance of men sportscasters who have had little exposure to women's athletics. While noting that attitudes about women's athletics are "still evolving" among the overwhelmingly male contingent of sportscasters, she offered a glimpse as to what the situation was like 20 years ago:

> AMD: At the Goodwill Games [in 1986], I was doing the announcing with Rick Berry and Bill Russell. Bill Russell was put on the women's games, I think, partly as a way to bolster the exposure of women's basketball. I understand why they did that, but it was disconcerting from a woman announcer's point of view because it seemed as if they did not have enough confidence in my credibility—or in the women's game in general. Things have changed, but back then

> Russell was saying things like, "Oh, these girls can really play! Look at that!" It was all so new.

Throughout television sport, and notably in the telecasting of the Olympics, there is a meager number of women sportscasters (described by Donna deVarona as "window dressing") in comparison with the number of men sportscasters. She went on to say that even though there had been some increased opportunities for women sportscasters and producers in recent years, their still tiny numbers have failed to make a noticeable difference:

> DdV: A chauvinist attitude towards women's sports permeates the industry. There has been tremendous progress made in respect to opportunities but one would never know it by watching the networks, listening to the radio or reading the sports pages let alone reading about women athletes in *Sports Illustrated*.

Donna deVarona noted that ABC sports pioneer, Roone Arledge, was instrumental in advancing women sportscasters by allowing her to influence him, asserting that "during the very successful 1984 Los Angeles Olympics, Roone made sure more women served as co-hosts and analysts than any other Games since".

Given that the Olympics frequently serves as the most salient, prominent outlet for conveying the breadth of women's athletic accomplishments, the depiction of women's pinnacle moments was also discussed within the theoretical construct of the dynamic spectacle (Real, 1975), which maintains that the communicative moments that wield the greatest influence are the apex instances that remain etched within people's psyches. When a sportscaster detects an epic moment that they feel almost certain will occur, it is difficult for him or her to distinguish how much of the "call" should be prepared in advance and how much should be spontaneously experienced firsthand. For example, Tom Hammond explains how he wanted to be prepared for the triumph of Australia's Cathy Freeman during the 2000 Sydney Olympics:

> TH: I knew it was going to be a big moment, so I wanted to be equal to that moment. There were 110,000 people in the stadium and I said that she had waited four years for this, and that Australia had waited since the first women's 400 meters in 1960, and the Aboriginal people had waited forever for this moment. You have to be part of a big moment. So you'd like to script it, but at that time I didn't know what

> I was going to say. On the other hand, if you know there's a chance there could be a big moment, you have to at least have thought about what you might say and say something meaningful.

Then there are the moments that few, if any, could have predicted. Hammond was also the announcer in 2002 when US figure skater Sarah Hughes stunned the world, skating the long program of a lifetime to improbably win the gold medal in Salt Lake City. Hammond describes this scenario as playing out in a much different way than with Freeman two years earlier.

> TH: I had no idea that would happen. None of us did. You couldn't be prepared. But that's one of those things where, hopefully, you laid enough groundwork in your preparation that, when that moment does occur, you can be equal to the moment. I had an underlying philosophy: the less you say, the better it plays. It is television, after all, so the pictures often tell the story, and there's hardly anything you can say as astute as the pictures that convey the scene of the moment. But I think you can make short comments to enhance the moment, to express your surprise or your concern. I had both hands held in the air to the other commentators that night [indicating] "do not say anything". Just don't say anything. Their first inclination is to pile on the words, so I just hold up my hands and let the moment play.

Hammond regarded some of the toughest storytelling moments to be when a sportscaster must balance the sport, the back story, and the legal story, as happened with Marion Jones in 2004. Jones, a highly decorated US track and field star from previous Olympics, was competing in Athens amid swirling accusations of performance-enhancing drug use. She had never tested positive at the time of the Games, but the story was sizeable because of her celebrity status. Hammond spoke of the equilibrium that had to be constructed when speaking speculatively about Jones, who later pled guilty and was stripped of her medals in 2007:

> TH: Every time she competed, it had to go in, but we also had to say she's never tested positive. That was a fine line to walk, but it certainly wasn't something you could ignore. We all agreed it had to go in, but how are we going to present it? She didn't want to be questioned about it, but we always had to bring it up in the interviews after the events in which she competed.

Also speaking about the Marion Jones controversy and the problem it posed in terms of inserting hard news within a fairly "Pollyannaish" sportscasting landscape, Donna deVarona characterized the dilemma as an unenthusiastic departure from the principal NBC themes:

> DdV: It was with reluctance that NBC, up against a devastating and news breaking story, finally decided to depart from its storybook coverage of Marion Jones's run for multiple golds during the Sydney Olympics to report the fact that her husband had quit the United States Olympic team because he had tested positive for the use of illegal substances.

Summarizing comments regarding the depiction of gender within the Olympics, NBC's Olympic sportscasters admit to minor shortcomings, believing that the overall portrayal of women athletes is similar to the portrayal of men athletes and that the telecast provides the most salient venue for enhancing women's athletics of any sportscast.

As with discussions of nationality and ethnicity, the true tests of how NBC does in this regard will lie in the content analytic examinations in Chapters 4, 5, and 6. Only then can we fairly compare how NBC feels it does with the actuality as borne out in the clock-time, mentions, and descriptors of men and women athletes that will be outlined in these later chapters.

Portraying ethnicity

Discussing ethnicity has always been a difficult topic for any sportscaster. Many sportscasters (e.g. Rush Limbaugh[9]) have lost their jobs because they failed accurately or coherently to discuss ethnicity in an appropriate manner. Issues of ethnicity are exceedingly difficult to convey in a Winter Olympics, as many contend that to discuss the lack of ethnic diversity would be to manufacture an issue at the Games when the focus should be on who is competing rather than who is not participating. In contrast to the discussion of gender, in which the interviewees argued that the telecast makes a concerted effort to highlight both men and women athletes, the discussion of ethnic issues tended to yield a different kind of response from the sportscasters, who collectively argue that ethnicity is nearly a non-issue. They contend that ethnicity is a subject that the visual aspect of the telecast can speak to and which should only be overtly discussed when the ethnicity of an athlete is unusual or if there is some sort of "first" for a given

---

9 Limbaugh was dismissed from the ESPN NFL preview show, *Sunday NFL Countdown*, for claiming Philadelphia Eagle quarterback Donovan McNabb was overrated largely because "the media has been very desirous of a Black quarterback to do well".

ethnicity at the Olympics. NBC sportscasters largely adopt the approach Tom Hammond advocates in which the sportscaster assumes that the visual image on the screen will speak volumes about ethnicity on its own:

> TH: There's no mandate for me to comment on that and I rarely do. It doesn't seem important. It's obvious most of the distance runners are Caucasian and most of the sprinters are Black, so it's not something that I delve into in any great measure to try to determine why that is. I've never had any mandate from NBC and no personal inclination to make any comments about it. It's all fairly neutral to me.

Ethnicity did become an issue in the 2006 Torino Olympics, though, primarily because HBO *Real Sports*[10] host Bryant Gumbel placed ethnicity in the forefront of his argument that the Winter Olympics were largely illegitimate. In some closing remarks on his February 2006 program, he stated:

> Try not to laugh when someone says these are the world's greatest athletes, despite a paucity of Blacks that makes the Games look like a GOP convention. And try to blot out all logic when announcers and sportswriters pretend to care about the luge, the skeleton, the biathlon and all those other events they don't understand and totally ignore for all but three weeks every four years. Face it: these Olympics are little more than a marketing plan.
>
> (Berry, 2006, p. 8C)

Not surprisingly, Gumbel's comments, harmonized with US speed skater Shani Davis attempting to become the first Black US Winter Olympian to ever win an individual gold medal, guaranteed that ethnicity *would* be an issue within NBC's 2006 Winter Olympics. Gumbel's comments signified that the Olympics is somehow supposed to be a unique sporting contest—a utopian model of fairness in every aspect but that the Winter Games, in reality, fail demonstrably to integrate Blacks into the competition. Some of the NBC sportscasters responded aggressively. Lampley felt that Gumbel "reflects a cynicism towards the Games that in some all-male circles probably feels very hip" but that in doing so, he "effectively insulted [Black gold-medal-winning bobsledder] Vonetta Flowers and Shani Davis". The usual media silence about the complete absence of Black competitors at previous Winter Olympics and the uncharacteristic presence of two Black competitors at Torino is in contrast to the high visibility of Blacks at Summer Olympic Games and their representation as "natural" athletes (Hoberman, 2007). Such

---

10 *Real Sports* is a sports news television program which has aired over 100 monthly newscasts, often investigating hard news issues that percolate within modern sport.

juxtaposition demonstrates how the media are implicated in the changeable nature of Black sporting identities. Costas felt ethnicity was important to mention in a story, but under set criteria that should be utilized when an issue appears important enough to warrant discussion:

> BC: If there's a valid first, whether it's Shani Davis or Vonetta Flowers, I think it's worth noting. It would also be worth noting in the Winter Games if the participation of non-Caucasians grows. I don't think you should harp on it, but it's noteworthy.

Again, Costas was able to draw a clear distinction between his role as host of the Opening Ceremonies and as host of the subsequent actual athletic events.

> BC: I mentioned in the Opening Ceremonies of the Winter Olympics that there were very few Middle-Eastern countries competing and very few African countries. Some of those things may be physiological, but many of them are just based on what the sporting culture and history of that country is: what they value, what they emphasize, what facilities they have in which to train. Very often you'll see a competitor from a Caribbean country or an African country, and now they race for the Netherlands or Canada. They've relocated to where there are better training facilities or they went to college someplace where they could compete at a high level. It's worth noting what their actual ethnicity is, regardless of what country they represent.

The most interesting case in the 2006 Winter Olympics was that of Shani Davis, a Black American speed skater from Chicago, Illinois, who became the first individual Black gold medalist by winning the 1,000 meters (previously Vonetta Flowers of the US had won gold as part of a two-person bobsled team in 2002 and Canada's Jarome Iginla won gold as a member of the hockey team). Davis was a highly controversial figure throughout the Olympic Games, characterized in the media as cocky and unlike other speed skaters. The media also focused on his feud with American teammate Chad Hedrick, who felt Davis should have competed in the team pursuit to enhance the opportunity for US gold. Davis countered that he was a solo athlete and that the pursuits would hinder his chances of winning in his individual events. Bob Costas commented on the complex case of Davis:

> BC: Shani Davis had multiple stories. Sometimes people are so simplistic that it has to be only one thing. He did noteworthy things athletically, regardless of what color he was. They were further noteworthy because they represent a first for an African-American competitor in a Winter sport that not too many Black kids in the United States would take up. He said it himself in the profiles—grew up in Chicago, all my friends wanted to be Michael Jordan, and I'm going to the skating rink.

Overall, though, Costas did not view the Olympic telecast as significantly shaping participation of ethnic minorities in the Olympic Games:

> BC: If there were barriers to African-American participation or non-White participation around the globe, that would be different. But if there's ten Shani Davises out there, they're welcome. The biggest barrier is climate and cultural patterns. Even if a Black kid grows up where Eric Heiden[11] grew up, it just doesn't follow that they'll want to be a speed skater.

Hammond corroborated the belief that climate and culture were the primary factors that hinder ethnic diversity in the Winter Games, not any overt biases that would specifically make a given ethnicity less likely to feel welcome at the Games. He felt the lack of ethnic diversity at the Olympics was more aptly a cultural phenomenon. As a result, he felt this problem was not something NBC's Olympic telecast could mend, given that "culturally and historically, black-skinned people were from warmer areas that didn't participate in Winter sports".

Peter Vidmar commented on the reasons why his sport, gymnastics, is not more ethnically diverse, believing that in the US, the barriers to participation are socioeconomic:

> PV: If you look at the demographics of our sport, the vast majority of gymnastics programs in this country are private clubs in middle-class and upper-middle-class neighborhoods. Demographically, there are fewer people of color in many of these neighborhoods, so we have a talent pool that hasn't really been tapped.

11 Heiden won a record five speed skating medals for the United States in the 1980 Lake Placid Winter Olympics.

Overall, all interviewees asserted that ethnicity did not shade their on-air dialogue in significant ways. This was interesting to note, as they seem to concede other biases at times with regard to nationality and gender. Researchers (Davis and Harris, 1998; Rada and Wulfemeyer, 2005; Wonsek, 1992) have found that athletes of different ethnicities have been treated in markedly different manners over the past several decades, although there is no evidence of bias specifically within the comments of Costas, Lampley, or Hammond. These sportscasters are knowledgeable about histories of discrimination in sport in relation to race and ethnicity, as well as nationalism and gender. They all avoid using ideologically loaded language and discriminating against athletes with certain identities or favoring those with others.

Profiles and promotion

Network hosts like Bob Costas and Jim Lampley also aid in promoting upcoming events and athletes who will be competing later on in a telecast or on subsequent nights.

NBC had dreadful promotional luck at the 2006 Torino Games when the most recognizable US star, Michelle Kwan, withdrew because of injury on the eve of the Games and the athlete that had received the most prominent media attention, skier Bode Miller, failed to win a medal in any of his five events. Lampley spoke of how the Olympics had some great stories, but how the lack of success from the heavily promoted athletes significantly influenced the perception of whether or not the telecast was a success. Lampley noted that "There was no escaping the sense that the thing had imploded" when Kwan withdrew and Miller failed to medal and that it was a "necessary, intelligent decision that met with disaster". Still, Lampley said such promotional decisions have to be made, even with the high potential for error, because athletes like Miller and Kwan "go to a way better audience". In addition, Lampley tried to assess fairly how the US performed in Torino, keeping in mind that the host nation (which the US was in 2002) usually wins 20 percent fewer medals four years later. Still, in a podcast during day nine of the Torino Olympics, he attempted to place American nationalistic pride into perspective:

JL: You're within your rights to think of the United States as a bit of a winter sports powerhouse. I like that; it makes me feel pretty good! Pretty good, that is, until I start to think of who it is we're losing to: Germany. It's a country whose land area is just a mountain or two smaller than Montana, with just about 80 million people. We've got almost four times that many Olympians, and they're still dusting us up on the slopes. Norway: four and a half million salmon-loving Norwegians live in a nation the size of New Mexico. Right now, they've got 17 medals; we have 15. If this were a boxing match,

> Norway would be about 14 weight classes below the United States, and they'd have us on the ropes. And then there's Austria. Austria is even with the United States, and they've gotten it done with about one-fortieth as many people.

In his personal interview, Lampley appraised the US performances another way:

> JL: This was another very representative performance by the United States, a nation that's growing and getting more competitive. Ted Ligety and Julie Mancuso's successes in Torino[12] demonstrate that ongoing evolution. But, attention falls on those people at the moment at which they succeed. Attention fell on Bode all summer.

The pre-produced profiles of athletes aid the storytelling process in immediate and crucial ways. Sportscasters indicated that the profiles enhance their story-telling abilities tremendously, particularly when an athlete is a lesser-known quantity with a remarkable background story. These athletes have little or no chance of winning a medal, yet are worthy of a modicum of clock-time because their stories are unique. For instance, in Sydney in 2000, Eric Moussambani of Equatorial Guinea competed in the 100-meter freestyle swimming competition after training in a hotel pool (his country only had two pools—both in hotels—and no swimming federation).

Donna deVarona reported that the pre-produced profile, then called the "Up Close and Personal" feature, was her idea that she had proposed to Roone Arledge when ABC held the rights to the Olympic telecast because "storytelling is key to painting each unique Olympic canvas". Hammond spoke of how this selection process takes place largely within a cognitive and subjective domain:

> TH: Sometimes it's someone who's overcome great adversity in order to just get there. They're not competing for a medal, they're not world-class, but they embody the spirit of the Olympics. The fact that they are there, competing even though they can't win any medals is a story. It's the process of competing that embodies the Olympic ideal and often those are the best stories.

12 Ligety and Mancuso won gold medals in skiing at Torino.

Nevertheless, the interviewees reported that such stories can become heavy-handed. To wit, John Naber claimed that the biggest difference between the Olympic telecast when he competed (1976 in Montreal) and what people see today is that "Olympic athletes have been allowed to become professional". Naber explains that the on-air profiles are only part of the packaging of an athlete and that the results are that "the boys and girls that used to represent 'us' have been replaced by professionals who are representing themselves". Naber continues:

> JN: ABC used to do "up close and personals" that showed the ordinariness of these people. Now they're shorter and they're also more sensationalized. If you're an Olympic athlete whose parents were alcoholics, you're more likely to get an "up close and personal" feature than if you come from a middle-class family and get 'B's on your report card.

Stigma-consciousness also applies beyond the depiction of identity issues because, as sportscasters know all too well, the Olympic telecast has traditionally been accused of being too "schmaltzy", or of focusing too much on the stories of overcoming great odds that Ebersol contends are central to the Olympic spirit and message. Tom Hammond indicated that he was well aware of the reputation NBC's telecast has had for over-hyping stories of personal achievement, particularly for the American athletes. Hammond even admitted that the telecast was once guilty of that, although he felt the issue has subsided to a great extent in recent years:

> TH: In Sydney [2000], I once said to the feature producer, does somebody have to die in order to make it to the Olympics? Can we have a feature that isn't all tears and gloom and doom? Can we have something uplifting and something funny? We sort of got in a rut there, but we've done a little better job [recently], going with less pre-produced features and more mini-features. Not as schmaltzy. But, yes, we've strayed too far in times past.

While Peter Vidmar claimed that profiles and storytelling are "really important to add a human element", Bob Costas was also sentient to the concerns that the storytelling could be manipulated or overdone for dramatic effect and storytelling arcs that possess ready-made conflicts, climaxes, and resolutions:

BC: Sometimes in sports—maybe more often in Olympic sports than others—you have dramatic stories, and you do have people who have overcome adversity. And when that's the case, I don't think you ought to shy away from presenting it. But neither do I think you need to trump it up.

Costas works hard to get the Olympic story "right" and to find comfortable ground about how stories are told and what stories should receive salient, vivid description and extrapolation. Speaking of his desire for balance, capturing legitimate highs and lows in the coverage rather than manufacturing them, Costas stated that:

BC: I try to maintain as even a keel as possible. That doesn't mean that you never highlight a dramatic story because there are dramatic stories! My approach is that I think I have a pretty good grasp of the difference between the legitimate drama and theatre of sports and issues that may seem contrived or overstated or cheesy. Everyone's sensibility is different. Overall, NBC's coverage has evolved to where, in recent Olympics, it's moved somewhat closer to my sensibility.

Costas also sought to clarify that one can strive for perfection without ever achieving it. He maintains that certainly within the biggest show on television, problems will occur, some stories will inevitably be over- or under-hyped, and others will not be told in a completely proper way. According to Costas, the goal is to minimize errors, making them as infrequent and diminutive as possible. Much like a golfer, who may only hit a few truly terrific shots over the course of the day, for Costas the key is controlling the other shots that can ultimately damage the final score, or, in this case, the assessment of the telecast:

BC: Can we capture legitimate drama instead of schmaltz? That's what I hope for. By and large, we're successful with that. But it's like, Sandy Koufax[13] goes out to pitch a game, but not every pitch was on the black. You can pitch a terrific game and you're still going to make some mistakes.

---

13 Koufax was a dominating baseball pitcher for the Brooklyn/Los Angeles Dodgers in the 1960s.

Jim Lampley seemed to adopt a more unapologetic approach, contending that it's a "matter of personal taste" and that comparing the Olympic telecast to any other sportscast is inequitable and a comparison that, in the end, proves fruitless:

> JL: It is what it is. It is a high-minded, self-consciously idealistic pageant about flags and anthems and individual stories of arduous pursuits and overcoming. If that's too good for you, go watch something grainier.

As a result of this mediated "pageant", some—such as Donna deVarona—argue that the sports and the athletes who compete in them become secondary to the storytelling mechanism:

> DdV: The athletes were more like pawns in this movement, and they still are in many ways. Too often they are merely a vehicle for everybody else's goals and aspirations.

Costas also spoke of the notion of personal taste when adopting storytelling approaches (and the exposure and emphasis variables that correlate with these overt choices), noting that the telecast can be produced by the same people with the same on-site reporters, yet the host is ultimately going to be a large factor in determining how the Olympics are received by the majority of viewers. He acknowledges that the host of the Olympics will always receive a disproportionate amount of credit when the telecast is deemed a success and more of the blame when it is regarded as a failure. In the end, all the primetime host can do is adopt the approach with which he is most comfortable, aspiring to create the best telecast he can:

> BC: You could take ten capable people, and make any of them host of the Olympics, and I'm sure they would all enjoy the assignment, be honored by the assignment, be proud to be associated with it. But because the Olympics are so vast, with so many different things, each of them would have to have some percentage of it that wouldn't quite be their cup of tea. Person B's list would be different from person A's or person C's. But it's impossible—no matter how well it's done in general—for every bit of it to perfectly match up with the point of view and the preferred approach, style, and sensibility of the host or of each viewer. It's too big with too many different sports, too many different stories, too many different announcers, too many different producers. And that means different sensibilities and different approaches.

Sportscasting "plausibly live"

If the premise of potential biases within the Games lies in the dissection of lin-guistic comments and choices made in an impromptu manner, a critical factor in understanding the origin of these comments is NBC's use of the live-to-tape format. Producers indicated that while some pieces (particularly in the studio) can be re-taped if egregious errors occur, they simply do not have the time or desire to reedit major portions of the Games for enhanced viewer consumption several hours later. The sportscasters were asked how frequently the "plausibly live" concept is altered to allow for different wordings, takes, visuals, and even overall storytelling arcs. Lampley admits that not everything in the host studio is done on the first take and that if Dick Ebersol "doesn't get what he wants out of take number one, then there's probably going to be a take number two". Costas confirms that there are instances of multiple takes, but that they are done spar-ingly and only in certain circumstances.

> BC: I like to do as much as possible live-to-tape or first take to tape. The only time that we would redo an on-camera would be if subsequent events meant that we had to change the order. Like the jigsaw puzzle got moved around and part D is now part K. Let's say we start laying stuff down and what you thought would be, let's say the beginning of the second hour, now they have to move it to the third hour because something happened that's so good, that we have to get it on nearer to the top of primetime. The lead to segment eleven now doesn't take into account what the viewers will already have seen when it now becomes segment nineteen. So we've got to do it over again. Other than situations like that, if—and luckily this doesn't happen too often—there was some egregious stumble, you do have the luxury of doing it over. But I've done so much live television, that if there is a stumble I hardly notice and it doesn't faze me very much. I make a joke about it; I correct it; I go on.

Costas contends that the Olympics are essentially produced live-to-tape and that the exceptions are not editorial in nature (in which the storyline or description changes) but rather for enhanced technical quality. Even so, another crucial dis-tinction for determining what is produced live, live-to-tape, and live-to-tape with the chance for multiple takes is the venue in which the Olympics takes place, as time zones dictate production schedules:

> BC: In Barcelona (in 1992), there was a seven-hour time difference, and a lot was done live-to-tape. I would tape live at a venue unless it was

something like skating or gymnastics that almost have to be pieced together because of the length of the competition. Most of what's done by Tom Hammond (at track and field) is calling a race live-to-tape, he doesn't voice it over afterwards, it's done live at the stadium. There it's possible for me, to say "All right, this is the situation, and let's go to Tom Hammond" and it's possible for me to tag it live-to-tape, too. When we're live-to-tape, the reaction at the result is immediate, spontaneous, and more authentic. But, if the jigsaw puzzle nature of it doesn't make it possible to do it that way, then the approach I take is to have an even-handed tone and try to be engaged and informative, but never be stunned and surprised or too excited, when in fact I've had time to absorb it. That's the best way to keep faith with the audience.

Frequently alluding to the metaphor of the telecast as a jigsaw puzzle (a concept referenced by Molly Solomon previously), Bob Costas spoke about a particular puzzle that occurred in 1996, when US gymnast Kerri Strug injured herself on her first vault, but managed to land a second vault on one leg, securing a gold medal for the US women's gymnastics team. Some criticism was levied later that Strug's vault had occurred after Russia had finished their final rotation, meaning that the US gold medal was assured before Strug's historic vault. But Strug's vault created an indelible image etched in the minds of millions of viewers long after the Atlanta Olympics were complete. Costas responded to the criticism of as follows:

BC: I'll tell you the way that jigsaw puzzle played out. That was my first live Olympics. I was not aware that the gold medal was secure prior to that jump. And I'm not even sure that everybody in the arena knew that. So, afterwards I heard those comments. Gymnastics, even in a live situation, has to be presented—even if it's a short turn-around—on tape. Otherwise it would be like going to the circus, where stuff is happening in all these different rings. There's no way you can let it play out in real time. Even gymnastics' buffs wouldn't watch it. It would be like watching gymnastics C-SPAN. You have to package it for some sort of narrative clarity and dramatic effect. I can honestly tell you as I sat there, I was not aware that the outcome was already assured at the time that Strug lifted off.

When discussing the way this puzzle was completed, a constant theme in the sportscasters' accounts was their level of trust in their producers and research staff, drawing a seeming correlation between increased belief in the abilities of the producers with decreased need for re-shooting a story or tag. Lampley spoke specifically of his collegial relationship with the producer with whom he worked most closely, Molly Solomon:

> JL: In 32 years of television, I've never worked with a producer whom I trust to the degree that I trust Molly Solomon. I've never had such an instinctive, chemical relationship with a producer. I trust her judgment, so the number of times that I'd jump in and say, no, I want to do it a different way [are very few]. Not only do I choose my battles, I say to myself before I go after her on a subject—even a small one—I say to myself, "Look at what you've achieved in her care. Look how superbly well she's chosen to manage you on the air". There's value in her detachment. Because she is the kind of person who will sometimes say to me, "No, you're wrong. Shut up. Go away".

Costas reports that there is little need for additional takes in large part because the questions or concerns about the storytelling process—in terms of both accuracy and tone—are usually addressed prior to taping, during the scripting process:

> BC: There's too much material for the anchor to write it all, so what I get are proposed leads or tags or bullet points, and then I make something out of it. Sometimes I change it; sometimes I'll substantially rewrite it; sometimes I'll just change a word or two here or there. I always ask questions. I'll say, "Do we want to say that this was 'incredible'? Or was it really just 'noteworthy'?" Part of the time I try to be skeptical. Even if I tend to agree, I try to ask the skeptical question. I want to make sure that the tone is right. I'm always saying, "What am I coming off of here?" If this is already on tape, what's the last few seconds? Is the last thing Lindsey Jacobellis smiling? Is the last thing somebody screaming in exultation? Are you sure Tim Ryan didn't say that earlier? And if he did, do I want to reiterate it or add to it? Then I'll say, "As Tim Ryan said ..." You want to make sure that not only are you good factually, but that you are in harmony in terms of tone, or at least that it's not discordant.

Overarching sentiments

Collectively, the sportscasters felt truly awed by the experience of being able to work on the biggest show on television. Nonetheless, the ability to decipher justifiable criticism from hyperbolic carping about the Olympic telecasts' shortcomings is an immediate imperative for these high-profile sportscasters.

Costas referred to the "spitball as argument" culture of modern sports, noting that some grievances about the Olympic telecast are often either exaggerated or misunderstood:

> BC: I respect, understand, and often agree with, reasonable criticism—even if it's tough—if it's insightful. But easy, glib criticism that begins with, "Oh, the Olympics will start tomorrow. More schmaltzy features and more bogus tape delay"? I mean, that's somebody who just intends to watch just to nitpick. There's too much worthwhile stuff that's done. Imagine an edit suite or a production truck trying to make narrative sense of something that played out over four hours, and now you've got to put this together in four 11-minute segments, or two 11s, an eight, and a four. You have to have it play out in a way that not only is narratively coherent, but has some theatrical and dramatic appeal, because, after all, this is a television program. And you're doing all this with changing circumstances, and camera three went down, and, you know, somebody only got three hours of sleep ... it's amazing to me! These people are putting together miniature movies on a nightly basis!

Costas admits that there will always be much that can be done to enhance the telecast, but that some media critics don't understand all of the intersecting issues that make the Olympics the most demanding sportscast to assemble. He provides the example of criticism that NBC's telecast is repetitive in telling the personal stories of athletes multiple times even in the same evening telecast. His counter-argument is as follows:

> BC: In the modern era when people are busy, even if they watch a lot of Olympics, they probably don't watch every minute in primetime. They certainly don't watch every minute on all the cable platforms and then every minute in primetime and when they're watching they may be channel surfing—especially this time around, when NBC faced significant competition from the other networks. A person who is a television critic who's watching it all or someone like you who's doing a scholarly work might say, "Well gee, they told this story about Lindsey, and they reiterated it. It's a good story, it's a valid story, but they told it four times". But you can't assume that every person watching heard it the first two or three times. You've got to bring them back in to what the story is and why they should care.

The notion that high or low ratings automatically correlate with the quality of the Olympic telecast is a spurious relationship, according to Costas. This correlation nonetheless is pervasive within the criticism. Costas explains:

> BC: Critics of the Olympics never assume that high ratings, such as in 1996, meant the programming was superior, but these same critics, when ratings fall, equate falling numbers with a decreased quality of the telecast. Quality should not be measured by ratings. Critics tend to employ whatever narrative is convenient for their arguments for or against the Olympic telecast.

Costas suggested that the most effective way by means of which the telecast could improve would be to include more technological advancement, which could embrace, for example, better utilization of other Olympic forums (most notably the Internet), high-definition formats on cable channels, side-screen rundowns (similar to ESPN's *Pardon the Interruption*) of upcoming events, and even showing the same program on two or three different channels (NBC plus cable options) but with each camera depicting the event from different camera angles for contrasting points of view.

Costas, Lampley, and Hammond are clearly very proud of their accomplishments with the Olympic telecast, even if widely criticized in the popular press. Lampley termed his work in Torino as "The 48 best hours of television collectively that I've ever done". Costas spoke of the immensity of the process, noting the pride he feels in being a part of the telecast, claiming that "anyone who really gets inside the belly of this beast comes away with a real appreciation for the high level of professionalism, talent, skill, and bulldog dedication" processed by the thousands of NBC workers.

There was a deep sense in all the interviews that the sportscasters were conversing about something much more personal and different with the Olympics than with, for example, the football playoffs or a championship boxing match. They "drink the Kool-Aid", as Lampley terms it, meaning that they buy into the Olympic experience. No comment summarizes more eloquently this contention that the Olympics are a larger-than-life event than Lampley's conclusion, as follows:

> JL: I think there's still a huge nucleus of us who would like to live in a better world and that's what the Olympics portray better than anything else I know. If there's something better on the planet, in terms of our hope for something more dignified in the future, than the opening or closing ceremonies, I don't know what it is. I truly don't.

4   The star-spangled Games?

Nationalism and the Olympic telecasts

> Nationality which is represented by any given expression of sporting nationhood is usually divisive in some way.
>
> (Allison, 2000, p. 347)

The gargantuan identity issue within the Olympic telecast continues to be overt (and covert) nationalism. Hall (1996) contends that the theorization of identity "is a matter of considerable political significance" (p. 16) and that we need to understand issues such as nationalism and the politics of identity because "identities are constructed within, not outside discourse" (p. 4). The discourses (and related frames) of NBC's telecast quickly inform even the casual viewer that NBC's telecast highlights US athletes at a higher rate than the 11–13 percent of medals that they typically win at an Olympic Games. Many reasons persist, most notably that the Olympics have historically been a channel for the construction and display of nationalisms, and the foregrounding of national identities within the overall construct of the Games. As Ann Meyers Drysdale indicated in her interview, in the Cold War era, the Olympic villains were easy to identify as they wore red and were assessed as television antagonists almost exclusively by their national affiliation. The Olympics highlight political tensions between different countries, usually exacerbating situations more than mollifying them because of the high-pressure "go for the gold" mindset that permeates the Olympic Games and, subsequently, the telecast as the mediated sport product also constructs and celebrates mythologies of nation (Allison, 1986; Kuper, 1994; Sugden, 1995) and political strife between nations. The concept of nationality incorporates a notion of a coherent community with common cultural beliefs and political values, but the reality is that within national boundaries there are divisions, inequalities, and oppositional ideologies (see Anderson, 1983), many of which have been reflected in the Olympics Games and telecast. These differences are certainly true of the United States, a country with deeply rooted differences in areas of gender, ethnicity, and economic class, just to name a few. Dubbing the term "sportocracy", Abdel-Shehid (2007) claims that:

it is no accident that the re-emergence of United States' imperialism has taken a ... tone ... of "Bush-speak", where people across the globe are asked to choose sides as a way to ensure ... something called "security" and "democracy" for what is called "the West".

(p. 196)

This chapter will certainly examine the degree in which NBC's Olympic coverage is "unabashedly American", yet it will also determine the extent to which these bifurcated nationalistic "us vs. them" differences are part of the overall Olympic product. The chapter will comment on the manners in which US athletes are highlighted and, inversely, describe NBC's stances when covering the presence and performances of athletes from other nations.

Depictions of nationality in televised sport

Sports and nationalism incessantly reside concurrently within a sportscast and in no place is this more evident than the Olympics (Bairner, 2001). Larson and Park (1993) claim that "Nationalism has plagued the modern Olympics since their inception in 1896" (p. 35) and while a country such as the United States has citizens who split their loyalties among dozens of professional teams and hundreds of colleges and universities, the large majority of its country's citizens unite to cheer on their national "team". Jarvie (1993) claims that sports enact a "uniquely effective medium for inculcating national feelings" (p. 74), with Anderson (1983) postulating that any form of nationalism involves an "imagined political community" because no nation is small enough for any single person to know even a measurable fraction of the general population (p. 6). Coakley (2004) suggests that governments use the Olympics, in particular, to promote nationalistic interests: "Government officials use international sports to establish their nation's legitimacy in the international sphere, and they believe that, when athletes from their nation win medals, their national image is enhanced around the world" (p. 449). But such partnerships between sports and countries provide governments with an additional outlet for arguing over international political issues (Houlihan, 1994), encouraging George Orwell to assert that international competitions resemble "mimic warfare" (Orwell, 1992, p. 38) and Larson and Park (1993) to contend that the combination of country and athletic event has hindered the Olympics repeatedly over the course of time. When Peter Ueberroth was president of the United States Olympic Organizing Committee for the Los Angeles Games in 1984—at the time when the two superpowers, the United States and the Soviet Union, had mutually boycotted attendance at a Games hosted by the other (Moscow in 1980 and Los Angeles in 1984)—he referred to the Games as an unambiguously "athletic-political event".

Assuming this is another situation in which one must "drink the Kool-Aid" of Olympism (a euphemism Jim Lampley incorporated in his interview in Chapter 3), presumably some sportscasters identify with the notion that national superiority is contested at these sporting venues, regardless of government structure, ideology, or economic status. Weber (1996) contends that many viewers embrace the joint-ventured nature of the pairing of nationalism and sport because they desire clear winners and losers, which international political disputes rarely provide but that sport does offer in terms of a definitive final score or placing.

Arguing that "sport and nationalism are arguably two of the most emotive issues in the modern world" (p. xi), Bairner (2001) contends that the power of sport-induced nationalism is vast, with the capability to influence millions of people internationally. To many countries, events like the Olympics are much more than mere sport, they are opportunities to raise the political standing of their nation (Espy, 1979). Athletes become "living, breathing representatives of national or racial characteristics" (Clarke and Clarke, 1982, p. 62), while national teams become banner bearers for socialism, democracy, communism, and myriad other social policies. Indeed, China's goals in hosting the 2008 Summer Olympics in Beijing run far beyond public relations and exposure; the Chinese have little reservation in stating that their goal is to lead the medal count in the Games to establish themselves as a superpower on the same level as the United States (Wang, 2005). In examining the top-ten countries in the medal counts of the 2004 Olympics, one can witness that many of the same countries that dominate the world economically and politically (United States, Russia, Japan, China, Germany) tend to dominate in the Olympics as well. Indeed, a country can suspend internal strife and other cultural tensions in favor of embracing a nationalistic "us vs. them" dichotomy within international sport (O'Donnell, 1994).

Sport nationalism is pervasive regardless of country (Hargreaves, 2000); indeed, the inherent connection between sport and culture feeds dominant ideologies about the role of a country and its politics within athletic enactment (Miller *et al.*, 2001). From England (Garland and Rowe, 1999) to Germany (Jutel, 2002) to Australia (Madan, 2000) to Canada (Mason, 2002), sports scholars have found elements of nationalism playing central roles within athletics and ubiquitous within media sport. The effects of nationalistic tendencies can be far-reaching; for instance, a recent study by Stempel (2006) who surveyed US television sports viewers, found a "televised masculinist sport–militaristic nationalism complex" that enhanced public support for military action in Iraq (p. 79).

Daddario (1998) particularly focused on the role nationalism plays in the Olympics, showing clearly that the top-ten countries in the medal counts are competing for more than just sports titles. Postulating that the Olympics is "particularly nationalistic" (p. 134), she maintains that Olympic telecasts construct transformative narratives that shape storytelling based on the athletes' country of origin. While many countries rely on an Olympic world video feed (that, for instance, provided over 900 hours of Torino Olympics commentary-free coverage (Hiestand, 2006c)) so that they can insert their own representation of the events, other nations such as the United States utilize the high-level production and expertise that networks like NBC provide. Consequently, "the presence of television ... can affect the course of events" (Buscombe, 1974, p. 21), shaping sporting events that have tremendous impact on society.

While NBC Sports President Dick Ebersol argues that his coverage is less "provincial" than that of other countries (Hiestand, 2006c), empirical analyses have indicated that virtually every host nation defers to various "cheerleading" tactics when mass-producing the Games, in an attempt to maximize ratings. Larson and Park (1993) referred to six different types of television segments that are pertinent to the analysis of national images: (1) sporting events, (2) torch relays, (3) ceremonies, (4) cultural features, (5) news and public affairs, and (6) commercials. All of these areas have proven to yield nationalistic biases. For instance, a study of three modes of English-speaking sportscasts (Australia, Great Britain, and the United States) of the 1988 Seoul Olympics indicated that announcer dialogue and gatekeeper choices (defined by clock-time) inevitably buttressed the home country of the telecast (Larson and Rivenburgh, 1991).

Several scholars (Collette, 1998; Puijk, 1997) have examined the role of the Olympic Opening Ceremony for fostering nationalistic pride as well as a sense of international understanding. The host country inevitably seeks to enhance its global standing within the international community, and the Olympic Opening Ceremonies halt the athletic competitions enough to do so. Nonetheless, this construction is then filtered through another construction: the network gate-keeping mechanism that seeks to provide an understanding of the host country with a strong link to how that affects the viewer at home. As a result, the Opening Ceremony specifically becomes a fairly translucent mechanism for bolstering nationalistic pride, potentially at the expense of other countries that fail to fit into this storytelling frame.

More contemporary analyses of NBC's coverage from Billings and Eastman (2002, 2003), Billings and Angelini (2007), and Billings *et al.* (in press) have indicated similar trends. For instance, Billings and Eastman (2002) found that 51 percent of all the athletes mentioned during NBC's coverage of the 2000 Sydney Olympics were American, yet Americans only won 11 percent of the medals at that Olympic Games. Two years later, Billings and Eastman (2003) established that in the 2002 Salt Lake City Games, American athletes were characterized as being more composed and courageous whereas non-American athletes were described as succeeding because of experience. The 2004 Athens analyses (Billings and Angelini, 2007) yielded eight separate differences in the character-izations of American athletes as opposed to non-American athletes, leading the authors to claim that the telecast was "unabashedly American" (p. 109). While Winter Olympic telecasts have proven to be a bit more "international" in char-acter than Summer Olympic broadcasts (presumably because of fewer events that produce a relative scarcity of American Olympic stars available to promote), all analyses have found that NBC covers US athletes at rates ranging from three to five times what participation rates and the overall medal count would suggest would be adequate for fair representation.

Furthermore, evidence exists suggesting that "American ideas have impacted upon the organization and packaging of sports throughout the world" (Bairner, 2001, p. 14). Undeniably, nationalistic biases are of major concern in a megasporting telecast (Billings and Tambosi, 2004), becoming what Sabo *et al.* (1996) refer to as the "fly in the ointment" of televised international sports.

Understanding content analytic methodology

Starting with an explanation of the methods that were employed, the following sections assess the extent and ways in which sport telecasts of the past six Olympic Games (three Winter Olympics and three Summer Olympics) produced and reproduced gender differences.

First, the data presented in this and the two subsequent chapters represents the compilation of data from several studies published over the past decade (Billings *et al.*, in press; Billings and Angelini, 2007; Billings and Eastman, 2002, 2003; Eastman and Billings, 1999). While I represent the lead contributor in all but one of these content analyses, it is important to recognize the immense contributions of my co-authors and over 200 student coders who aided the data collection process.

Second, 347 primetime hours from the 1996–2006 Olympics were videotaped for this mega-analysis, representing 100 percent of NBC's (and, in 1998, CBS's) coverage over 102 Olympic evenings (Jul. 19–Aug. 4, 1996; Feb. 6–22, 1998; Sept. 15–Oct. 1, 2000; Feb. 8–24, 2002; Aug. 13–29, 2004; Feb. 10–26, 2006). Since NBC recently expanded their coverage to one hour beyond primetime, the 2004 and 2006 analyses incorporated this expanded coverage as well (eight–midnight EST Monday through Saturday, seven–midnight EST the first two Sundays, seven–11 EST during the Sunday closing ceremony). In sum, 55 primetime hours were aired in 1996, 51 hours in 1998, 54 hours in 2000, 52 hours in 2002, 70 hours in 2004, and 65 hours in 2006—resulting in the 348 hours that are included within this longitudinal analysis. The choice of exclusively primetime hours is warranted given that the most prominent events and athletes are reserved for the primetime telecast and the evening hours are used to determine overall Olympic ratings and are the most appropriate subset of the total coverage for comparison with analyses of previous Games.

Third, only comments spoken by network-employed individuals were analyzed for descriptors and mentions of athlete names as this is a study of the on-air speech of Olympic employees, which can be largely scripted and supervised by NBC editors and producers (see Eastman *et al.*, 1996). Those network employees included host commentators (such as Bob Costas), on-site reporters (such as Tom Hammond), special assignment reporters (such as Jimmy Roberts), and color commentators (such as Mary Carillo). For cases in which an NBC employee was interviewing a non-NBC employee (such as Mary Carillo's interview with Michelle Kwan during the first night of the Torino coverage), only Carillo's comments were subject to analysis.

Fourth, regarding the measurement of clock-time (to determine gender differences in Chapter 5), stopwatches were utilized to determine the amount of coverage devoted to each sport in each sportscast. Each night was coded at least twice, with the results compared for accuracy and, if necessary, coded a third time. All coverage by the hosts, on-site reporters, pre-produced profiles, and promotions were included in the database.

Fifth, coders documented each name mentioned within the primetime broadcasts as they were trained to record (a) the name of the athlete, (b) the nationality of the athlete [American or non-American], (c) the gender of the athlete [male or female], (d) the ethnicity of the athlete [White, Black, Hispanic, Asian, other], and (e) the position of the NBC employer or the type of broadcast it appeared in [host, on-site reporter-male, on-site reporter-female, profile, or promotion].

Sixth, for the athlete descriptors, each descriptor (defined as any adjective, adjectival phrase, adverb, or adverbial phrase), was recorded by at least two of over 200 coders over a ten-year period and subsequently classified using the Billings and Eastman (2003) 17-item taxonomy, which used comments pertaining to the athlete's (a) concentration [e.g. "focused"], (b) athletic skill relating to strength [e.g. "weak"], (c) athletic skill relating to talent or ability [e.g. "fast"], (d) composure [e.g. "lost his cool"], (e) commitment [e.g. "hard-worker"], (f) courage [e.g. "gutsy"], (g) experience [e.g. "two-time Olympian"], (h) intelligence [e.g. "smart play"], (i) consonance [e.g. "it was just her night"], (j) outgoing/extroverted [e.g. "openly opinionated"], (k) modest/introverted [e.g. "quiet"], (l) emotional [e.g. "hot-head"], (m) attractiveness [e.g. "easy on the eyes"], (n) size/parts of the body [e.g. "huge hands"], (o) other/neutral [e.g. "weighs 185 pounds"], (p) odd/but interesting [e.g. "doesn't have enough swash in that swashbuckling"], and (q) background [e.g. "former college football player"]. Any discrepancies between a pair of codings for clock-time, mentions, or descriptors resulted in the footage being coded a third time.

Finally, once all data was analyzed and tables were created, chi-square (χ^2) analyses were employed to determine significant differences between groups by using the percentage of overall comments as expected frequencies. For example, if 45 percent of all attributions for success were about American athletes, it was expected that roughly the same proportion (45 percent) of comments about concentration, skill, composure, commitment, attractiveness, and so on should be established as expected frequencies for American athletes, meaning that significant deviations from this baseline would be meaningful.

Nationalism Olympic measures

Athlete mentions

One gains a more accessible understanding of disparities in athlete mentions when examining the most mentioned athletes of each Olympics. Table 4.1 reports these results for each Olympic Games from 1996 in Atlanta to the most recent Games, 2006 in Torino.

As one witnesses in Table 4.1, US athletes receive an inordinate proportion of the coverage. Overall, from 1996 (Atlanta) to 2006 (Torino), each time an

Table 4.1 Sources and distribution of athlete mentions by nationality in the 1996–2006 Olympics

Source (nationality, year)	N	% per night	Host	Reporters Male	Female	Profiles	Promos
US, 1996	3030a	57.2	390	2196b	71	302c	71d
Foreign, 1996	2268a	42.8	332	1661b	55	197c	23d
US, 1998	1991	47.0	237	1474	50	186	44e
Foreign, 1998	2242	53.0	342	1659	53	164	24e
US, 2000	3749	51.5	533f	2809	126g	154	127h
Foreign, 2000	3496	48.5	274f	2823	213g	128	58h
US, 2002	2835i	39.2	351j	2119k	122l	122	121m
Foreign, 2002	4388i	60.8	236j	3735k	235l	108	74m
US, 2004	7094n	54.9	703o	5522	381	294p	197q
Foreign, 2004	5839n	45.1	341o	4973	366	60p	98q
US, 2006	7097r	40.2	352s	2523t	136	65	151u
Foreign, 2006	5838r	59.8	131s	4434t	151	46	40u
Total	44963	100.0	4222	35928	1959	1826	1028

Note: Paired letters indicate χ^2 significant differences at the 0.05 level.

athlete was spoken about by an anchor, sportscaster, profile, or promotion, there was a 48.8 percent chance the athlete competed for the United States. Such a finding is hardly surprising; even the interviews with producers and sportscasters from NBC in Chapters 2 and 3 seemingly conceded that their goal is often to achieve 50/50 equilibrium between US and non-US athletes, which was more than accomplished over the ten-year period. Nonetheless, such results must be tempered with the notion that 48.8 percent is well over four times as many mentions as the amount of medals won by the US would warrant. To date, there are no studies that address how other countries fare in this specific regard.

Table 4.1 also allows one to determine where US athletes were prominently featured. Overall, on-site reporters devoted more mentions to non-US athletes, while pre-produced promotions for upcoming events were the most blatantly American. Such findings are cogent when one hypothesizes that much of the US viewing audience tunes in specifically to watch their home country do well; in Torino, for instance, promotions primed the audience for coverage of US figure skater Sasha Cohen and then on-site reporters discussed the performances of all six of the final skaters, with only two of the finalists being from the United States. The host/anchor also appeared to be primarily serving promotional functions here, as Nantz and Costas more frequently highlighted Americans than did on-site reporters. Indeed, it is clear that the anchors' job is to make the critical stories more salient and that the foremost of these stories involved US participants.

A longitudinal perspective, which Figure 4.1 provides, pinpoints the percentage of coverage devoted to US athletes for both the Summer and Winter Olympic Games from 1996–2006.

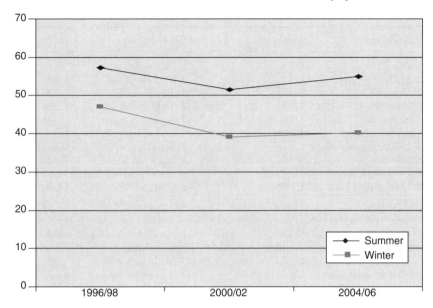

Figure 4.1 Percentage of coverage devoted to US athletes in the 1996–2006 Olympics

As the line graph shows, biases toward covering Americans peaked in the 1990s, lessened four years later, and then slightly increased most recently. The Winter Olympics has always highlighted a greater percentage of foreign athletes, most likely because—as producer Molly Solomon indicated in Chapter 2—little is left on the cutting-room floor for these Games. NBC is able to highlight all the prominent American athletes and yet still have a substantial amount of time to promote prominent athletes and stories from foreign countries. In the Summer Games, there are three times as many events, meaning the coverage can more directly focus on the American athletes that excel in the events that are deemed to be most worthy of primetime attention. In addition, the slight increases in US athlete coverage in 2004 and 2006 could be explained in two interrelated ways: (a) patriotism/nationalism was likely considered to be slightly more acceptable when the country was at war, which it was in both Games after the onset of the Iraq war of 2003, and (b) at least in the Winter Games, the US team is becoming increasingly more successful, meaning that events like snowboarding (which was not even offered ten years earlier) were allowing NBC the opportunity to high-light more US success stories.

   In terms of mentions, another useful heuristic is to examine the ten most-mentioned athletes in each of the Games, to understand who were pinpointed as subjects for the key stories of any Olympic coverage. Table 4.2 lists the top-ten athletes in terms of the number of times each was mentioned within the prime-time Olympic telecast.

Table 4.2 Most-mentioned athletes in primetime Olympic telecasts (1996–2006)

1996 (Atlanta)	Nation	1998 (Nagano)	Nation
1 Dan O' Brien	USA	1 Picabo Street	USA
2 Michael Johnson	USA	2 Michelle Kwan	USA
3 Vitaly Sherbo	Belarus	3 Tara Lipinski	USA
4 Kerri Strug	USA	4 Todd Eldridge	USA
5 Shannon Miller	USA	5 Hermann Maier	Austria
6 Alexei Nemov	Russia	6 Louis Zamperini	USA
7 Li Xioushuang	China	7 Elvis Stojko	Canada
8 Carl Lewis	USA	8 Ilya Kulik	Russia
9 Dominique Moceanu	USA	9 Masahiko Hirato	Japan
10 Dominique Dawes	USA	10 Chris Witty	USA

2000 (Sydney)	Nation	2002 (Salt Lake City)	Nation
1 Marion Jones	USA	1 Apolo Anton Ohno	USA
2 Cathy Freeman	Australia	2 Bode Miller	USA
3 Lenny Krayzelberg	USA	3 Michelle Kwan	USA
4 Michael Johnson	USA	4 Kim Dong-Sung	South Korea
5 Alexei Nemov	Russia	5 Christine Witty	USA
6 Maurice Greene	USA	6 Casey Fitzrandolph	USA
7 Jenny Thompson	USA	7 Kjetil Andre Aamodt	Norway
8 Blaine Wilson	USA	8 Chris Klug	USA
9 Svetlana Khorkina	Russia	9 David Pelletier	Canada
10 Brooke Bennett	USA	10 Jennifer Rodriguez	USA

2004 (Athens)	Nation	2006 (Torino)	Nation
1 Michael Phelps	USA	1 Apolo Anton Ohno	USA
2 Misty May	USA	2 Chad Hedrick	USA
3 Kerri Walsh	USA	3 Bode Miller	USA
4 Paul Hamm	USA	4 Shani Davis	USA
5 Ian Thorpe	Australia	5 Ahn Hyun-Soo	South Korea
6 Carly Patterson	USA	6 Shaun White	USA
7 Justin Gatlin	USA	7 Sasha Cohen	USA
8 Shawn Crawford	USA	8 Joey Cheek	USA
9 Laura Wilkinson	USA	9 Anja Pareson	Sweden
10 Maurice Greene	USA	10 Lindsey Jacobellis	USA

This table reveals interesting findings regarding the frequency of athlete mentions. A total of 44 of the 60 most-mentioned athletes in these six Olympic Games were from the United States, a whopping 73 percent. In addition, the number one most-mentioned athlete was always an American and, specifically in the Winter Games, the top three most-mentioned athletes were from the US despite the fact that US athletes fared slightly worse in terms of proportional medal achievement in the Winter Games than in the Summer Games. Sometimes the mentions could be attributed to the length of their competitions (e.g. Dan O'Brien led the list in 1996 partly because he was a decathlete, meaning NBC could show him competing in ten separate events) and other high frequency totals could be ascribed to brilliant athletic achievement (e.g. Michael Phelps clearly warranted being the most-mentioned athlete in 2004 if one considers he became the first Olympian from any country since 1980 to win eight medals in a single Olympic Games). Still, some of the athletes were undoubtedly mentioned frequently as the result of excessive hype of American athletes, none more so than Bode Miller in 2006, who was the third most-mentioned athlete despite the fact that he failed to win a medal in any of his events. Ironically, Miller was competing in five events, making the tracking of his failures touchingly long-winded.

Sportscaster descriptions

Using a database of 24,950 descriptors that encompassed attributions of success/failure or personality/physicality, conclusions can be drawn as to how NBC depicted the US Olympians as opposed to the characterizations of Olympians from other countries. While such a broad "us vs. them" dichotomy brings all non-US countries under a single rubric, previous research has found that such a two-pronged approach is useful in illuminating issues of network host country/home team biases (Billings and Tambosi, 2004), particularly as they explicate (and, subsequently, implicate) differential treatment based on self-identification status (Hogg and Reid, 2006; Hogg and Tindale, 2005; Turner *et. al.*, 1987).

A total of 10,228 (41 percent) descriptors were of US athletes, leaving 14,722 (59 percent) descriptors of athletes from all remaining countries. These frequencies were applied to all taxonomical categories as statistically anticipated frequencies, meaning that 41 percent of all comments about concentration or athletic skill would be expected to be applied to athletes from the US, with any significant deviation presenting a worthy heuristic for the study of nationalistic difference. Categories were subdivided by two main rubrics: (a) explanations for success and/or failure, and (b) personality/physicality descriptors.

Regarding explanations for the success or failure of an athlete, six significant differences emerged in at least two of the six analyzed Olympics. First, American athletes were more likely than foreign athletes to be depicted as succeeding because of superior concentration. US athletes received comments such as "on a mission" and "another determined effort for this US skier". In contrast, foreign athletes were depicted as lacking concentration with utterances including "forgot what the phrase of music was", "confused", and "distracted". These differences were uncovered in three Olympic Games (1996, 2004, and 2006), meaning that they existed in the earliest analysis and in the most contemporary Summer and Winter Olympic telecasts.

Second, the greatest number of comments rendered in any Olympics pertain to the athletic abilities of each participant and these comments skewed toward foreign athletes in the 2000 and 2004 Summer Games. US athletes who failed to perform as well as expected were described in derogatory terms—for example, as "physically under par", "not technically sound", and in one case, with the peremptory exclamation, "would be a shock if she could contend!" When US athletes did excel, the comments frequently claimed that their performances offered no room for athletic error (e.g. "used every bit of power"). Supreme athletic ability was also the reason attributed to the successes of many athletes hailing from countries outside the US, and there were many dialogues that veered toward the innate supremacy of a foreign athlete, arguing that their athletic skills were replete to the point of flawlessness. Foreign athletes were described as a "physical force", "a tank", "immaculate", "invincible", and "rock solid", implying a machine-like entity whose athletic skills trump any sense of emotion or outside influences.

Third, in the past two Winter Games, US athletes received copious comments about their superior composure. Such comments were particularly applied to members of the successful US figure-skating team who were described as "poised", "relaxed", "with no nerves", and having "statuesque, calm demeanour". It should be noted that while US athletes were characterized as succeeding because of their composure, foreign athletes were not inversely illustrated as failing because they were lacking in this area, although they did receive many negative comments, such as "looks terrified" or "tight". It was the repetitive nature of the positive evaluations of American composure that triggered significant differences in this area, whereas dips in the composure of US athletes were used as the explanation for failure.

Fourth, Olympians from the US again received a disproportionately high number of comments in portrayals of athletic commitment. Both in the 2004 and 2006 Games, US athletes received numerous comments about their triumphs arising from dedication at the highest level, receiving descriptors such as "scrapper", "fighter", "unrivaled tenacity and intensity", and "knows how painful it is going to be". Even in the 2006 Torino Games, when US downhill skier Bode Miller seemed to embody a lack of commitment to victory, the attributions for failure did not yield significant pejorative comments in relation to foreign athletes who were described as voluntarily relinquishing the Olympic dream—specifically that they "didn't care" and were "throwing it away".

Fifth, US athletes were also described by NBC as possessing greater courage, at least as measured by the number of descriptors. In the 1996, 2000, 2002, and 2006 Olympics, foreign athletes were less likely to have their achievements attributed to this variable. Sometimes one could point to a singular figure (such as US gymnast Kerri Strug's one-legged vault to secure gold for the US women's gymnastics team in 1996 or US alpine skier Lindsey Kildow's return from a devastating crash to compete again in Torino) as a rationale for the higher figures, but given that four of the six analyses generated these differences, the trend appears clear and perfunctory. There is a noticeable tendency in the storytelling process to focus on overcoming obstacles of great magnitude, with expressions such as "pushing through the pain", "brave return", and "gutty". Courageousness was also associated with many support stories about athletes overcoming illness and adversity, from asthma to lung cancer. The breadth of the stories revealed the preparedness of the NBC commentators.

Finally, one area in which foreign athletes received more comments than US athletes was in the taxonomical category of experience. Olympians from countries other than the United States were more likely to be ascribed labels such as "veteran", "mature", and "highly decorated". Even when these athletes were less successful than in the past, they were characterized as dealing effectively with the impediments to their achievement—for example, they had "learned how to deal with success as well as failure". Meanwhile, US athletes were more frequently depicted as failing because they simply had not "been there before" causing a "meltdown based on inexperience", while others simply "need maturity". Such differences were found in 1996, 1998, 2002, and 2004, all in the same direction favoring experience as a reason for foreign athletic successes and, consequently, the lack of US successes.

When making the transition to the analysis of personality and physicality of the athletes, the results shift dramatically. While six categories yielded significant differences in two or more Olympics when studying the attributions of success and failure, only one of the personality or physicality categories offered significant differences in more than a single Olympic Games. The single taxonomical area in which there were documentable nationalistic differences was regarding the discussion of the background of athletes, specifically regarding the geographical area from which athletes came, with Americans receiving increased frequencies of these comments. But whereas American athletes were associated with their local region as, for example, when one of them was dubbed as an "impetuous New Hampshire rebel", foreign athletes were allied to their countries as a "German star" or a "Croatian wonder". In addition to the athletes' backgrounds, the personality/physicality classification also included the areas of introversion, extroversion, emotionality, attractiveness, and size/parts of body, totaling over 5,000 comments. Despite this large sample, no significant differences were found between American and foreign athletes in any of the areas apart from athletes' backgrounds, indicating that nationalistic differences in these areas cannot be viewed as primary biases.

Overall, these findings can collectively offer insight into the evaluative differences imparted by sportscasters about US and foreign athletes in the Olympic telecast. Foreign athletes were more often characterized as succeeding because of two quantifiable variables: (a) athletic ability [which can be assessed by a score or clock] and (b) experience [which can be determined by consulting the résumé of each athlete]. In contrast, subjective measures seemed to inordinately favor athletes from the United States, as they were more frequently depicted as winning because of immeasurable determinations such as concentration, composure, commitment, and courage. It appears that when athletes from the United States succeeded, it was more likely to be explained as due to some innate determination or Olympic spirit, whereas foreign athletes were said to have won because they were technically superior and had been perfecting their craft for longer durations.

One can witness these dual dialogues in many ways, but a comparison between the pre-produced profiles of alpine skiers in 2002 provides a useful exemplar. Two decorated skiers, Lasse Kjus and Kjetil Andre Aamodt, hailed from Norway. They were profiled jointly by NBC, with the following opening to the pre-produced profile, narrated by Tim Ryan:

> TR: Lasse Kjus and Kjetil Andre Aamodt took to the slopes as two-year-olds, growing up in the suburbs of Oslo, just 50 miles apart. As boys, they would measure their abilities at local club races. Kuis, eight months the senior, was the natural talent; Aamodt, the tireless worker.

The profile subsequently flashes on-screen text to display their achievements (i.e. experience), indicating that they were the winners of "9 Olympic medals" going into the Salt Lake City Olympics. Descriptions of these athletes are clearly focused on their innate talents and unrelenting spirits. The performances of these athletes were also focused specifically on their skills, with comments such as "likes the ice", "one of the most powerful skiers, and he can really rip through it" and "rides the edge so beautifully, so cleanly".

In contrast, the US skier Bode Miller was depicted with much more personality, arguing that he was an atypical skier who relied on assets other than technical skills. One short pre-produced package for him offered just his own narrative voiceover that aided the shaping of this different picture:

> BM: I would say, pretty close to all out is how I ski. It just seems like, to me, the most honest way to do it. And my style is definitely not normal. When I'm skiing my fastest, it looks different. I would say I pretty much go for it.

One easily identifies the differences between the two narratives with the Norweigan skiers sharing a profile, having the opening narrated by an NBC broadcaster, and indicating that technical skills combined with commitment yielded Olympian results; US skier Bode Miller is a stark contrast—a solo profile, narrated by Miller himself, that focuses on how he wins medals without the fundamental aspects typically ascribed to Olympic medal winners. These types of dual dialogues show how the US/non-US distinction was frequently employed.

Nationalistic conclusions

In this examination of six Olympic telecasts, the seemingly crude dichotomous measure of US vs. non-US athletes resulted in significant findings at many levels, signaling that sportscasters treat US national athletes in a particular way that is significantly different from the treatment of non-US athletes. Both the mention and descriptor analyses illustrated that 41–44 percent of the time is devoted to the coverage of US athletes, a spike of 300–400 percent compared to the 11–13 percent of the medals US athletes won in these Games over the ten-year duration.

NBC's focus on American nationals is driven by mass media ratings and advertising rates—a practice that is replicated in other countries. There is an inherent question in this process about a necessary balance between highlighting athletes from the home country and representing the full breadth of Olympism. It would seem that America's NBC sports telecast carries a greater burden in this regard than the telecasts of other countries, as much of the world regards the NBC Olympic telecast as the grandest, most thorough, and most intricate of all. Given NBC's status as the foremost global media juggernaut, expectations are higher that the network will be able to chronicle a sport history that would be relevant to future generations of countries across the world.

Longitudinal trends in the percentage of coverage devoted to US athletes in NBC's coverage provide additional insight. NBC accelerated the international-ization of television sport coverage at the turn of the twenty-first century, making stories and coverage of foreign athletes and teams more salient than in previous Olympic telecasts. Still, these percentages traversed back to the foundational baselines of the 1990s at the Athens and Torino Games. Additionally, the Summer Games appear to highlight US athletes at a rate significantly higher than in the Winter Games. It is true that more US athletes win medals in the Summer Games, but the number of medals won remains relatively in proportion to the dramatically increased number of events offered in a Summer Olympiad. Instead, the difference is likely the result of increased framing techniques. The Summer Games may offer three times as many events as the Winter Games, but primetime hours are finite, meaning that NBC has more events from which to select the athletes/stories to highlight in their evening telecast. Inevitably, NBC can fill the Summer primetime telecasts with high-profile events that almost uni-versally feature medal-winning US athletes. In contrast, the Winter Olympics of 2006, for instance, produced only nine US gold medal winners, making it impos-sible for NBC's coverage to continually show US Winter Olympians winning gold each of the 17 nights of the Torino telecast. Future studies should continue to interrogate NBC's primetime telecast for issues of identity portrayals; however, an analysis ripe for comparison would be to examine issues such as nationalistic salience on NBC's other telecasts in different time slots and on their other cable networks. One would likely surmise that the international stories receive greater focus within these other network outlets that do not inherently require gigantic Nielsen ratings to be considered programmatically successful.

Table 4.2 reports the most-mentioned athletes in each of the six Olympics that were studied, suggesting that American athletes are the ultimate focus of the telecast. Not only were nearly three-quarters of the most-mentioned athletes from the United States, but the remaining athletes on the list were nearly uni-versally competing with other top-ten American athletes, serving as foils to the competition. Indeed, it is not easy to imagine that an athlete such as South Korea's Kim Dong-Sung would have been mentioned nearly as frequently if he had been without the rivalry he had with US short-track speed skater Apolo Anton Ohno. Some foreign athletes clearly transcended the focus on US athletes (such as in 2000, with host Australia's swimmer Ian Thorpe and sprinter Cathy Freeman) and others were highlighted because they were the best athletes in the most popular Olympic sports (such as gymnasts Li Xioushuang and Alexi Nemov). Although 73 percent of the most-mentioned athletes were from the US—substantially more than the 44 percent of the total mentions ascribed to US athletes— the overall medal chart indicates that many countries do as well if not better than the US in the Winter Games and are fairly close to the US in the Summer Games. And although no NBC commentator or anchor ever indicated within any telecast that the US team was vastly superior to any other Olympic team competing, NBC has made it a policy to not air overall medal counts by country, which can serve to construct a false picture that US athletes are more successful overall than they really are.

Conceptions of self-categorization (Turner *et al.*, 1987) also appear primary to any discussion of nationalism in NBC's telecast. The very strong US orientation is further strengthened since the overwhelming majority of NBC's sportscasting talent are US citizens and/or former US athletes. However, without question, most of them are trying their absolute best to render the fairest, most accurate accounts of athletes from both home and abroad (as witnessed in Chapter 3), but with foreign athletes they face substantially more difficulties as language barriers, for instance, make interviews more arduous and a lack of knowledge about, and understanding of, unfamiliar cultures and societies could cause a sportscaster to revert to discussing what he or she knows best: American athletes, American culture, and American sensibilities.

Interestingly, only one personality/physicality difference was uncovered in more than a single Olympic telecast. Using the theoretical frameworks established earlier, one could surmise that foreign athletes would receive fewer comments in the personality-driven categories and increased comments in the physicality classifications (which are more readily observable by sportscasters). Still, no entrenched deviations emerged, leaving future scholars to explore and explain why nationalistic biases did not permeate commentary in the same manner as the dialogue regarding athletic successes and failures. The reason for the lack of significant findings may reside in the difference between the evaluation of an athletic performance and the evaluative nature of characterizing the athlete individually.

The descriptors also imparted knowledge as to what these differential sportscasting group identities could inflict upon actual on-air dialogue. Perhaps the most valuable insight in this chapter arises from the types of comments that were more likely to explain the successes and failures of US and non-US athletes. The external/subjective measures were the areas in which US athletes were more frequently characterized as mastering, but one must take these findings within the theoretical frameworks discussed previously. Undoubtedly American sportscasters can more effortlessly communicate with US athletes and are more familiar with their back stories, but they have a comparatively rudimentary understanding of the intricacies of foreign athletes. It is, therefore, easier for them to comment on the number of years a foreign athlete has competed or the high-scores or personal-best times they have achieved than to make more personal comments regarding character and personality, as they do with US athletes. The result is a two-pronged approach to commentary that could feed notions of foreign athletes being emotionless cyborgs whose purpose is to conquer athletic competitions, a stereotype repeated in other areas of mass media, such as the depiction in the cinematic *Rocky IV* of Russia's Ivan Drago—a character who possessed vastly superior athletic skills to the American challenger, Rocky Balboa, but who ultimately lost because Rocky possessed more commitment, focus, and courage.

The sense of familiarity with "one's own" athletes dovetails well with arguments specifically regarding in-group and out-group communication patterns. Given that a US network's depiction of the Olympics uses predominantly US sportscasters and is framed for a primarily English-speaking US audience, it is not surprising that the divisions between in-groups and out-groups are evident. Chapters 2 and 3 on NBC's production and sportscasting highlighted that the biggest mistake sportscasters could make was to refer to the United States using personal pronouns, differential voice inflections, or other ways to indicate that a favorite athlete or personal hero had emerged and should be supported because of his or her citizenship above any notion of the Olympic spirit. But the sportscasters' construction of US athletes as insiders can have a contradictory effect as it can both damage the credibility of the sportscast and encourage and intensify US nationalism and xenophobia (Allison, 2000).

5 Competing on the same stage
Gender and the Olympic telecasts

After 30 years of Title IX and surging female athleticism, the sport world we know barely resembles the world many of us were born into.

(Messner, 2002, p. xii)

To begin an examination of the interaction of gender and language as they relate to power structures, one must first evaluate how gender is constructed through language.

(Crawford and Kaufman, 2006, p. 185)

When Title IX was implemented in the US in 1972 with the aim of removing sexual discrimination in educationally based athletic programs receiving federal funds, there was a dramatic increase in female participation in school and college sport. In spite of contradictory effects in the following years (Hargreaves, 1994; Hult, 1989; Billings, 2000), Messner (2002) observes that there continues to be a surge of female athletic participation and correlative interest levels, something O'Reilly and Cahn (2007) describe as a "spectacular transformation ... in which the right to play sports and receive resources commensurate with men's sports is rarely disputed" (pp. xi–xii). Nonetheless, there is a notable discrepancy between active female participation in sport and the portrayal of girls and women within media sport. In the US, for example, ESPN's *SportsCenter*[1] routinely focuses on women's athletics at a less than 2 percent rate (Adams and Tuggle, 2004; Eastman and Billings, 2000); and even in mainstream newspapers, such as the *New York Times*, less than 10 percent of their sports space is devoted to women (Eastman and Billings, 2000).

---

1 *SportsCenter* is ESPN's flagship television program, offering breaking sports news, analysis, and highlights at various points throughout the day. The sports newscast has been shown since ESPN's inception, with over 30,000 programs airing since 1979.

Men's team sports remain the most popular of all media sport in the United States; American football, basketball, and baseball continue to form the foremost triumvirate of male sporting interests, blanketing all 12 months of the calendar year and dominating sports coverage, news programs and talk radio. Conversely, women's sports are largely regarded as a niche market, with the exception of some individual sports, such as tennis, golf, and figure skating. Taken as a whole, the sports media continue to be overwhelmingly male-dominated.

However, NBC's Olympic telecast represents one of the most progressive outlets of all American sports media in terms of its awareness of the long history of gender inequalities in sport and its commitment to make female Olympians more visible. The telecast showcases women's athletics with unprecedented salience when compared to any other media outlet. Even so, it still highlights more men than women, even at times when women win the majority of the US medals (Billings and Eastman, 2002, 2003; Billings and Angelini, 2007; Eastman and Billings, 1999; Higgs and Weiller, 1994; Tuggle and Owen, 1999; Tuggle *et al.*, 2007). But the issue of equality between the sexes in the Olympic telecast is just one part of a thorny, intricate question. In order to better understand the character and effects of gendered differences, a scrutiny of the language used to describe the social backgrounds and performances of men and women athletes and the construction of their sporting masculinities and femininities has been useful to complement the documentation of the unequal exposure of men and women on television.

Given that the Olympics includes many diverse events, it is also significant to ascertain which sports are more likely to receive air-time, and if, for example, men are viewed in powerful, dominating sports, while woman are shown predominantly in swimsuits and leotards. In other words, it matters fundamentally what transpires within the sports media, who and what are represented, how gender is portrayed, and, as Crawford and Kaufman (2006) signal in the earlier quotation, the particular role of *language* in these processes. For instance, what is said about women athletes when they are portrayed? How does commentary fluctuate between men and women athletes?

There is an important link between the participation of women in sport and their representation in the media, and so this chapter very briefly outlines first the historical growth in participation and approval of women in sport, including the history of gender portrayals in the sports media, and it subsequently interrogates potential gender biases in the Olympic telecast through three related, yet distinctive, measures: (a) clock-time devoted to men's and women's sports, (b) mentions of men and women athletes, and (c) specific dialogues employed to describe men and women athletes by Olympic sportscasters. Such interrogations are critical because, as Hall (1986) emphasized, "It matters profoundly what and who gets represented, what and who routinely gets left out, and how things, people, events, relationships are represented" (p. 9).

Women in sport: a historical overview

From their inception in the nineteenth century, modern sports have been organized in ways that have systematically discriminated against women through the separation of the sexes into classifications such as dominant and inferior, powerful and weak, aggressive, and pretty (Davis, 1997; Jones *et al.*, 1999; Nelson, 1994; Toohey and Veal, 2000; Tuggle *et al.*, 2002; Ward, 2004). Toohey and Veal (2000) argue that gender disparity in sport has been based on scientifically and morally based assumptions that "women are physically inferior to men and that it is unbecoming for them to indulge in certain activities, many Olympic sports being included on the list of inappropriate pastimes" (p. 179).

Hargreaves (1994) catalogs three phases of women's participation in the Olympics. The first, she suggests, was from the dawn of modern sports in 1896 to 1928, which was largely an era of exclusion and dismissal of women's sports; the second spans from 1928 to 1952—a period when primarily "feminine-appropriate" sports received recognition and then standards of skill and international competition accelerated; and the third ranges from 1952 to the present day, during which time women's sports have pushed the boundaries of traditional masculine hegemony, and female athleticism is celebrated. But it has only been since the 1970s that there has been a systematic challenge to the overwhelmingly negative stigmas of the past about female sport. American women who have been influenced by the wider feminist movement—specifically those who have grown up during the post-Title IX era in the United States—have staked a claim to athletic legitimacy, as have those women from other contexts who have been influenced by sports development programs and the women's rights movements in their own countries. The strengthening of women's sports spread from countries in the West, to those in the old Eastern Bloc and to developing nations across the world (Hargreaves, 2000; O'Riordan, 2007). Women participated in greater numbers over the years, pushed their athletic abilities to unprecedentedly high achievement levels, and shattered records again and again (Kane, 1989; Lenskyj, 1994, 2002). Consequently, women have often become pawns in the war for Olympic medals, heroines both inside and outside their own countries, with their accomplishments spectacularized and honored in the media (Hargreaves, 2000).

Depictions of gender in televised sport

However, and ironically, the mass media have served as willing enablers of gender discrimination in sport through the generation of a dual communication culture (Maltz and Borker, 1982)—one aspect of which is masculine, focusing on athletics being played at purportedly its highest level, and the other aspect of which is feminine, targeted to a niche audience, and continually reinforcing the "supposedly crucial biological differences" between males and females (Williams *et al.*, 1985, p. 643)—in print (Claringbould *et al.*, 2004; Daddario, 1992; Lumpkin and Williams, 1991; Theberge, 1991) and on television (Antcliff,

2005; Billings, 2007; Billings and Eastman, 2002, 2003; Daddario and Wigley, 2007; Duncan *et al.*, 1990), in the United States (Adams and Tuggle, 2004; Fuller, 2006; Tuggle and Owen, 1999) and beyond (Capranica and Aversa, 2002; Urquhart and Crossman, 1999). Over the years, programming strategies by sports television network executives have reinforced the belief that the airing of men's sport is the surest way to secure solid ratings.

Stephenson (2002) contends that female athletes have been characterized in novel yet perplexing ways and these gender differences in media coverage can have profound effects, even subtly influencing men and women about what sports they should or should not play (Matteo, 1986). Although the gap between men's and women's athletic achievements (as defined by world records) is closing over time (Dyer, 1989; Simri, 1977) and Hargreaves (1994) claims that "women have exploded the myths surrounding female biology and are engaged in a process of reinterpretation of physical ability" (p. 284), Trujillo (1991) neverthe-less contends that "perhaps no single institution in American culture has influenced our sense of masculinity more than sport" (p. 292).

The popular practice in the media of making direct comparisons between men's and women's achievements in sport tends to solidify masculine hegemony (Davis, 1997; Pelak, 2002) and male superiority (Messner, 1988). For instance, when I ask my sports media class to name the top auto racing driver, they fre-quently cite Tony Stewart, Jeff Gordon, or Dale Earnhardt, Jr.—all of whom compete in the NASCAR circuit, a form of stock car racing. When I inform these students that there are dozens of other drivers on the Indy car circuit who drive much faster (often 50 miles per hour or greater), they feel duped by the ini-tial question. Indeed, they are correct that there were two ways to answer the question: who is the *best* driver and who is the *fastest* driver. Conceptions of sporting achievement tends to privilege speed and power over finesse (McKay, 1997), agility, or other trained athletic skills, reinforcing hegemonic gender dis-tinctions in the process. Dyer (1989) contends that:

> Physiological differences are undoubtedly responsible for some of the perfor-mance differential between sexes but it is simply flying in the face of evidence to label physiology the sole cause. To do that directs attention from what those other causes might be.
>
> (p. 97)

The immense volume of coverage of men's sports vis-à-vis the substantially lower volume of coverage of women's sport clearly sends a message to the reader and/or the viewer of media sport that men's sport is more significant—a reason why Harry (1995) argues that sports lag behind modern attitudes on gender. For example, Lumpkin and Williams (1991) found that just 9 percent of all *Sports Illustrated* articles were specific to women's sports, which is four times more gen-erous when compared to televised sports (Adams and Tuggle, 2004). The results of another analysis found that the National Spelling Bee received more *SportsCenter* coverage than the total coverage of women's sports for an entire week (Eastman and Billings, 2000). Still, it is not just the lack of coverage given to women's sports that suggests that they are unimportant; it is also *what* sports are covered that is significant. Kane (1988) found that women were three times as likely to be shown in *Sports Illustrated* in sex-appropriate sports, findings that are consistent with other sex biases found in *Sports Illustrated* studies (Bishop, 2003; Cuneen and Sidwell, 1998; Daddario, 1992; Fink and Kensicki, 2002).

There are also deep-seated biases in terms of the gendered language that is used by sports journalists and announcers (Messner *et al.*, 1993). The preeminent form of gender bias within televised sport has been the single-minded spotlight on the attractiveness of female athletes (Bryson, 1987; Hilliard, 1984). Not only are "feminine appropriate" sports (like golf, tennis, and swimming) more likely to be shown than less glamorous sports (like softball and hockey), but the media favor the athletes playing these sports who are of near supermodel status (e.g. tennis players Anna Kournikova and Maria Sharapova). When conventionally heterosexually attractive athletes play at very high levels, a media "perfect storm" emerges, such as the multiple hours of primetime coverage devoted to women's beach volleyball in the 2004 Summer Olympics because of the widespread appeal of exceptional US athletes Kerri Walsh and Misty May winning the gold medal while donning alluring swimsuits (Billings and Angelini, 2007). Relatedly, although it was claimed that the gold medal won by the 1999 US Women's Soccer World Cup team was the primary reason for increased coverage, the physical attractiveness of the team undoubtedly also impelled media attention (Christopherson *et al.*, 2002), with Brandi Chastain's removal of her jersey providing the most enduring image of the Cup.[2]

Analyses of individual sports have proven useful heuristics for the understanding of gender in televised sport. Much focus has been placed on basketball, which has received a groundswell of support in past decades through increased women's college basketball coverage and the inception of the US professional league, the WNBA. All studies reported substantial differences in the ways in which men's and women's basketball games were aired (Kane and Parks, 1992; Theberge and Cronk, 1986). Hallmark and Armstrong (1999) focused on the television production of the men's and women's NCAA basketball championships (1991–1995), concluding that the women's championship game employed far fewer cameras and fewer graphics than the men's championship telecast, a discovery that correlates with the arguments of Messner *et al.* (1996) who concluded that the men's Final Four was constructed by the sports/media complex to be a "must see", while the women's Final Four was constructed largely as a "non-event". Differences in dialogue were also identified (Blinde *et al.*, 1991; Duncan and Brummett, 1987), with Duncan and Hasbrook (1988) noting that commentators were frequently describing women's play as "very pretty" and

---

2   Chastain scored the winning penalty kick in the United States' 1999 defeat of China, removing her jersey and celebrating in her sports bra.

"beautiful"—comments which were never applied to men athletes. During the 2000 college basketball men's and women's championships, Billings *et al.* (2002) uncovered a disproportionate number of observations about men players' physical abilities and high tallies of comments about their positive consonance (i.e. luck), physical beauty, and personality. While these traits are not considered to be inherently masculine, such differential dialogues underscore how dialogue is often segmented by gender. Even promotions for the WNBA reinforced gender hierarchies and masculine dominance (Wearden and Creedon, 2003).

Sports such as golf and tennis persistently yield gender disparities in sportscaster dialogue (Vincent, 2004; Weiller and Higgs, 1999). Billings *et al.* (2005) applied a pre-tested and refined content analysis taxonomy to uncover two dozen critical differences in the ways men and women golfers were portrayed on television. For instance, women were more likely than men to be described in terms of why they succeeded or failed, whereas men were more likely than women to be depicted with personality or physical attributes. Additionally, women were significantly more likely to be deemed "lucky", consistent with the findings from Billings *et al.* (2006) who even documented a male golfer receiving a favorable bounce and the sportscaster adjudicating the shot to have received an "Annika bounce", a reference to Annika Sorenstam, who competed admirably in the men's tournament that weekend, but who the sportscasters considered to have benefited from a disproportionate amount of luck. Tennis analyses (e.g. Billings, 2003a) have uncovered gender differences as well, including Halbert and Latimer's (1994) finding that an exhibition match between Jimmy Connors and Martina Navratilova yielded many more lauded comments about Connors than Navratilova, even when the score was tied.

Media analyses specifically of the Olympics (Duncan, 1986; Higgs *et al.*, 2003; Lee, 1992; Lenskyj, 2002) have also revealed gender discrimination in terms of both quantity and quality of coverage. In terms of clock-time, interesting trends have been uncovered (Higgs and Weiller, 1994; Tuggle and Owen, 1999). While the Olympic Games are the only megasporting event that draws more women viewers than men viewers (Sandomir, 1992; Toohey, 1997), the US telecast concentrates on men's sports more than women's sports (Billings and Angelini, 2007; Billings and Eastman, 2002, 2003). For example, in 1994, all of the gold medals won by the United States were won by women, yet CBS's coverage showed men the majority of the time. In fact, Eastman and Billings (1999) found that in the 1996 Atlanta Games, although women athletes were promoted more than men, it was men who were given the majority of the clock-time. Even in terms of the most-mentioned athletes, the top-20 most mentioned athletes have been overwhelmingly men, with gymnasts and figure skaters only slenderly aiding the women's total (Billings and Angelini, 2007).

Focusing on the language used in Olympic telecasts and the descriptions applied to men and women athletes, Farrell (1989) asserted that the mass media like their Olympic heroes to be male, boyishly charming, and brash at times; Eastman and Billings (1999) found that women were more likely to be portrayed in stereotypical ways (e.g. failing because they lack experience with terms like "youngster" and "immature"). Similarly, when Daddario (1994) contrasted the assessment of slalom skier Bianca Fernandez as, a "linebacker ... very aggressive with those big pads on her shoulders", with the description of figure skater Nancy Kerrigan's "elegant presence", she was pinpointing the male-like, butch character-izations of women taking part in traditional male sports and the conventionally feminized heterosexual images of women taking part in those sports that have been characterized as "feminine appropriate" (Kane, 1989; Tuggle and Owen, 1999). The practice of assigning the characterizations of compulsory heterosexu-ality (e.g. Anderson, 2005; Connell, 1987) to female athletes results in more comments like those alluding to Kerrigan in the overall discourse, than to those that masculinize female athletes, since women competing in field hockey, softball, shot put or discus, for example, are relegated to short segments between main events, if they are covered at all. Indeed, the entire telecast is geared toward attractive athletes doing attractive things, as NBC President Dick Ebersol stresses that "every minute we showed boxing, we lost a minimum of 25 percent of the audience. The Olympics are driven by female-appeal sports, and we lost all the women". In underscoring these demographic concerns, Ebersol emphasizes how the Olympics often function outside of the traditional domain of the sports media, which is less concerned about losing the woman viewer. Indeed, the continued high ratings of the Olympics in a time of general television ratings erosion (arising from increased channels and Internet offerings) indicates that the loyalties of women viewers are typically more fickle than those of men, who will be ensconced in front of sport on television even when the event is not defined in traditionally masculine terms. Kane and Greendorfer (1994) argue that the media hold the power to challenge predominant gender ideologies—and also to succumb to them. It appears that the bulk of sports telecasts yield to the pressures to lend preference to men's sports, even at a time when the public appears to be more ready to embrace women's sport (Toohey, 1997).

Gender Olympic measures

Clock-time

Understanding the gendered character of the Olympic telecast stems initially from comparative clock-time measures of men's and women's sports. One way in which stories are framed is through mere exposure and, more cogently, what is selected to be shown, what is emphasized, and what is excluded (Gitlin, 1980; Tankard, 2001). Agenda-setting theory also relates to such notions. While the first agenda-setting studies examined political campaigns (McCombs and Shaw, 1972), there are parallels to the Olympic telecast. Both events offer myriad stories in which gatekeepers must decide what content is shown and what issues—because of time/budget constraints—are relegated to secondary status or are not mentioned at all. Given that such agendas are negotiated in a much more deliberate manner, with multiple people negotiating clock-time decisions weeks and often years in advance within interpersonal interactions (Yang and Stone,

2003), agenda-setting functions are more attributable to NBC's production frame-work than to other identity measures of mentions and sportscaster descriptors.

Since the 1996 Games (which Dick Ebersol and Bob Costas dubbed the "Title IX Games" because most of the female Olympians at these Games were the first female athletes who had lived their entire lives in the Title IX era), my co-oper-ative work with several other scholars (most notably Susan Eastman at Indiana University) has provided longitudinal insights into the amount of clock-time devoted to men and women athletes. First, the relatively good news: the Summer Olympic results. Tables 5.1 and 5.2 tally the total amount of time given to men's and women's sports within NBC's primetime telecasts.

Table 5.1 Clock-time for men in the 1996, 2000, and 2004 Summer Olympics

Event	1996	%	2000	%	2004	%	Total	%
Archery	0:08	0.8	0:00	0.0	0:00	0.0	0:08	0.2
Badminton	0:00	0.0	0:00	0.0	<0:01	0.0	<0.01	<0.1
Baseball	0:07	0.7	0:12	1.2	0:03	0.2	0:22	0.7
Basketball	2:49	16.3	1:50	11.2	0:09	0.7	4:48	8.6
Beach volleyball	n.a.	n.a.	0:14	1.4	0:01	0.1	0:15	0.4
Boxing	0:00	0.0	0:00	0.0	0:01	0.1	0:01	<0.1
Canoe/kayak	0:13	1.3	0:00	0.0	0:03	0.2	0:16	0.5
Cycling	0:21	2.0	0:19	1.9	0:40	3.0	1:20	2.4
Diving	1:25	8.2	1:10	7.1	1:59	8.9	4:34	8.2
Equestrian	0:00	0.0	0:18	1.8	0:01	0.1	0:19	0.6
Fencing	0:00	0.0	0:00	0.0	<0:01	0.0	<0:01	<0.1
Field hockey	0:00	0.0	0:00	0.0	<0:01	0.0	<0:01	<0.1
Gymnastics	5:51	33.9	3:58	24.2	5:50	26.1	15:39	28.0
Handball	0:00	0.0	0:00	0.0	<0:01	0.0	<0:01	<0.1
Judo	0:00	0.0	0:00	0.0	<0:01	0.0	<0:01	<0.1
Marathon	0:00	0.0	0:39	4.0	0:00	0.0	0:39	1.1
Mountain biking	0:00	0.0	0:04	0.4	0:00	0.0	0:04	0.1
Rhythmic gymnastics	0:00	0.0	0:00	0.0	0:00	0.0	0:00	0.0
Rowing	0:00	0.0	0:31	3.2	0:15	1.1	0:46	1.4
Sailing	0:00	0.0	0:00	0.0	0:02	0.1	0:02	0.1
Shooting	0:00	0.0	0:00	0.0	0:01	0.1	0:01	<0.1
Soccer	0:06	0.6	0:12	1.2	0:06	0.4	0:24	0.7
Swimming	0:46	4.4	2:31	15.4	4:49	21.5	8:06	14.5
Synchronized swimming	0:00	0.0	0:00	0.0	0:00	0.0	0:00	0.0
Table tennis	0:35	3.4	0:00	0.0	<0:01	0.0	0:35	1.0
Taekwondo	0:00	0.0	0:00	0.0	<0:01	0.0	<0:01	<0.1
Tennis	0:05	0.5	0:00	0.0	0:01	0.1	0:06	0.2
Track and field	3:45	21.8	2:49	17.2	6:47	30.3	13:21	23.9
Trampoline	n.a.	n.a.	n.a.	n.a.	0:00	0.0	0:00	0.0
Triathlon	0:00	0.0	0:35	3.6	<0:01	0.0	0:35	1.0
Volleyball	0:00	0.0	0:19	1.9	0:57	4.2	1:16	2.3
Water polo	0:00	0.0	0:00	0.0	0:01	0.1	0:01	<0.1
Weightlifting	0:09	0.9	0:19	1.9	0:03	0.2	0:31	0.9
Wrestling	0:54	5.2	0:22	2.2	0:30	2.2	1:46	3.2
Men's total	17:14	100.0	16:22	100.0	22:22	100.0	55:58	100.0
% including women		50.7		52.5		52.3		51.9

Table 5.2 Clock-time for women in the 1996, 2000, and 2004 Summer Olympics

Event	1996	%	2000	%	2004	%	Total	%
Archery	0:00	0.0	0:00	0.0	<0:01	<0.1	<0:01	<0.1
Badminton	0:00	0.0	0:00	0.0	<0:01	<0.1	<0:01	<0.1
Basketball	0:17	1.7	0:15	1.6	0:03	0.2	0:35	1.1
Beach volleyball	n.a	n.a	0:00	0.0	2:00	9.8	2:00	3.9
Canoe/kayak	0:13	1.3	0:00	0.0	0:15	1.2	0:28	0.9
Cycling	0:18	1.8	0:00	0.0	<0:01	<0.1	0:18	0.6
Diving	2:35	15.3	2:04	14.0	3:08	15.4	7:47	15.0
Equestrian	0:06	0.6	0:00	0.0	<0:01	<0.1	0:06	0.2
Fencing	0:00	0.0	0:00	0.0	0:05	0.4	0:05	0.2
Field hockey	0:00	0.0	0:00	0.0	<0:01	<0.1	<0:01	<0.1
Gymnastics	9:34	57.2	5:04	34.3	6:09	30.2	20:47	40.1
Handball	0:00	0.0	0:00	0.0	<0:01	<0.1	<0:01	<0.1
Judo	0:00	0.0	0:00	0.0	<0:01	<0.1	<0:01	<0.1
Mountain biking	0:25	2.5	0:00	0.0	0:00	0.0	0:25	0.8
Rhythmic gymnastics	0:02	0.2	0:00	0.0	<0:01	<0.1	0:02	0.1
Rowing	0:00	0.0	0:07	0.8	0:14	1.1	0:21	0.7
Sailing	0:00	0.0	0:00	0.0	<0:01	<0.1	<0:01	<0.1
Shooting	0:00	0.0	0:00	0.0	0:00	0.0	0:00	0.0
Soccer	0:23	2.3	0:00	0.0	0:14	1.1	0:37	1.2
Softball	0:30	3.0	0:00	0.0	0:00	0.0	0:30	1.0
Swimming	0:55	5.5	2:06	14.2	3:00	14.7	6:01	11.6
Synchronized swimming	0:21	2.1	0:00	0.0	0:19	1.6	0:40	1.3
Table tennis	0:00	0.0	0:00	0.0	<0:01	<0.1	<0:01	<0.1
Taekwondo	0:00	0.0	0:04	0.5	<0:01	<0.1	0:04	0.1
Tennis	0:03	0.3	0:02	0.2	0:01	0.1	0:06	0.2
Track & field	1:02	6.2	3:39	24.7	4:05	20.0	8:46	16.9
Trampoline	n.a.	n.a.	n.a.	n.a	0:11	0.9	0:11	0.4
Triathlon	0:00	0.0	0:40	4.5	0:22	1.8	1:02	2.0
Volleyball	0:00	0.0	0:46	5.2	0:12	1.0	0:58	1.9
Water polo	0:00	0.0	0:00	0.0	<0:01	<0.1	<0:01	<0.1
Weightlifting	0:00	0.0	0:00	0.0	<0:01	<0.1	<0:01	<0.1
Women's total	16:44	100.0	14:47	100.0	20:22	100.0	51:53	100.0
% including men		49.3		47.5		47.7		48.1

As these tables reveal, the difference between men's and women's athletics is relatively meager, with an overall split of less than four percentage points. Men's dominance in clock-time was reinforced in each of the three Olympic telecasts, yet many more men compete in a Summer Games, providing one justification for the modest split. However, the notion that the larger number of men athletes vis-à-vis women athletes entered in the Games should equate to more clock-time is arguably misleading. The primetime telecast nearly always highlights the final rounds of any event so that athletes pre-determined to not be in contention for a medal are rarely (if ever) shown in primetime. In sum, one could resolve with a rudimentary glance at the Summer Olympic tables that the telecast comes close to gender parity—certainly closer than virtually all other modern sportscasts.

When delving deeper into the numbers of men and women athletes at the Summer Olympics, the results showed that the five most-shown men's events— in order of popularity—were gymnastics, track and field, swimming, basketball, and diving. For women, the top five were quite similar: gymnastics, track and field, diving, swimming, and beach volleyball. But while gymnastics was number one on both lists, the gap between gymnastics and track and field was less than two and a half hours for men, but was over 11 hours for women. Eight men's events (basketball, cycling, diving, gymnastics, swimming, track and field, volleyball, and wrestling) received at least one hour of coverage while only six women's events (beach volleyball, diving, gymnastics, swimming, track and field, and triathlon) received an hour or more. Such exemplars underscore how lopsided the Olympic coverage can be toward highlighting a small number of favorite women's events at the exclusion of secondary events that are traditionally aired in men's athletic coverage.

Then we must make the transition to the less heartening news: the Winter Olympic tables. Tables 5.3 and 5.4 report the primetime clock-time in the 1998, 2002, and 2006 Winter Games. The 1998 Games were broadcast by CBS; the 2002 and 2006 Games were contracted to NBC.

As evidenced in Tables 5.3 and 5.4, the gap between men's and women's athletics is much larger at the Winter Games. Ice dancing and pairs skating (two events that, by their very nature, denote gender equity in terms of clock-time) are excluded from this analysis, but the comparison of solo sports yields a cavernous disparity of over 23 percentage points (compared to the four-point gap in the Summer Games). Eleven different men's events received at least one total hour of airtime, compared to just five women's events. Alpine skiing, bobsledding, cross-country skiing, luge, short-track speed skating, and speed skating all

Table 5.3 Clock-time for men in the 1998, 2002, and 2006 Winter Olympics

Event	1998	%	2002	%	2006	%	Total	%
Alpine skiing	5:16	39.5	1:40	11.4	3:53	18.4	10:49	22.4
Bobsleigh	0:41	5.1	1:16	8.6	1:30	7.4	3:27	7.2
Cross-country	0:00	0.0	0:27	3.1	1:21	6.7	1:48	3.7
Curling	0:00	0.0	0:00	0.0	0:00	0.0	0:00	0.0
Figure skating	3:10	23.8	3:41	25.1	2:51	14.1	9:42	20.1
Freestyle skiing	0:11	1.4	0:34	3.9	1:34	7.7	2:19	4.8
Ice hockey	0:16	2.0	0:50	5.7	0:00	0.0	1:06	2.3
Luge	0:44	5.5	0:46	5.2	0:16	1.3	1:46	3.7
Nordic combined	0:00	0.0	0:49	5.6	0:00	0.0	0:49	1.7
Short track	0:18	2.3	0:29	3.3	1:27	7.2	2:14	4.6
Skeleton	0:00	0.0	0:23	2.6	0:13	1.1	0:36	1.2
Ski jumping	0:43	5.4	0:54	6.1	0:43	3.5	2:20	4.8
Snowboarding	0:12	1.5	1:06	7.5	2:25	11.9	3:43	7.7
Speed skating	1:49	13.6	1:45	11.9	4:01	19.9	7:35	15.7
Men's total	13:20	100.0	14:40	100.0	20:14	100.0	48:14	100.0
% including women		61.1		64.7		60.0		61.6

Table 5.4 Clock-time for women in the 1998, 2002, and 2006 Winter Olympics

Event	1998	%	2002	%	2006	%	Total	%
Alpine skiing	2:17	26.9	1:51	23.1	3:00	22.2	7:08	23.7
Bobsleigh	0:00	0.0	0:21	4.4	0:25	3.1	0:46	2.6
Cross-country	0:00	0.0	0:00	0.0	0:00	0.0	0:00	0.0
Curling	0:00	0.0	0:00	0.0	0:00	0.0	0:00	0.0
Figure skating	3:18	38.8	2:06	26.2	4:49	35.6	10:13	34.0
Freestyle skiing	0:18	3.5	0:53	11.0	0:58	7.1	2:09	7.2
Ice hockey	0:19	3.7	0:12	2.5	0:00	0.0	0:31	1.7
Luge	0:00	0.0	0:00	0.0	0:01	0.1	0:01	<0.1
Nordic combined	0:00	0.0	0:28	5.8	0:00	0.0	0:28	1.6
Short track	0:11	2.2	0:13	2.7	0:30	3.7	0:54	3.0
Skeleton	0:00	0.0	0:08	1.7	0:11	1.4	0:19	1.1
Ski jumping	n.a.	n.a.	n.a.	n.a.	n.a.	n.a.	n.a.	n.a.
Snowboarding	0:37	7.3	0:41	8.5	1:37	11.9	2:55	9.7
Speed skating	1:30	17.6	1:08	14.1	2:01	14.9	4:39	15.5
Women's total	8:30	100.0	8:01	100.0	13:32	100.0	30:03	100.0
% including men		38.9		35.3		40.0		38.4

were shown significantly more for men than women, all representing serious long-term deficits against women's events.

One Winter event, ski jumping, is not offered for women, yet this event did not receive substantial airtime for men athletes anyway, so the effects were negligible. The Summer Games offers synchronized swimming for women but not for men, yet, again, the women received less than a minute of airtime in primetime for this event in the three Olympics combined. The most plausible explanation for the Winter Games focusing much more on the men lies with ideas about traditional male and female sports, which reinforce women as being athletes only in gender-appropriate sports (Kane, 1989, 1995). The Summer Olympics certainly offer more athletic events in which women have been traditionally "allowed" to compete.

Athlete mentions

Another salient way to determine how men and women athletes are portrayed is through frequencies of athlete mentions. Over the course of the past decade, scholars have counted the number of times each athlete is mentioned within an Olympic broadcast (Billings et al., in press; Billings and Angelini, 2007; Billings and Eastman, 2002, 2003; Eastman and Billings, 1999). NBC policies often dictated fairness in this regard, but what has been found is that as commentary becomes less scripted, it is also more likely that men's names will be used at greater rates than women's names. As an exemplar, the host of an Olympic broadcast (in these studies predominantly Bob Costas but also CBS's Jim Nantz in 1998) has continually maintained far greater gender equity in terms of mentions than their field-reporting counterparts. Some studies even found that men were mentioned more than women by an expansive 2:1 ratio in some telecasts. Table 5.5 reports the mentions in each of the six Olympics for hosts, reporters, profiles, and promotions, and highlights nearly two dozen significant differences between the number of times men athletes are mentioned when compared to women's mentions. The only time these numbers favor women athletes over men are in mentions by women on-site reporters (2000–2004), suggesting a stacking (Cashmore, 2000) function in which women sportscasters are specifically designated to cover women's athletics. It should also be noted that expected frequencies for chi-square analyses were set at 0.50, meaning that equal gender treatment was used as a baseline. This is the most prudent method for determining where deviations are located within the on-air dialogue.

By scrutinizing the extensive data that has been gathered over an extended period of years, it has been possible to verify that men received substantially more mentions in all six Olympic telecasts, but that the magnitude of these differences tended to be larger for the Winter Olympics than for the Summer Olympics, a likely corollary of the clock-time differences. An overwhelming portion of the database (84.2 percent) consisted of commentary from on-site reporters, with significant differences reported in each of the six Games. As mentioned earlier, hosts fared much better in achieving equitable treatment given that men were mentioned more than women in only three of the six Olympic telecasts. Additionally, the pre-produced profiles yielded gender differences in three of the six sportscasts and the pre-produced promotions (usually shown at the beginning or end of a programming segment) produced only one significant difference, indicating that the less scripted the coverage becomes, the more gender biases are likely to occur. However, significant differences were more likely to

Table 5.5 Sources and distribution of athlete mentions by gender in the 1996–2006 Olympics

Source Gender/ Year	N	% per night	Host	Reporters M	F	Profiles	Promos
Men, 1996	3360a	63.4	404b	2519c	70	320d	47
Women, 1996	1938a	36.6	318b	1338c	56	179d	47
Men, 1998	2413e	57.0	313	1832f	45	185	38
Women, 1998	1820e	43.0	266	1301f	58	165	30
Men, 2000	4044g	55.4	424	3248h	99i	162j	111k
Women, 2000	3176g	44.6	387	2351h	241i	121j	76k
Men, 2002	4595l	63.6	326	3901m	91n	168o	109
Women, 2002	2626l	36.4	261	1953m	266n	62o	84
Men, 2004	7042p	54.4	607q	5818r	234s	213t	170
Women, 2004	5893p	45.6	437q	4677r	513s	141t	125
Men, 2006	5012u	62.4	323v	4397w	141	55	96
Women, 2006	3017u	37.6	160v	2560w	146	56	95
Total	44936	100.0	4226	35895	1960	1827	1028

Note: Paired letters indicate χ^2 significant differences at the 0.05 level.

be detected with the increased sample size and increased clock-time devoted to covering the actual, enacted athletic performance.

Sportscaster descriptions

The final way gender equity has been measured in the Olympics has incorporated the actual on-air dialogue of sportscasters—not just *who* they talk about, but *what* they say about each of these athletes. Masculine hegemony is most entrenched in on-air comments as sportscasters tend to learn from what they have witnessed in other sportscasts, providing a useful heuristic tool for refining the art of sports commentary, but concurrently providing opportunities for the reinforcement of traditional athletic patriarchal discourse.

Given that over 90 percent of sportscasters are men, it is not surprising that the gender gap is evident from the onset of any analysis of on-air dialogue. A taxonomy for coding Olympic descriptors has been refined by myself and co-authors dividing Olympic commentary into three main categories: (a) attributions of success and failure, (b) depictions of physicality/personality, and (c) factual/neutral/unclassifiable categories (Billings *et al.*, in press; Billings and Angelini, 2007; Billings and Eastman, 2002, 2003). Gender differences are most likely to be located in the first two of these categories, as they represent a substantial percentage of all comments in any Olympics and involve the interpretation of the athletic event that was just witnessed. In essence, the first two categories usually constitute the "color" commentary, while the third is largely "play-by-play". Color commentary is particularly pervasive in the Olympics because so many of the events are relatively short. For instance, a 200-meter sprint takes 20 seconds to complete; a figure-skating routine in a long program is completed in four minutes. The remaining time is largely spent describing the athletes or deciphering why an athlete or team was successful or unsuccessful in their performance—a form of storytelling that draws attention to the nuances and drama of the event. This language-oriented measure joins together qualitative and quantitative procedures classifying the comments within a taxonomical structure. By investigating the dialogue, gender biases were found that have provided a critical dimension in the analysis.

First, when examining each of the previous Olympics (1996–2006), a substantial number of significant differences were detected using chi-square analyses. Because chi-square is influenced by sample size, disparities were more likely to be exposed in the categories explaining athletic success than explanations of athletic failures or physicality and personality depictions. This skewed distribution of athletic descriptors makes sense when considering that the Olympic telecasts usually show the top athletes in each sport, meaning that, inevitably, more of the comments are positive than negative. In all, the same database of 24,950 descriptors that was reported in Chapter 4 for the analyses of nationalism was also incorporated here to determine gender differences along the lines of attributions of success or failure and personality/physicality illustrations.

The most common difference in the on-air dialogue of announcers regarded attributing athletic success to the superior skill of men athletes. Three of the six Olympics (1998, 2000, 2002) yielded statistically significant differences with substantially more comments in this category for men than for women. In addition, many other significant differences were uncovered in at least one of the six Olympic sportscasts, most notably in accrediting men athletes for succeeding because of superior (a) composure [in 1998 and 2006], (b) experience [in 1998], (c) consonance [in 2004], and (d) commitment [in 2000]. One of the most intriguing differences was that men athletes were also found to succeed in 1996 and 2004 because they were courageous; however, this difference was transposed in 2006, as suddenly women athletes were ascribed significantly more comments about their courage.

In terms of uncovering explanations for athletic failure, three differences were detected within an individual Olympics. For men athletes, the categories that inordinately were attributed to their downfall were lack of athletic skill (in 1998) and lack of concentration (in 2000). Not surprisingly, commentators also argued that athletic skill, more than any other category, was a reason for men's triumphs. In contrast, there were significantly more comments about inexperience being a significant reason for failure assigned to women than to men in both the 1998 and 2002 Olympic Games.

Concerning comments about the athletes' personalities and physical appearances, three differences were uncovered. In 2000, men were described more than women in terms of their size and/or shape of body and—quite interestingly—in 2004, in terms of being more introverted. Women had one dominant descriptor that was attributed to them an inordinate number of times: attractiveness. Attractiveness was cited most especially in 1996 and 1998, but, remarkably, not in the four subsequent Olympic telecasts.

When one aggregates the six Olympic descriptor databases, four significant differences remain. First and second, over the course of the entire decade, the sportscasters suggested that men were most likely to succeed for reason of (1) athletic skill and (2) courage. Both of these descriptor categories correlate with prototypical masculine qualities. For example, sportscasters' commentaries that men would prevail if they were stronger and tougher than their counterparts from other countries were fairly commonplace. Third, women's failure because of perceived inexperience remained a factor in the aggregate database, a finding that is not surprising as the two women's sports with the most clock-time, gymnastics in the Summer Olympics and figure skating in the Winter Olympics, frequently involve teenagers competing at the highest levels. Particularly in the case of gymnastics, the mean age of women is considerably younger than for men. The final aggregate difference detected the predominance of comments about the attractiveness of the women athletes. Still, this overall difference was principally the result of gender differences found in the coverage of the telecasts of the 1990s. For example, the 1996 and 1998 Games yielded significantly more comments about female attractiveness than male attractiveness while the most recent four Olympics between 2000 and 2006 did not yield these same differences. Future studies will need to determine whether this bias is truly diminishing, which the lack of significant differences in the past four Games seems to suggest.

Frequency deviations inform us as to the ways in which dialogue differs as a whole, but specific comments offer supplementary insights into the qualitative impact of differential discourse. For instance, the most prevalent bias regarded a disproportionately high number of comments about men's athletic skills. Short, single-word descriptors such as "conquering" and "battling" elements of men's performances modified athletic skills such as "fast" or "talented", but other comments included "cool, smooth skater" or "amazing acrobat". In contrast, women received comments such as "gasping, trying to catch her breath" or they were described as "physically sub par". While none of these comments were exclusively relegated to one gender (for instance, in 2006 a male was described multiple times as being "fatigued" and "gassed"), when correlated in conjunction with the significant differences detected within the taxonomy, there was notable repetition of such comments for one gender much more frequently than for the other.

A second major area of difference was in comments about success because of courage. Men received more comments regarding how they were "fearless" and "gutsy", but there were also comments implying that men's courage amounted to risk-taking, and that great risks amounted to great rewards with comments such as "risking injury on one ski" or "taking an outrageous line". Women received more comments relating to courage, but they were qualitatively different with some examples being "fantastic that she even tried it", "never quitting", and "heart as big as the skating rink". Several of the comments about women were imbued with an element of sportscaster surprise, while courage for the men athletes was regarded as much more commonplace.

The third difference was in relation to the continual comments about the inexperience of women athletes. Understandably, at age 14, US gymnast Dominique Moceanu was described as a "youngster" when she competed at the 1996 Summer Olympics, but there were countless variations of the youth variable applied to young female performers in general, such as: "kid", "immature", "young lady", "teenager", "rookie". The magnitude and frequency of such comments constitute a stereotype of young sporting femininity which could have the effect of diminishing the credibility of female athletic performance.

Finally, there were also comments about attractiveness that were skewed towards women more than towards men. These comments provided the greatest variation in the abundance and nature of dialogic descriptions ranging from women athletes who take a person's "breath away" or are "easy on the eyes" to other characterizations such as a "sweetheart" or "adorable". When men were described in terms of their attractiveness or sex appeal, the manner of these comments was starkly different, calling a male athlete a "heart-throb" or noting that "ladies like him". Some comments about masculine attractiveness lent strength to the notion that men are well-trained athletic machines (for instance, one male was described as having a "Darth Vader look"). In sum, women were not only more frequently defined in terms of heterosexual attractiveness, but also were depicted as being more interested in their own looks, exemplified by a comment in Torino that the "US women are determined to be the best-dressed team".

Single descriptor analyses are telling, yet another way to add context to the comments is through the examination of language on a more holistic basis. Frequently, language would adopt a gendered tone through prolonged passages, providing additional examples of the ways in which male and female Olympians are depicted differently. For example, take two passages from the 2000 Sydney Summer Games. Both were pre-produced "lead-ins" to the beginning of the all-around gymnastics competitions; both began with descriptions of Russian gymnasts who had failed to win team gold; both were spoken by NBC sportscaster John Tesh. Yet, the two tones are unmistakably in contrast to each other. First, the men's lead-in from September 20, 2000:

> JT: Russia's Alexei Nemov remembers Atlanta and the duel he lost to China's Li Xioushuang. The bitterness sent him back to the gym for payback in Australia. In the team competition this week, Nemov unveiled his brilliance, but the team couldn't keep up. Bronze was once again unfulfilling. Tonight, he's on his own.

Despite Nemov's personal and team defeats, the language is loaded with powerful terms: the competition is a "duel"; he seeks athletic "payback" because of this profound "bitterness". Certainly, this language surrounding Nemov could be defined as determined and focused. Contrast that with the lead commentary to the women's gymnastics all-around final on September 21, 2000:

> JT: Life took away the fathers of Elena Zamolodchikova and Elena Prodounova while replacing them with gymnastics. Prodounova simply never knew hers, but came to find her coach was someone who could bring discipline and success to her life. Zamolodchikova's father was a soldier who cleaned up the radioactive disaster at Chernobyl. In April, after years of illness, it cost the army major his life. In spite of a country's support, this week, the Russians fell. And then, later, the team stepped to the podium for a silver that, based on expectation, was an insult ... Today, a second chance.

In this case, the two Russian women gymnasts were depicted in much more sympathetic, emotional ways. Indeed, both were defined by their relationships (or lack thereof) with their fathers, even intimating that Prodounova succeeded because of the pseudo-father status of her coach. There is no question that tone is impacted by each personal story; it is also important to note that the female gymnasts were teenagers, whereas Nemov was not. Nonetheless, what is critical to the understanding of sportscaster dialogue is that the language is gendered in some way. It is likely that a male gymnast who had been orphaned would have been portrayed differently.

Stories that are constructed about Olympic athletes in all sports typically include references to the family, to the influence of other key figures during their development into elite athletes, to their struggles and successes in sport, and so on. The gendering of language—sometimes manifest in obvious ways and at other times quite subtly—is a common thread that runs through the storylines of all major sports telecasts. Still, because of the grander storytelling nature in which NBC conveys the Olympic telecast, the gendering of language becomes more important and salient within sportscaster dialogues.

Gendered conclusions

Van Sterkenburg and Knoppers (2004) noted that "relatively little is known about the way media users read media representations [of] gender" (p. 304). NBC producers and sportscasters appear to be particularly proud that their Olympic coverage provides women athletes with greater prominence than other telecasts. NBC notes that, by far, they provide more clock-time to women's athletics than any other sporting event and, by all raw measures, this is predominantly affirmed. Still, with women receiving 48 percent of the Summer coverage and 38 percent of the Winter coverage, the case can certainly be made that women could be highlighted with even greater frequency, particularly when showing a US team that, in recent Olympic competitions, has yielded more female gold medal winners than male gold medal winners.

Entrenched notions of gender remain a significant obstacle to offering sportscasts that jointly respect men and women athletes. Agenda-setting scholars would further argue that the emphasis on men's athletics in terms of clock-time is the cornerstone for ascertaining why the mentions and descriptors subsequently yielded substantial gender differences. In many ways, it appears that a glass ceiling may be in effect as the gaps between the coverage of men's Olympic sports and of women's Olympic sports ten years ago are similarly pervasive today, and divergent dialogues for men and women athletes also appear to be just as pervasive today as in the mid 1990s. Although women athletes continue to receive increased respect for their athletic accomplishments, they are described in notably different manners than are the men athletes.

Gender disparities within sports media are merely one cog in a social world in which gender is an organizing principle (Sagas and Cunningham, 2004; Staurowsky, 1995; Wolfe *et al.*, 2005) and the mass communication negotiation of gender often pervades interpersonal and other communicative arenas (Bernstein and Blain, 2003; O'Sullivan, 1999). Given the immensity of the Olympic telecast, differential treatment of men and women (including a paucity of women sportscasters and a substantially lower visibility in clock-time) can significantly influence attitudes about the role of women in sport generally, and in the Olympics specifically.

6 Dialogue differences in black and white?

Ethnicity and the Olympic telecasts

Social meanings and experiences associated with skin color and ethnic background influence access to sport participation, decisions about playing sports, and the ways in which sports are integrated into everyday life.

(Coakley, 2004, p. 284)

In contrast to gender differences, which may be effortlessly pinpointed within any sportscast because of the division of sports by gender, ethnic differences are multi-layered, complex issues in which sportscasters have lost jobs because they failed to appreciate the complexities and sensitivities of interpreting and analyzing them. For instance, CBS National Football League analyst Jimmy "The Greek" Snyder (who, in the 1980s claimed Black slave breeding was a reason for Black athletic successes) was fired from his job because his comments were regarded as racist. In 2003, Rush Limbaugh was hired as ESPN's political commentator for their National Football League Studio Show, only to be fired several months later for claiming that the media embraced Philadelphia Eagles' quarterback, Donovan McNabb, because they were "very desirous to see a Black quarterback do well". Interestingly, Olympic producers and sportscasters in this research had devoted the least analytic introspection to issues of ethnic identity. For example, Dick Ebersol admitted that he had never been asked questions about ethnicity issues in the Olympics and several sportscasters indicated that visual imagery was largely left to do the storytelling, thus reducing the intricate issues of ethnicity to the observation of skin pigment. Several sportscasters indicated that ethnicity should only enter the equation if a "valid first" was achieved for an athlete of a certain race. Tom Hammond's comment in Chapter 3 that it is "all neutral" to him reflects a general trend of avoiding, rather than addressing, issues of ethnicity.

Recurrently, sportscasters describe athletic engagement with stereotypical dichotomous distinctions (most notably Black/White, but nearly equally White/Non-White), reducing an amalgamation of disparate ethnicities into overarching, supposedly homologous categories defined solely by skin color.

Thus, athletes such as Fijian golfer Vijay Singh, Cablinasian golfer Tiger Woods, and French basketball player Tony Parker are frequently subjected to biases applied to "Black" athletes, even though each has a distinctively different ethnic (and nationalistic) background. Furthermore, when ethnicity cannot be summarized into a simple one-word description (e.g. "Black" or "Hispanic"), sportscasters would rather ignore discussions of ethnic divisions or issues rather than make an egregious error in the very public context of a sportscast. Tiger Woods actually created the word Cablinasian largely because sports commentators had no idea how to mention his ethnic roots in a simple way.

There are extremely sensitive and interlocking issues relating to ethnicity in sport (see Carrington, 2007; King *et al.*, 2007; Staurowsky, 2007) and which appear to be more marked in telecasts of the Summer Olympics (when the majority of African and South America countries compete) than in telecasts of the Winter Olympics (when far fewer countries participate and Caucasians win the vast majority of medals). This chapter examines the role of ethnicity in both the Summer and Winter Games, focusing in both cases on media framing—with reference in the Summer Olympics to how athletes of different ethnicities are framed, and in the case of the Winter Olympics whether ethnicity is even framed at all.

Depictions of ethnicity in televised sport

While ethnicity may be difficult to pinpoint and concisely define within a sportscast, it is critical to an athlete's self-concept and perception of social identity. Tajfel (1972) defines social identity as "the individual's knowledge that he or she belongs to certain social groups together with some emotional and value significance to him or her of the group membership" (p. 32). Suzuki (1998) examines in-group and out-group communication patterns as they relate to social identity, concluding that when a person becomes aware of a certain group membership, that individual is likely to find justification in maintaining social distance from an out-group (see also Ashforth and Mael, 1989; Smith, 1983).

Ethnicity is an important expression of individual and group identity which in sport is both complex and contradictory. Historically, ethnicity has been linked to and has defined national identity, and in elite sport, and above all at the Olympic Games, both ethnic identities and national identities are simultaneously foregrounded. It is also the case that the Olympic telecast generates feelings of community and solidarity—as well as difference and opposition—and channels them through visual representation and language for the viewers' consumption. With regard to the United States, Olympic sport has been a channel for the celebration of a manufactured all-American culture, but it is one which also incorporates the tensions and inherent contradictions that frequently arise from a false sense of belonging. The African-American "Black Power" salute at the 1968 Olympics by Tommie Smith and John Carlos was an overt example decades ago that, in contradiction to the construction of America as a United Nation, in fact it remained a divided society incorporating acute racial conflicts. Smith brought attention to the discrimination of African-Americans in their own country when he said:

> If I win, I am American, not a Black American. But if I did something bad, then they would say I am a Negro. We are Black and we are proud of being Black. Black America will understand what we did tonight.
>
> (Hartmann, 1996)

The politics of race and ethnic conflict at the Olympics Games—both within and between nations—inevitably shape and color the Olympic telecast. For example, scholars have argued that White commentators do not give sufficient credit to non-White athletes because of racial sensitivities (e.g. Eastman and Billings, 2001; Edwards, 1969; Rada and Wulfemeyer, 2005; Rowe, 2003) and have assessed the scope and variety of racism in the sports media. Legendary NFL player Reggie White once spoke to the Wisconsin legislature with an implausible list of racial group attributes (i.e. Native Americans excel at "sneaking up on people" and Asians can "turn a television into a watch"; Ford, 2004, p. S6). In a similar vein, FOX network broadcaster Steve Lyons was fired following a comment during a baseball playoff game in which he stated, "Lou [Piniella] is habla-ing some Espanol, and I'm still looking for my wallet. I don't understand him and I don't want to sit close to him, now" (Mushnick, 2006, p. 81).

Traditionally, Winter Olympic coverage has skimmed over issues of ethnicity because the athletes are predominantly (over 80 percent) White. King (2007) believes the paucity of non-White athletes competing in the Winter Games aids the entrenchment of White Power. In his essay, he contends that:

> Sport matters to White power because of the manner in which it confirms and challenges myths about race and power, grounding assessments of character and indeed the ordering of entire social fields within the bodies of a few extraordinary individuals. For White nationalists, White separatists, and White supremacists, the 2006 Winter Olympics offered a safe space to underscore a set of "truths", which to their minds anti-White gatekeepers work to ridicule, malign, and silence.
>
> (King, 2007, p. 93)

The lack of ethnic diversity in the Winter Games is typically a non-story within the mass media. But, unusually, the 2006 Torino Games returned ethnicity to the media's stage for several reasons including, most notably, the rise (albeit paltry) of the successful Black athlete within the Winter Olympics. If anyone thought issues of ethnicity would somehow be skirted around in media coverage (and subsequent media criticism) of the 2006 Olympics, HBO *Real Sports* host Bryant

Gumbel ensured this would not be the case. However, Gumbel's blistering critique (cited in Chapter 3) is plainly simplistic and relies on a bias of its own—that any sporting event that does *not* include Black athletes is inherently prejudiced. But when one asks questions about why certain ethnicities participate in and are more likely to dominate a given sport than others, then different conclusions can be drawn. The lack of ethnic diversity at the Winter Olympic Games is influenced by the climates of the countries that participate, the politics, economics, and cultures of those countries, and their sporting infrastructures, as well as ethnic demographics. Not surprisingly, for example, athletes from Scandinavian countries fare exceedingly better at the Winter Olympics than those from African nations.

But the issue of Black athletic superiority in other sports—notably, but certainly not limited to, track events, especially sprints—is highly controversial and has forced a choice between genetic and environmental explanations (Hoberman, 2007). Notably during the 1970s, at a time that was paralleled by the rise of the Civil Rights Movement, the idea that African-Americans were "born athletes" was opposed as racist ideology (Whannel, 1992; Jackson, 1989; Staples and Jones, 1985). But by buying into the idea of natural athletic superiority, "the White race" according to Harry Edwards, "thus bec(ame) the chief victim of its own myth" (1973, p. 197) and, in order to rise above inadequacies in athletic talent, it was argued that White athletes need intelligence, diligence and determination to succeed (McCarthy and Jones, 1997; Birrell, 1989).

The fact that Blacks are disproportionately represented in explosive running events and in positions that require speed and power in other popular sports is used to bolster the credibility of genetic explanations for their supreme athletic talent. As Hoberman (2007) has pointed out: "No sprinter the modern world would classify as 'White' has ever run under ten seconds in the 100-meter dash under legal conditions. All those who have done it are (wholly or partly) of West African origin" (p. 221). Referring to the turn of the century and the Human Genome Project, Hoberman goes on to state that "the idea of biological race is already making a comeback after spending decades in disrepute" (p. 224).

In his controversial book, *Taboo: Why Black Athletes Dominate Sports and Why We're Afraid to Talk About It* (2000), Jon Entine argues that outstanding physical ability (an attribute of the usual Black stereotype) and intellectual supremacy (stereotypically attributed to Whites) have historically been associated as key positive attributes of strong athletes, and that there is no scientific support for the belief that athleticism and intelligence are not inherently related. The "dumb jock" stereotype, Entine argues, has only recently materialized within sports telecasts and modern social beliefs. Hoberman (2007) predicts that:

> Sports' racial dimension in the 21st Century will retain both its social and genetic aspects. Black dominance within important sectors of the sports

entertainment industry will continue to emphasize the identification of Black people with the capacities of their bodies rather than their minds.

(p. 224)

Much discussion of ethnic stereotyping in sport has focused on leadership positions such as "natural" point guards in basketball or quarterbacks in football (Wonsek, 1992). More directly, dialogue about the rise of the Black quarterback has been the focus of several studies (e.g. Billings, 2004; Byrd and Utsler, 2007; Murrell and Curtis, 1994) because of the perceived disconnect between myth (White athletes are the smart, born leaders) and reality (many Black quarterbacks [e.g. Michael Vick and Donovan McNabb] currently dominate the professional game). Rainville and McCormick (1977) found blatant biases against Black quarterbacks and Rada (1996) found many of these biases were still in play decades later. Examining NFL telecasts, Rada reported that sportscasters had vastly different focal points for commentary about athletes of different ethnicities. He found that if the player was White, sportscasters spotlighted the cerebral aspects of the player (e.g. cognitive qualities) but, if the player was Black, sportscasters concentrated their attention on describing the body size, type, and strength of the athletes (e.g. physical qualities). While Billings (2004) found many of these differences in commentator discourse had diminished in recent years, there still were significant differences between the attributions ascribed to White and Black quarterbacks when succeeding as opposed to when they were failing, most notably that Black quarterbacks were more likely to succeed because of perceived athletic skill and that White quarterbacks were more likely to fail because they lacked these skills. It is noteworthy that the leader of the Philadelphia National Association for the Advancement of Colored People, J. Whyatt Mondesire, appeared to be ill-at-ease discussing the play of Philadelphia Eagle Black quarterback, Donovan McNabb. He went as far as to purport that McNabb's decline in play was the result of his becoming a pocket-passer[1] in order to avoid the image of being an athletic, running quarterback that would befit the Black football stereotype (Fitzgerald, 2005).

Discussions about ethnicity and sport have focused on an ideological notion of biological difference between innate Black athletic physicality compared to athletic skills that are developed by White sportsmen and sportswomen as a result of practice and repetition over time (Denham *et al.*, 2002). The debate has centered on the physical makeup of athletes of different races, with Bass (2002) contending that "sport exists as a realm where Black masculinity and physicality are visually represented. When applied to the athlete, the appellation "Black" implies a variety of inherent or, more directly, *inherited* traits and abilities" (p. 47). Rada (1996) points to inequities between the ethnic diversity (or lack thereof) of sportscasters

---

1 Pocket-passers run less than mobile quarterbacks, staying in the same general area of the field for the entire play and relying on a quick release of a football pass to avoid being tackled.

(the majority of whom—within US television media—are White) when compared to the athletes being described at an athletic event, a contention that Denham *et al.*(2002) corroborate in their analysis of Final Four basketball telecasts. In the study, the investigators found that while many stereotypes of Black players persisted (such as perceived innate athletic gifts), the one variable that did matter was the ethnicity of the sportscaster. Sports booths continue to become more ethnically diverse, but remain the domain of predominantly White males, even in athletic venues such as basketball that are dominated by non-White players. Dewar (1993) suggested that White broadcasters did not sufficiently credit Black athletes for their accomplishments.

The result is that sportscasters sometimes either (a) do not talk about ethnicity, or (b) discuss ethnicity in a slapdash, inaccurate fashion. In highlighting the former point, Entine (2000) gives us the scenario in which aliens came down from space to witness an NBA basketball game. Given that the large majority of the players on the court would be Black and the large majority of the fans watching the game would be White, Entine asks the question: Would the aliens not consider ethnicity an issue? He retorts that of course they would. Yet, most discussions of athletic achievement are implicitly colorblind—a misguided stance that serves to gloss over ethnic backgrounds and diminishes the identity of an athlete and a culture.

One the other hand, there may be good reason why ethnicity is rarely discussed within the modern sportscast—many broadcasters are not comfortable with or adept at dialogue and analysis of ethnic issues. Bass (2002) chronicles the following story in her role as an NBC broadcast research supervisor in 2002:

> On February 19, 2002, Vonetta Flowers became the first African-American to win a gold medal at an [Winter] Olympic Games ... All agreed that she was not the first Black medalist; Debi Thomas assumed that title when she won a bronze medal in figure skating in 1988. The more difficult question was whether a Black athlete had won a medal since Thomas. Everyone seemed certain that a Black face had not graced a skiing or skating victory podium, but who could be absolutely sure that the fourth member of the Swiss bobsleigh team in 1994 was not Black by some definition? Deeming Flowers the first African-American, then, seemed the most precise route to follow, and it was the one that I—in my capacity as a broadcast research supervisor—helped NBC settle on for its coverage of the event, thinking that the word *Black* might be too ambiguous for the television audience. I did not foresee, with this decision, that a commentator at the bobsleigh venue would then erroneously describe Flowers as the first African-American *from any country* to win winter gold".
>
> (Bass, 2002, p. ix)

Anecdotes such as these accentuate the need for greater understanding of ethnic diversity (Drzewiecka, 2003), incorporating a shift away from the controversial

White/Black dichotomy to a recognition of complexity. Scholars have also tapped into the intricate issues of ethnic identity in sport (Billings, 2003b; Billings *et al.*, 2007) with particular focus on golf. Billings (2003b) examined the unique case of Tiger Woods, finding that Woods was often classified in terms of Black stereotypes when he was failing, but received commentary more befitting a White athlete when he was successful. Sportscasters had a difficult time describing the play of Woods, who labels himself as "Cablinasian" (Eagan, 2001), a mixture of his Caucasian, Black, Indian, and Asian backgrounds (Nordlinger, 2001). Through this example, one witnesses the tendency in televised sport for multifaceted identities to be misleadingly reduced to one-dimensional distinctions. The very structure of Olympic sport, with the identification of athletes with specific national allegiances/alliances, militates against ideas of ethnic and cultural diversity. Hargreaves (2000) concurs with Hall (1996) that the conception of a "unified identity" is misleading:

> Identity embodies sameness and difference … The politics of difference and identity have led to a questioning of the essentialist notion of a single and fixed identity and a recognition that identities are diverse and fluid, affected by changing political, cultural, and social conditions.
>
> (Hargreaves, 2000, p. 7)

Ethnic disparities in televised sport are not relegated to stereotypes of non-White athletes and certainly are influenced by more than the concepts of clock-time, mere exposure, and framing. Specific, identifiable dialogic differences have been uncovered by many researchers as well (e.g. Denham *et al.*, 2002; Rada, 1996). When disparate treatment is applied to the depiction of an athlete of a certain ethnicity, mischaracterizations hurt not only the ethnic group with which the athlete self-identifies but also the ethnic group with which it is being compared. For instance, a website is now devoted to the fallacious dialogue applied to Caucasian wide receivers in American football (www.cwraa.blogspot.com), the Caucasian Wide Receivers of America. Ninety percent of the time, the wide receiver position is secured by a Black player, but the website highlights comments ascribed to White athletes playing this position. They are depicted as "deceptively fast", "gritty team players", and "possession receivers". The blog postulates the oppression of White athletes while simultaneously marginalizing Black wide receivers in the process.

With reference to sports telecasts, because of the complexities and sensitivities surrounding ethnicity, it is sometimes very difficult to assess whether or not commentaries are overtly biased. For instance, Denham *et al.* (2002) analyzed college basketball, finding that one Black player in particular (Michigan State University's Mateen Cleaves) received an inordinate number of comments about his leadership ability, an attribute typically attached to White athletes. The authors contended that this was a sign of progress—and perhaps it was. However, one could alternatively contend that Cleaves' leadership was regarded as atypical and, consequently, noteworthy. In other words, athletes and events are often considered to be newsworthy if they are unusual and fail to match the sports-caster's expectations.

In sum, assessing ethnic portrayals involves arduous analysis of thorny, multi-faceted issues. Nonetheless, ethnic analyses are crucial to comprehending the impact of sports television. Olympic telecasts are particularly convoluted, as no other sportscast offers the breadth and depth of ethnic diversity. Even the overly Caucasian Winter Olympics are replete with performances by athletes from multiple ethnic groups across the whole spectrum of events. The remainder of this chapter reports on the results of the content analysis of the 1996–2006 Olympic sample (Billings *et al.*, in press; Billings and Angelini, 2007; Billings and Eastman, 2002, 2003; Eastman and Billings, 1999). Clock-time is not a plausible measure for ethnic identity as it is impossible to determine, whereas mentions and descriptions provide meaningful heuristics for an examination of the significance of ethnicity in the Olympic Games.

Ethnicity: Olympic measures

Athlete mentions

Athlete mentions are operationalized as the raw measure of the number of times each athlete's name is uttered within the Olympic telecast. However, assessing differences regarding ethnicity is demonstrably more complex for several reasons. First, with gender, there is a reasonable baseline of 0.50 (50 percent) as an expected frequency in each category; with ethnicity, it is not logical to expect each ethnic group to be mentioned an equal number of times when the athletes competing (particularly in the Winter Games) are predominantly White. Thus, we return to the notion mentioned in the production and sportscasting chapters—that one cannot assess what is not present at the outset. This is not primarily a function of media framing—if anything, networks like NBC actively seek out stories of unique ethnic diversity (e.g. a Black speed skater or a Middle Eastern sprinter). Instead, the lack of ethnic diversity is interpreted as a result of cultural, social, and political pressures and obstacles that can cause the non-participation of entire countries and, sometimes, virtually entire continents.

Second, mentions are difficult to assess by ethnicity because the categories are not dichotomous but rather offer a complex multiplicity. For the purposes of this study, perceived ethnicity/preexisting knowledge of the athletes' backgrounds was used to aid classification into six categories (Asian, Black, Hispanic, Middle Eastern, White, and other). When the ethnicity of an athlete was in question, the Internet and other research tools were used to determine his or her classification. Such classifications may appear crude, but provided a guide for the investigation of significant production and dialogic differences. For instance, originally, Tiger Woods was described in the sports media as a Black golfer, misleadingly implying that he had exclusively African-American heredity and marginalizing his very mixed identity (Cablinasian, see Eagan, 2001 and Nordlinger, 2001). The fashion in which a casual viewer assesses ethnicity on a daily basis is through the examination of outward appearances. Employing the recurring example of Tiger Woods, if a person views him for the first time, they are much more likely to label him as Black than as Cablinasian. Given that these outward labels are the intended measure in this study, perceived ethnicity is the appropriate independent variable to assess. Using these external informational databases, agreement between the coders using Cohen's kappa exceeded 97 percent.

Table 6.1 reports athlete mentions across the six ethnic categories constructed for the analyses of the six Olympic broadcasts (1996–2006). First, regarding the overall percentages, one can witness how White athletes are mentioned well over two-thirds (72.1 percent) of the time within an Olympic telecast. The overall proportion of White athlete mentions unsurprisingly skews to a higher percentage in a Winter Games (well over 80 percent) than for a Summer Games (closer to the actual two-thirds margin). Black and Asian athletes are mentioned 13.1 percent and 9.5 percent of the time respectively, with Hispanics and Middle Eastern athletes rarely shown, constituting less than 1 percent of the database.

Two significant source differences are highlighted in Table 6.1 as the pre-produced profiles and promotions yielded significantly more divergent ethnic proportions than the overall percentages (used as anticipated frequencies) would suggest. Profiles were slightly more diverse than the overall totals (overwhelmingly derived from on-site reporters), but promotions, in particular, provided more ethnic diversity. White athletes were promoted 63 percent of the time (compared to an overall 72 percent total), while Asian and Black athletes received modest yet significant jumps (13.5 percent instead of 9.5 percent and 16.4 percent instead of 13.1 percent, respectively). Given that the profiles and promotions are the two sources that are entirely pre-produced by NBC, one must conclude that ethnic diversity was more likely to be highlighted in structured, pre-generated work than in the more spontaneous coverage that on-site reporters and producers provide, which is often the part of the jigsaw puzzle that is pieced together in a matter of several hours (or in some cases, minutes) between actual athletic performance and taped primetime coverage.

Additionally, it is important to recognize that within Table 6.1 significant differences are statistically more difficult to detect when one measured group

Table 6.1 Sources and distribution of athlete mentions by ethnicity in the 1996–2006 Olympics

Source Ethnicity	N	% per night	Host	Reporters M	F	Profiles	Promos
Asian	4269	9.5	370	3365	202	193a	139b
Black	5847	13.1	553	4546	278	301a	169b
Hispanic	440	0.9	33	317	38	35a	17b
Middle Eastern	316	0.7	6	287	6	6a	11b
White	32415	72.1	3053	26139	1335	1237a	651b
Other	1649	3.7	211	1241	101	55a	41b
Total	44936	100.0	4226	35895	1960	1827	1028

Note: Paired letters indicate χ^2 significant differences at the 0.05 level.

represents the overwhelming majority of the database. In this case, the fact that Whites were mentioned twice as frequently as all other ethnicities combined made it difficult for the mentions to be parsed out in a substantially different way within each source-based analysis. Still, the significant differences uncovered with regard to the profiles and promotions provide a baseline for comparisons and trends to be articulated.

Sportscaster descriptions

Results in this area are qualitative in nature, resulting from the interpretation and extrapolation of meaning from the actual on-air dialogue of the NBC sportscasters.

First, regarding the perceived level of concentration of the athletes within the actual sporting competition: White athletes were considered to have excellent concentration in comparison with Black athletes in particular. For example, a White female athlete was said to have had "the focused presence of mind" to have won the gold medal in her event and a White male was described as successful because of his "meticulous" approach to the competition. The bulk of comments about the superior concentration of White athletes dealt with their resolute "focus" (e.g. "started to focus", "focus in her eyes", "wants to focus on making the top six"). Black athletes certainly received similar comments about focus, but not as many proportionally as expected frequencies would predict. Moreover, Black athletes received a fair number of comments about lack of focus (e.g. "needed to concentrate on that one"). Asian athletes also were more likely to be perceived as succumbing to the immense pressure (e.g. "so worried that she lost concentration"), feeding the notions that (a) the Far East places the most pressure on athletic successes as measures of nationalistic pride and (b) Asian athletes possess such a single-minded work ethic that the stress of the situation is more likely to influence the final product.

There were no substantial differences in the number of comments devoted to the perceived strength of each athlete, but the comments varied in character according to the ethnic backgrounds of the athletes. For instance, White athletes received many comments that inferred that failure was the result of superlative athletic endeavor (e.g. "looked fried", "fatigued", "collapsed"), whereas other athletes received comparatively reserved comments, such as "hurting here" (for a Black athlete) or "starting to fade" (for an Asian athlete). In other words, when White athletes failed athletically there were times when their skills were not simply diminished, but were characterized as evaporating almost instantaneously as a result of extraordinary effort.

There were also differences when determining whether each ethnic group possessed the necessary athletic ability. Limited ability was more likely to be viewed as a reason for the downfall of White athletes, who received comments such as "tightening up", "way under-revolving", "physically not equivalent", and, tellingly, the disclaimer that the athlete "is human after all". These comments can be contrasted with descriptions of the seemingly exceptional Black athletes (e.g. "aerodynamic proficiency", "effortless") and the perceived meticulously trained Asian athletes (e.g. "strong technically", "phenom", "he floats").

Yet another characteristic of commentaries was the comparison of composure variables. White and Black athletes received proportionally fewer "composure" comments than did Asian athletes. Asian athletes were often ascribed terms like "patient", "Zen-like zeal"; even while having difficulty with composure, whereas White athletes were attributed relatively moderate comments such as "tough for him to compose himself" and "feeling the Olympic pressure". Black athletes received different types of comments about their composure, incorporating more powerful and hyperbolic terms, such as an athlete possessing the focus of a "pit bull", or overwhelming the competition with such confidence that exuded a "signature swagger". Indeed, one Black athlete was alleged to have the innate demeanor of a champion, with the sportscaster claiming he was "born to be great". In contrast, Asian athletes received a greater frequency of negative comments regarding composure, ranging from an Asian athlete who "has a tendency to crack under pressure" to another Asian participant who failed because she "had a meltdown".

The final taxonomical area in which there were documented ethnic differences was regarding the personal background of athletes. White athletes received comments that made them appear more colorful (e.g. "plays the pole like a guitar", or "has a repertoire of celebrations") while Black athletes received most comments regarding their home environment (e.g. "youngest in the family" or "from the streets of Chicago"), which aid the telling of stories about overcoming great obstacles that has become an Olympic trademark.

Overall, it is most accurate to claim that ethnic differences took place in two distinctive and divergent forms: (a) disparities in the frequencies of the comments employed [as compared to relative chi-square expected frequencies], and (b) qualitative distinctions between the types of comments offered within each taxonomical area. Although White and Black athletes received an approximately equal proportion of the comments in a given area, the character of the comments varied in relation to the ethnicity of the athletes to whom they were applied.

The clearest example of how NBC negotiated issues of ethnicity occurred with the first Black US individual event gold medal winner in a Winter Games, Shani Davis in 2006. The elite speed skater was discussed prior to his gold medal run in an extended profile on February 18, 2006, which ran twice the length of Ebersol's desired two-minutes per profile. The profile led with the story of Davis's perceived "selfishness" for declining to compete in the team pursuit competition, saying he needed to focus on his individual events, even opening with NBC sportscaster Tom Hicks's voiceover that "The first headline Shani Davis made at these Games wasn't about why he skated. It was about why he did not". Another US speed skater, Chad Hedrick, had openly blamed Davis's non-participation as a reason why the US failed to even qualify for the finals. After this opening, the profile then brought ethnicity into focus, providing a context for Davis's athletic achievements and objectives:

Tom Hicks:	Davis, himself, is a complete outsider. He's an only child, raised by a single mother in inner-city Chicago. The sport's first bona fide Black star.
Shani Davis:	Every once in a while if it was cold outside, I'd wear a Bonnie Blair[2] sweatshirt. And everyone else would kind of make fun of it because it was out of the norm. No one had ever seen a Bonnie Blair sweatshirt before. So they were like "Why are you wearing that White girl on your shirt? What's wrong with you?"

The atypical nature of Davis's Olympic dream was again documented at the end of the profile:

Hicks:	As Davis's star rose, so too, did the level of conflict between Cherie Davis [Davis's mother] and US Speed Skating.
Cherie Davis:	They rule by intimidation and I'm not to be intimidated, so it's always going to be a problem. When Shani earns it, then I make sure he gets what he's earned and that's about it.
Hicks:	After the fallout from his non-appearance in team pursuit, Davis has chosen to be silent. He has repeatedly turned down NBC's requests for interviews here, and in the absence of comments from Davis, Chad Hedrick, the winner of the 5000 in Torino, has already had enough of being asked to talk about Davis ... the two have nothing in common, except the fact that they are each exceptional. One a former in-liner from Houston, the other a short-tracker at heart, who emerged from Chicago's gang-infested streets. It is clearer than ever; they are not at all teammates— merely opponents.

In an Olympic Games in which nationalism usually trumps all other identifications as a means for bonding together people of differing backgrounds, the narrative of two athletes from the same country with "nothing in common" is, indeed, a rarity. The original dispute over competing in the team pursuit provided a pretext for the sportscaster to point to the different ethnic and social backgrounds of the two speed skaters as a reason for the antagonism between them.

Ethnicity conclusions

Although sportscasters understand the need to avoid ethnic stereotyping, the data from this study indicates that there is a definite trend for subtle ethnically

---

2 Blair is a speed skater who won five gold medals collectively in the 1988, 1992, and 1994 Winter Olympic Games.

based generalizations and assumptions in Olympic telecasts. Referring to the United States, Turley (2006) contends that, "we remain a highly race-conscious society with highly segregated neighborhoods, schools, prisons, and—yes—entertainment" (p. 13A). He goes on to claim that if ethnic divisions are apparent in popular cultural activities such as sport, it reflects a greater truth about modern society.

There has been a general failure in modern sport broadcasting to discuss ethnic issues in a sensitive and informative way. Rhoden (2006) places some of the responsibility on the shoulders of Black athletes themselves when he claims that they need to develop long-term memories in order to comprehend the role of minority athletes in sport during a long history of White privilege. The sports media have certainly become sensitive to racially ignorant and even racist comments of prominent American athletes and sportscasters such as Jimmy "The Greek" Snyder and Reggie White, but, as we have observed in this chapter, most media professionals are White. In 2005, the African-American sportswriter Michael Wilbon perceived differing responses to a charge of racism arising from someone's endorsement of racial athletic aptitude, and commented as follows:

> "I've heard some Black dissent, but mostly I hear objections being raised by White administrators and media colleagues, a sort of misplaced liberal guilt, if you ask me" (cited in Hoberman, 2007, p. 221).

Controversy about explaining sporting prowess in terms of innate biological characteristics that are supposedly common to all people within one particular ethnic group continues in the media. For instance, calling a Black athlete "speedy" is no overt faux pas, particularly if they have just won a race; the problem is instead the implication of a blanket attribution of characteristics to other Black athletes. Hoberman (2007) points to the evolutionary narratives that surround athletes, the basic premise of which is that Blacks are "endowed with a biological toughness and resiliency that constitute an enduring racial trait" (p. 213). He later extrapolates that "pointing to racially segregated athletic events carries its own message about distinct racial biologies" (p. 214).

But drawing implications from ethnically specific commentaries can be misleading. The differences between different ethnicities uncovered in this chapter are—at least in part—a function of varying sport participation ratios. Is it any surprise, for instance, that Black athletes receive more comments about speed given that they represent the overwhelming majority in track and field sprinting events and the overwhelming minority in gymnastics (where speed is not a primary issue)? Without question, each event brings inherently nuanced descriptions to the commentary simply because each sport necessitates different skills.

Overtly racist sportscaster dialogues (Harris, 1993; Long and McNamee, 2004) were not noted within any of the NBC commentary; instead, the analysis uncovers the varied discourses that are employed for athletes of varying ethnicity (Buffington, 2005). The repeated comments within given taxonomical categories collide with the politics of omitted comments (Bryant and Raney, 2000) of ethnicity in sport that alter the way Whiteness (McDonald, 2005), Blackness (Staples and Jones, 1985), and otherness are understood and interpreted within modern sport.

It is also important to comprehend what the analyses in this chapter do not confirm in addition to what differences were detected. To wit, the significant findings in this research only measured differences; there was no evidence of overt bias, prejudice, stereotyping, or overgeneralizations (Wigboldus *et al.*, 2000). The interviews with producers and sportscasters indicate that there is certainly no intention to portray athletes of different ethnicities in markedly different manners. Even if a stereotype is being employed within the coverage, it does not necessarily follow that negative prejudices are being enacted as well. Moreover, this study cannot uncover why there are apparently ethnically based references to athletes in Olympic sportscasts. The very character of each sport compels a different set of comments by sports commentators and there are participatory effects related to social and cultural patterns, economic and political structures, as well as structures and discourses of racial prejudice—a mixture of effects that influence sports participation and commentary, making the analysis very complex indeed.

Relatedly, it is important to comprehend that each Olympics yields different ethnic demographics that can alter content analyses. Certainly, the Summer Olympics consistently offers greater ethnic diversity than the Winter Olympics, but there are numerous other factors influencing participation as well. Ethnic stereotyping within mediated sport has a storied and troubled history since the inception of television and even before that in newspaper and radio coverage. This chapter offers more questions and areas for future research than clear answers. Part of the reason for this is that American society has progressed to the point that attributions specifically directed at the ethnicity of an athlete are no longer acceptable and/or tolerated. Furthermore, ethnicity is nearly impossible to define or quantify. Complexity may bring greater cultural sensitivity, yet it also results in less concrete guidelines for commentary and for measuring progression or regression in terms of the media's response to the ethnic diversity and controversy. The result, quite frequently, is that sportscasters fail to address ethnic issues at all, realizing that to do so would entail a more sophisticated discussion than they are prepared to instigate. Consequently, media sport often lets the camera do the work, which places the definition of ethnicity squarely in the lap of the home viewer. Chapter 7 will explain how viewers interpret these mediated cues, delving into the nebulous but fascinating world of media effects.

7 What do American Olympic viewers *think* happened in Torino?

Examining media effects

> The ideas the mediated sports produce are hammered home repeatedly. These moral lessons are cleverly integrated into our cultural psyche.
>
> (Boyd, 1997, p. viii)

Content analyses of multiple Olympic telecasts have shown strong indications that the depiction of an athlete can change depending on his or her nationality, gender, and ethnicity. But there is also evidence that biases in media content do not necessarily mean that the audience embraces the mediated version as Olympic "reality" (Billings and Angelini, 2007; Tuggle and Owen, 1999).

This chapter is designed to examine questions regarding the effects of NBC's Torino Olympic telecast on "light" and "heavy" viewers of the Games. Gerbner *et al.* (1986) provide insights into understanding how media consumers process messages, arguing that there are potential effects of light and prolonged exposure to biased messages such as the ones that are prevalent within the Olympic telecast. They argue further that mediated stimuli can negotiate the terms of debate, depict boundaries of discourse, and increase argument salience, bringing certain topics to the fore of public debate (Gerbner *et al.*, 2002). Consequently, heavy television viewers will be more likely than light viewers to see reality as closely matching what is exhibited on television.

Media coverage of megasporting events, such as the Olympics, serves the dual purpose of entertaining the masses while providing a sense of historical background. But it is the supreme human endeavor, the triumphs and failures, the danger and daring, and the sheer spectacle that provide a sense of the transcendence of everyday sport and life. Many viewers acknowledge that they watch sports as a form of escapism, or, as Morse (1990) terms it, a "partial loss of touch with the here and now" (p. 193). Sports communication scholars (see Kassing *et al.*, 2004) have found that viewers do, in fact, exhibit altered behaviors as a result of watching sports programs on television (Gantz and Wenner, 1991) and that consuming sport can even alter a fan's self-identity (Dietz-Uhler and Murrell, 1999).

Previous media effects studies have canvassed a relatively vast landscape of topics (e.g. Aday, 2007; Banning, 2007; Bryant and Miron, 2002; Mehus, 2005;

Muschert and Carr, 2007), with many studies confirming stereotyping effects (e.g. Hansen and Hansen, 1988; Power *et al.*, 1996; Sherry, 2004). For example, it is argued that gender influences the public's attitudes and actions in both subtle and overt (e.g. Harrison and Cantor, 1997; Herrett-Skjellum and Allen, 1996) ways. Both Bandura (1986) and Potter (1986) claimed that the two key determinants in classifying the power of the media are (a) prolonged exposure and (b) perceived realism. When applying these variables specifically to NBC's Olympic telecast, there is clearly potential for dramatic attitudinal shifts. First, no other telecast affords the opportunity for prolonged exposure to the extent that the Olympic telecast does. The overwhelming majority of Americans watch portions of the Olympic telecasts and millions watch multiple hours per day, compared to many other television programs that air 30–60 minutes of the Olympics per week with considerably smaller audiences.

Second, as previously discussed, many regard the NBC telecast as the documentation of history, which closely relates to the concept of perceived realism. Indeed, none of the events are scripted in the same manner in which most television is rendered (i.e. dramas, comedies, or other forms of fictional entertainment) and many viewers watch exclusively because even when an athletic ending seems inevitable, the best moments in sport are when the inevitable is trumped by the unbelievable. Viewers tune in for the all-too-human drama of real people in real situations with unpredictable results. If the Olympics were a movie, the great heroes would be exalted and the villains vanquished, yet the allure of sport is the reality that this does not necessarily occur. Indeed, sport usually does not follow any predictable script. The Olympic telecast is perhaps the most ripe for media effects of any sports event and it may exact more influence than any other television program in the United States. After all, it is the biggest show on television.

Over a decade ago, Larson and Park (1993) argued that it was imperative to examine the media effects of Olympic broadcasts, postulating that "questions about media audiences and media effects ... must be answered in relation to the various Olympic messages constructed by television and the other major media" (p. 52). The following assumptions provided a starting point for investigating the consequences of watching the Olympic Games carried out for this chapter: (1) that the majority of Olympic viewers will overestimate the achievement of Americans, Whites, and males because the Olympic content favored these identity groups; and (2) that heavy viewers of the Olympic telecast will be more likely than light-to-moderate viewers to equate the NBC Torino Olympic experience as representing the "accurate/complete" Olympic experience played out in Italy.

We already know that NBC telecasts are to some extent skewed—for instance, in NBC's coverage of the Olympics outlined in the previous chapters, American men athletes are shown more frequently than American women athletes. A casual viewer may watch parts of a few Olympic events and assume that US men achieve at a proportionately higher level than US women, whereas a person who watched a greater proportion of the Olympic events (including every single American medal-winning performance) would be more likely to rightly deduce that women actually won the majority of the US medals in Torino.

Take a non-Olympic example. Let us say both light and heavy golf viewers are asked to guess the names of professional golfers on the PGA Tour that are "Black". Even casual sports fans would be likely to suggest Cablinasian Tiger Woods and Fijian Vijay Singh—both of whom were among the very best golfers in the World Rankings in 2006. However, the casual viewer might also assume that there must be more Black golfers, while the avid golf fan would know that Woods and Singh are the only two golfers in the top 100 of the world rankings that could be identified as Black. The heavy viewer, because of his or her enhanced expertise, should be able to predict a more accurate percentage of golfers that could be identified as Black.

The same would presumably hold true for the Olympics. The casual viewer is still subjected to biases, but the millions of Olympic viewers who followed every event and medal ceremony that is televised may have a different perspective. To test media effects, 232 respondents were asked a series of questions at three different time periods. Seventy-six respondents were surveyed the day after the Opening Ceremonies (February 27, 2006), 79 responded two weeks later (March 13, 2006), and 77 more responded one month after the Opening Ceremonies (March 29, 2006). The respondents ranged in age from 18–90 and were jointly recruited from a mid-sized Southeastern US university and from the general public within this Southeastern community. All respondents took less than 25 minutes to complete the survey.

The survey instrument was designed using a combination of bogus information scales [scales in which respondent guesses are compared to verifiable known facts] with an example being: "What percentage of the total number of overall medals do you think were won by athletes from the United States?" In addition, closed-ended fixed response items (e.g. "On average, how much did you watch NBC's evening (7–12 p.m.) Winter Olympic telecast this February?"), and open-ended response items (e.g. "What moments do you remember most about the Winter Olympics?") were incorporated to create a measure that could accurately answer all proposed hypotheses and research questions. The survey was pre-tested on a small group of college students (N = 8) three months prior to the Games, with adaptations from this pre-test being incorporated into the final measure. The only item that was determined to need additional clarification for a scant number of respondents was that even if they had not watched much (or any) of the Olympic Games, they should still provide their best percentages in terms of the amount of medals won by athletes of different genders, ethnicities, and nationalities. In terms of items in which respondents were asked to make their best estimates regarding gender, ethnic, and nationalistic achievement, the results of the 2006 Winter Olympic Games were statistically analyzed, yielding specific actual percentages to compare to the average guesses from respondents.

Fiction meets "reality": the results

Nationality results were quite imprecise as the US respondents wildly overestimated the success of their country's athletes. The 25 medals actually won by the United States represent only 11 percent of the total number of medals awarded at the Games. Nonetheless, the Ameri-centric focus of the viewers (and, indeed, the NBC telecast) presumably resulted in the divergent approximations reported in Figure 7.1.

In Figure 7.1, we gain several important insights. First, collectively the respondents believed that the US won approximately 30 percent of all medals—nearly three times as many as in reality. Such findings overwhelmingly support the notion that the Olympic telecast can feed overt nationalism to the point that people will overvalue their country's achievement. In this case, heavy viewers were slightly more realistic in their estimations that US athletes won 25 percent of the medals, whereas light viewers assessed that US athletes won 31.8 percent of the medals. Approximations became even less accurate as time passed after the Games were complete. While all answers were immensely off-target, the most accurate responses came from the group that was tested immediately after the closing ceremonies (27.7 percent). Two weeks later, the proportion of medals perceived to be won by US athletes jumped to 30.1 percent; two weeks after that, the percentage was 33.9 percent. Given that the US team did not fare as well as four years before in Salt Lake City, one could assume some of the more accurate numbers came from the feeling that the Torino Games were a letdown in comparison. As time passed, the specifics of the Olympic results likely dropped from most memories and entrenched feelings of nationalism may have caused the percentages to increase. However, in spite of these slight variations, US respondents universally overestimated US achievement.

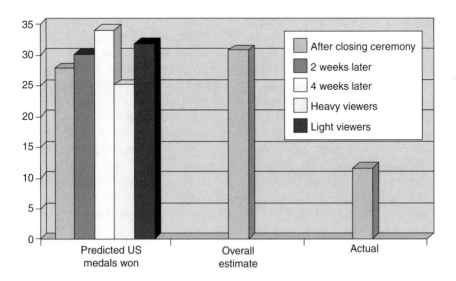

Figure 7.1 Estimations of US achievement in the 2006 Torino Winter Olympics

Regarding gender, respondents offered estimates of the percentage of NBC's coverage that was devoted to men's and women's sports and the percentage of medals won by men and women athletes. Groups tested in all three time periods almost uniformly provided the proper distributions for amount of coverage, as the 232 people speculated that 59.5 percent of the coverage was devoted to men's sports, leaving 40.5 percent of the coverage for women's sports. This was remarkably close to the actual results from primetime (when excluding pairs skating competitions): 59.2 percent for men, 40.8 percent for women. These numbers also were fairly consistent for light (less than one hour of coverage watched per day) and heavy (one hour or more watched per day) viewers, with light viewers predicting a 62 percent/38 percent gender gap and heavy viewers predicting the gap to be 59 percent/41 percent. There were no notable differences between the predictions of light and heavy viewers as both groups estimated that approximately 60 percent of NBC's coverage was devoted to male athletes.

The subsequent query for participants to forecast the percentage of medals won by men and women American athletes yielded more fascinating results. There was an assumption that the reason for the gap in clock-time was because US men athletes were considerably more successful than their women counterparts, which was not the case in reality. Overall, the respondents believed that US men were responsible for 54.5 percent of the medals won for the United States, when the real figure was only 44 percent (in both individual and team competitions). Respondents polled immediately after the closing ceremonies believed this number to be 56 percent and the two subsequent survey groups estimated US men won 53 percent of the time. Both light and heavy viewers gave the same responses on this item within a +/-1 percent margin of error. Thus, the amount of coverage did not significantly alter the predictions which were all skewed appreciably in favor of men athletes. It appears that viewers know they are watching a telecast that highlights men at a higher frequency than women, yet they assume a quite mistaken causal relationship between clock-time and athletic success (defined by medals).

The most dramatic contrast between perception and actuality was uncovered in the ethnicity results, with an amalgam of invalid calculations permeating the responses of all respondent groups. While formal data regarding the ethnicity of the Olympic athletes is not readily available (and practically impossible to attain), there are benchmarks that can be used for comparison with the educated guesses yielded from respondents. Using information on ethnicity found on Internet databases, fairly consistent estimates can be realized and are reported in Table 7.1. Additionally, the compilation of reports and statistics serve as reliability checks for these actual percentages. For instance, we know that speed skater Shani Davis was the only Black athlete to win a medal (two of them) for any country in Torino, meaning that less than 1 percent of all medals were won by Blacks. We also know that major Hispanic countries (such as Spain and Mexico) failed to win a single medal in 2006. The only other non-White/non-European ethnicities to win a noteworthy percentage of the medals were Asian athletes who did quite well in figure skating and speed skating. Without question, at least 80 percent of the medal winners in Torino could be identified as White.

Table 7.1 Estimated percentage of medals won by each ethnic group in the 2006 Torino Winter Olympics

	After closing ceremony	2 wks later	4 wks later	<1 hr/nt.	>1 hr/nt.	Overall	Est. Actual
Caucasian	48.8	50.6	49.4	48.5	50.7	49.6	85
Black	16.0	15.5	16.2	16.2	15.6	15.9	<1
Hispanic	6.4	4.9	4.9	6.0	5.2	5.6	<1
Asian	11.2	12.6	12.6	12.1	11.7	11.9	8
Middle Eastern	6.3	5.9	5.9	6.8	6.8	6.8	<1
Mixed/Other	11.2	10.5	10.5	10.4	10.0	10.2	5

When these figures are compared to respondent estimates, a chasm of difference is uncovered. Table 7.1 reports the estimated percentage of medals won by each ethnic group in the 2006 Winter Olympics. As witnessed in this table, even if one concedes that the actual totals for each ethnic group could fluctuate several percentage points in either direction based on one's operational definition of ethnicity, there is no question whatsoever that Americans perceived the Olympics to be much more ethnically diverse than actual database results indicate. Perhaps because of Black successes in other sports (including the Summer Olympics), viewers believed that Blacks must have experienced at least a modicum of success in Torino, predicting that Black athletes won approximately one-sixth of all the medals awarded. Articulated another way, this means that participants predicted that for every two medal ceremonies, at least one winner on the podium would have been Black.

Whereas African-American athletes were vastly overestimated in terms of Winter Olympic participation (16 times their actual numbers), ironically, White athletes were approximated to win only half the number of medals—far fewer than the 85 percent they actually won. The estimated figure for Hispanic medal winners was 5.6 percent and for Middle-Eastern athletes was 6.8 percent—the latter being a particularly odd finding when considering that virtually all Middle-Eastern countries opted not to compete in the Torino Games. Again, there were no significant differences between the estimates of the heavy and the light viewers. None of the participants in this study seemed to have a grasp of the exceptionally White and Western character of the Winter Olympic Games and the NBC telecast clearly did little to quell misconceptions about, or to comment on, questions of ethnicity.

Combining the nationality, gender, and ethnicity results, one can also determine whether two independent variables (date of survey and amount of exposure) significantly impacted results. Date of survey had three measurement levels (after the closing ceremonies, two weeks later, and four weeks later) while exposure was bifurcated into light (less than one hour per day) and heavy (one hour or more per day) viewers.[1] No significant interactions were uncovered with

1 A 3 × 2 ANOVA was utilized to determine significant effects with *F* values.

regard to the date on which the respondent completed the survey, but the quantity of exposure did alter overall responses about ethnicity with regard to predictions about the successes of White athletes and Black athletes. Additionally, quantity of exposure significantly altered views of nationalistic achievement. Thus, the overall effect of testing dates was negligible, but the amount of exposure to NBC's telecast did significantly matter.

Respondents were also queried about the moments and people they most vividly recalled from the Games, providing a qualitative dimension to the analysis. The results are shown in Table 7.2. Regarding categorization, broad coding applications were used in order to classify similar comments. For instance, one of the moments that were described was of "Ted Ligety coming out of nowhere to win the gold in the men's combined skiing", while other respondents equated people's names as moments, simply citing "Ted Ligety". Both of the above comments were classified in a "Ted Ligety" category.

The date of the test did appear to have a substantial effect. For instance, the group tested immediately after the Opening Ceremonies named the failure and/or media saturation of Bode Miller as the fourth most memorable moment of the Games; two weeks later he was the third most-frequently mentioned memorable moment; four weeks later he was number one. A similar trend occurred with the story of Michelle Kwan, whose injury kept her from competing in Torino. She was the ninth most-mentioned moment for the group responding after the Closing Ceremonies, and then jumped to sixth two weeks later and fifth two weeks after that. One can conclude that these two heavily hyped athletes had staying power in the eyes of the viewers. Promotional impact outlasted actual athletic performance. For instance, Ted Ligety—a surprise skiing gold medalist in Torino who was a virtual unknown until the moment of his tremendous achievement—made the top ten most memorable moments in the first test immediately after the event, but not in the subsequent tests. Evident as well in the individual comments were ingrained beliefs that viewers held before the 2006 Olympic telecast even commenced. Regarding nationality, many comments referred to the "disappointing

Table 7.2 Top ten most-remembered Olympic moments by testing frame

After closing ceremony	*Two weeks after closing ceremony*	*Four weeks after closing ceremony*
1 Figure skating	1 Figure skating	1 Bode Miller
2 Sasha Cohen	2 Sasha Cohen	2 Sasha Cohen
3 Apolo Anton Ohno	3 Bode Miller	3 Figure skating
4 Bode Miller	4 Apolo Anton Ohno	4 Apolo Anton Ohno
5 Shaun White	5 Shaun White	5 Michelle Kwan
6 Lindsey Jacobellis	6 Michelle Kwan	6 Shaun White
7 Davis/Hedrick feud	7 Downhill skiing	7 Davis/Hedrick feud
8 Curling	8 Lindsey Jacobellis	8 Downhill skiing
9 Michelle Kwan	9 Davis/Hedrick feud	9 Bob Costas
10 Ted Ligety	10 Curling	10 Speed skating

performances" of the US team, yet these same respondents continued to report overall percentages of medals won by the US team to be substantially higher than in actuality. For instance, one person believed that the US team needs to "stop showboating and start focusing", but also felt the US team won 25 percent of all the medals awarded, which would have more than doubled the winnings of any other country had it been true. Another respondent felt the performance of the US team was "disappointing", yet believed the US team had won 30 percent of all the medals awarded. Another felt "more Americans should be shown because that's what I care about", but also estimated that 50 percent of the coverage was already devoted to athletes from the United States. In a related vein, another noted that "NBC should stop showing us losers like Bode Miller ... no one wants to see Americans get beat".

Moving to gender, one male—typifying a chauvinist, anti-woman stance—posited a 50/50 gender split in terms of clock-time, and noted that NBC's Olympic telecast continually showed "too much women when ... they are inferior to the men [in athletics]". Conversely, a female (who projected a 70/30 gender split in favor of the men) inferred that "women always get the shaft" within televised sports. Other respondents saw the positive value in showing women's events, exemplified as follows: "[Growing up], I knew the Olympics were the only place I could see women who took being an athlete seriously". These comments reflected the very mixed opinions that viewers espoused about gender equality—directly in favor of, or directly opposed to, equal exposure for athletes of both sexes. They typify the general awareness among the viewers of gender divisions in Olympic sport and of their own gendered attitudes.

There was also an awareness among the participants' comments of ethnic divisions and racial tensions in the Olympics. For example, one participant claimed that the Winter Olympics are for White people because "everyone else knows they [the Winter Olympics] are racist", whereas another participant objected that when an aberration like Black speed skater Shani Davis was televised, his ethnicity was the focus of the discussion too frequently: "Shani Davis is Black. We get it. Isn't there more to this story than being Black?"

On the subject of memorable moments, many spoke about the specific role of NBC as the storyteller within the broadcasting process. Indeed, Bob Costas was one of the top-ten most mentioned "moments" reported by the final test group, even though no specific Costas moment was noted. In addition, the changes that NBC had installed into the telecast were not recognized. For instance, most profiles were reduced from three minutes to 60–90 seconds, yet one person recalled that "whenever a sob story comes on, I know I can channel surf for a while", indicating that the pre-produced profiles were too long. There were mixed messages about NBC's choices and reputation (e.g. "I know if I just watch the nights' coverage everything important will be on"; "No one watches the Olympics anymore. *American Idol* rules now"). There was also a noteworthy number of responses about ways in which the telecast could improve. The most common comment was that time-delayed events were no longer acceptable, or, as one person articulated, "I'm supposed to avoid watching sports news, surfing the Internet, and talking about the Olympics with my friends so I can watch something on tape that night? Get real!" Other comments dealt with the selection of sports that were offered for primetime viewing (e.g. "I watch every single skier but can't find a hockey game"), or they related to the amount of coverage not devoted to showing the actual sporting event (e.g. "The Olympics are the only thing I know that can hype something like Bode Miller skiing for hours when [Miller will only actually] ski for two minutes [that night]").

It is clear from the viewers' responses to NBC's telecast that they begin watching the Games with definite ideas about what the telecast will be like and what they will like and/or dislike. Attitudes are increasingly influenced by mass media spins on how the ratings and countries are faring in comparison with other programs (in terms of ratings) and countries (in terms of medals). Understanding media effects is always a complex endeavor, yet there were unmistakable instances of influence by the two independent variables as well as mistaken predictions concerning Olympic participants and winners.

Implications of media effects

While cultivation theorists frequently contend that the media have the power to shape people's perceptions about the reality in which they live, media framing (Goffman, 1974) procedures can be used to explain many of the media effects uncovered in this study. Notably, the exclusion function (Gitlin, 1980) could have altered respondent answers. For example, NBC never informed the viewers of the overall medals table which would, relatedly, inform viewers of the percentage of medals that the United States was earning. NBC is also ignoring social divides by avoiding many overarching questions of nationality, gender, and ethnicity. Cultivation theorists have previously analyzed the effects of omission (Shanahan *et al.*, 2004), arguing that television can influence a viewer as a result of both what is shown and also what does not make the air. Such claims relate to the fundamentals of the agenda-setting theorists of the 1970s, who claimed that media outlets such as television shape what we think about (McCombs and Shaw, 1972; McQuail and Windahl, 1993).

In his 2005 book, *The Wisdom of Crowds*, James Surowiecki (2005) articulates a thesis that "when our imperfect judgments are aggregated in the right way, our collective intelligence is often excellent" (p. xiv). He incorporates dozens of social examples to argue that a group of novices will often formulate wildly inaccurate guesses, but that, collectively, the average is almost always quite close to the actuality. However, the findings of this study appear to counter his claims. The viewers that were selected from the general public were, collectively, inaccurate in several of their assumptions, including the numbers of medals won by American athletes and Black athletes. They were certainly not smarter than experts, such as Olympic scholars or NBC anchors or producers who would know the correct figures.

When viewers come to watch the NBC Olympic telecast, they always bring with them long-held beliefs (such as the US being the sporting epicenter of the world, men being better athletes than women, and Blacks having greater natural aptitude as athletes than Whites), and if the sportscast does nothing to counter those views, it is probable that they will stay in place. Critics who postulate that NBC should do more to correct identity-oriented entrenched cognitions (e.g. Tuggle *et al.*, 2007) should also note the double-edged sword that would concurrently arise. If NBC opted to mention repeatedly that US women were faring better than the men, they could be perceived as pitting men against women. Would it really be progress for NBC to note in their coverage of a swimming event that all finalists are White, and then move to the track and remind the viewers that all finalists in a 100-meter sprint are Black? Perhaps this would open lines of dialogue, but it would also infuse a new set of identity-laden issues that would support stereotypes that Blacks cannot swim well, or that Whites are not fast sprinters.

Furthermore, the main imperatives in the production of the Olympic telecast remain the pressures for ratings and corresponding advertising dollars. What is perceived to be what the audience desires is fundamental. Wenner and Gantz (1989) found that, above all, the top motivation for watching sports television was to determine the fate of their favorite team, followed by the compelling drama and tension that sport provides. Whannel (1992) connects to this study, explaining that his own sense of sport viewing is that "for most people, the desire to know what happens next, to follow a narrative and to discover the final resolution is a central and indispensable part of the mechanism of identification" (p. 200).

The following quotation, again from Whannel (1992), serves as a useful conclusion to this chapter, outlining the inherent problems of understanding the effects of the Olympic telecast on the viewing public:

> But of course research in this area faces problems both of theory and of method. You cannot adequately explore the nature of popular pleasures solely by asking direct questions; people are not necessarily reliable sources on the nature of their pleasures, which cannot always be easily comprehended.
>
> (Whannel, 1992, p. 202)

8 Looking forward by looking back
Reflections on the Olympic telecasts

At the Games, a complete picture is never possible.

(Jim Lampley)

A lie can travel halfway around the world while the truth is putting on its shoes.

(Mark Twain)

Dichotomies such as "fairness/unfairness", "equitable/inequitable" and "unbiased/biased" permeate much of the literature about media production, content and effects (e.g. Higgs and Weiller, 1994; Rada, 1996; Sabo et al., 1996; Staurowsky, 1995). NBC's Olympic telecast performs yeoman's work in highlighting the global and diverse nature of sport; yet others claim critically that much more must be done to remedy a broken paradigm within all megasporting telecasts in the United States, with the Olympic telecasts being merely exemplars (e.g. Lenskyj, 2000; Tuggle et al., 2002). However, it has not been the intention of this book to contend that Olympic telecasts are deficient or to suggest a way to "fix" them, but, rather, to document features of their production, with particular regard to the portrayal of nationality, gender, and ethnicity. The contention that NBC's coverage is currently imbued with identity-laden differences that could alter viewers' perceptions of what they are watching is significant when considering the possible direction of NBC's coverage in future sports television airings.

"Negotiation" aptly describes how identity issues such as nationality, gender, and ethnicity are portrayed, conveyed, determined, bandied about, altered, influenced, and ultimately received. While no formal "back and forth" style of construction occurs, the research for this book has shown how the media gatekeepers—specifically, the producers and sportscasters—while aiming to be accurate and "fair", are aware of some of the nationalistic, gendered, and ethnic imbalances within NBC's Olympic telecasts. They are also aware of the truly massive audiences to which their telecasts are conveyed. In 2006, an estimated 168 million Americans viewed the Winter Olympics; it is predicted that the 2008 Beijing Summer Olympics will draw a viewership of over 200 million

Americans (Ryan, 2006). The construction of Olympic telecasts is determined in large part by the different ways in which the NBC professionals negotiate "factual" information about athletes, events, and circumstances; by their storytelling techniques and personal interpretations of events; and by the imperatives that are continually tied to ratings and advertising rates. Viewers respond to what they see in different ways and, as witnessed in Chapter 7, their versions of the relative prominence and success of participating athletes, teams, and countries vary widely from the documented, official "facts". But perceptions can change in the blink of an eye and can be determined, refined, and reinforced by what is seen, discussed, and interpreted within the Olympic telecast.

Regarding the interviews with the media professionals, it was clear that identity issues were taken into account in NBC Olympic telecasts in a more overt way than in other megasporting telecasts. Jim Lampley unhesitatingly stated that "this [the Olympic broadcast] is not like anything else", referring to the augmented degree of earnestness that the producers and presenters had for their occupations. The viewers' confidence that NBC's media professionals had a dedicated sense of duty and responsibility emanated from the majority of the audience interviews. Decades ago, the sports division of any newspaper or television network was routinely admonished as the "toy department" of news (Rowe, 2003), yet the super-professionalism that the NBC producers and sportscasters exhibited is a modern contradiction of this belief. The NBC professionals that were interviewed all understood that they were conveying more than mere sport by commenting on social, cultural, and political factors as well. That said, NBC's Olympic telecasts still highlight Americans, men, and White athletes—these groups were found in many instances to receive various forms of differential and preferential treatment.

The negotiation of nationalism

The notion of "feeding the beast" is most evident within the first identity variable that was investigated in this analysis: the negotiation of nationalism. If Dick Ebersol decided to show US athletes for less than one-eighth of the broadcasting time (as relative medal winnings would warrant), he would certainly no longer have a job at NBC Sports as the ratings would inevitably be dismal. Thus, the question becomes, "how might NBC provide a comprehensive Olympic experience for US viewers while satisfying their foremost desire to see athletes from their own country do well?" Referring to exposure and characterization, most producers and sportscaster interviewees conceded that US athletes had to be shown at a considerable rate to maintain a large viewing audience; at the same time, they adamantly purported to show no overt bias in terms of the characterizations of US athletes and those competing from all other countries. In other words, US athletes are shown a lot, but the interviewees did not feel they were depicted within on-air dialogue any differently. This analysis indicates otherwise. As witnessed in Chapter 4, foreign athletes were more likely to be depicted on purely objective assessments such as athletic skills (measured by speed, distance, height, weight, etc.) or experience (measured by whether they had previously competed in an Olympics or garnered world honors), while American athlete characterizations seemed to be more rounded, capturing more nuanced notions of concentration, composure, courage, and personality. One can postulate many reasons for the differences in descriptors, but the most likely correlate would appear to be sportscaster familiarity with the athletes. As Tom Hammond and other sportscasters noted, their preparation for the Games begins with the national Olympic trials, which provides ample opportunity to get to know each US athlete's story more vividly. Coupled with language barriers arising with many non-English-speaking athletes from other countries, it is understandable that sportscasters feel more at ease rendering multifaceted stories and descriptions of US athletes.

Clock-time differences may also have interacted with viewer perceptions of American athletic achievement. The participant viewers overestimated US medal winnings by nearly 300 percent in many cases, and light and heavy viewers had largely the same distorted responses in this regard. Interestingly, the bloated perceptions of American dominance within the Games steadily increased as weeks passed after the closing ceremonies, a troubling finding when considering how American senses of athletic superiority can bleed into other aspects of societal consciousness (Billings and Angelini, 2007) so that people most certainly correlate athletic superpowerdom with the nation's status within the world strata. NBC has attempted to avoid pitting countries against each other in the overall structure of the Games, shunning medal counts and charts that highlight the most successful countries. Still, virtually all other media outlets ubiquitously provide these tables, meaning that most nations are conscious of their ascendancy or failure on these charts and can equate their position with nationalistic pride and power. Take the following utterance from Jim Lampley's final podcast from the Torino Games:

> JL: Beijing, China is the next destination for the Olympic torch. The Olympic Games, in many ways, will serve as a coming-out party for this nation of a billion people. In every way, they are looking to compete with the United States on the world stage, and the playing field may once again be lined with the subtext of competing ideologies. I hope not. In Torino, the youth of the world came and competed without rancor, without hostility. We shall hope for the same when the cauldron is lit again in one of the world's most fascinating nations—a place which will play an enormous role in shaping the future of the planet.

This comment highlights the way Lampley wishes the Olympic Games to be (a pure athletic celebration devoid of nationalism) and what he concedes is the reality (China announcing itself as a world power by hosting and aiming to lead the medal count at the 2008 Summer Olympics). By avoiding the reporting of overall medal winnings by country, NBC endeavors to avoid chauvinism and nationalistic competition, yet by doing so fails to educate its audience with regard to how diverse the Olympics are in terms of the number of medals won by each country. John Naber points out that, "If you publish a list of nations in [ranked] order of number of medals, someone will use that information for political purposes". Naber also believes that inserting identity more overtly in the Olympic telecast can present problems, revealing his feelings that, "On an idealistic note, I'd love to see the Games revolve around what we have in common, and not what we have that separates us".

However, the separation of nations already regularly occurs, and most news outlets report on the overall competition in permeating global terms, so that sporting results have ramifications for the national pride and power of other nation states across the world as well as for the home country. Take the report in *USA Today*, published immediately after the Torino Olympics, in which US Olympic Committee Chairman Peter Ueberroth compares the increasing Olympic global competitiveness with the commercialization and globalization of business, education, and medicine. Ueberroth goes on to state that the 2008 Summer Olympics in Beijing "will be the most important sporting event in history ... the reasons for that have to do with culture and politics and sport and the very impressive emergence of the Chinese people in sport" (Michaels, 2006, p. 3D). The article contends that China is viewing the Beijing Games in ultra-competitive terms, seemingly to announce itself as a second world superpower. Even Canada, after a strong showing in the 2006 Torino Games, is deemed a "direct threat" by United States Olympic Committee (USOC) chief executive officer, Jim Scherr. The global competition within the overall medals table is already being waged, regardless of whether NBC reports it or not.

One other potential way to assuage the nationalistic biases encountered within sportscaster dialogues would be to exchange sportscasters with those from other Olympic telecasts from around the globe. While language barriers would limit the exchange possibilities, such arrangements are possible, as evidenced by coverage of the men's British Open golf tournament in which Amerian Broadcasting Company (ABC) and the British Broadcasting Company (BBC) periodically trade sportscasters (namely, the US's Mike Tirico and England's Peter Allis). In a small way, some home nations would experience different storylines and points of view from presenters from other countries thus mitigating nationalistic biases and increasing the diversity and global character of megasporting stories.

The negotiation of gender

With regard to gender, clock-time differences reported in Chapter 5 illustrated that men athletes were more likely to be shown than women athletes, but considerably more so in a Winter Olympics (62 percent men; 38 percent women) than a Summer Olympics (52 percent men, 48 percent women). Molly Solomon was surprised by this finding as she noted that for a Winter Olympics, virtually nothing is left on the cutting room floor (because of the immense number of hours to fill and the dramatically decreased number of medal events).

If one is to presume that NBC's focus will be placed most directly upon US medal winners, this finding is even more surprising, as the majority of the gold medal winners for the US are more often women than men and, for instance, 56 percent of all US medal winners in the 2006 Torino Games were women. Both NBC employees and at-home viewers incorrectly assumed that the division of clock-time by gender closely resembled the relative successes of the men and women athletes from the United States. Yet, interestingly, NBC's Olympic telecast highlights women's sports at a much higher frequency than any other megasporting event on US television (Eastman and Billings, 2000, 2001; Hallmark and Armstrong, 1999; Tuggle *et al.*, 2007).

In terms of the salience of men and women athletes (defined by mentions), the one unmistakable trend was that the less scripted the coverage was, the more likely men were to receive increased coverage. However, promotions and pre-produced profiles provided virtually equivalent coverage of both sexes, just as lead writer Joe Gesue contended in Chapter 2. The host/anchor also fared well (see Chapter 5). However, the on-site reporters were significantly more likely to mention the names of men athletes than those of women athletes. Future research could usefully focus on whether this is the consequence of a lack of reporter familiarity with women's names or a correlate of clock-time, and whether there are gendered differences defined by the visual (measured by the amount of screen-time each athlete receives) as well as by the verbal (measured by athlete mentions).

With regard to the gender descriptors, there was no evidence of blatant sexism or stereotyping. However, there were significant divergences between the types of dialogue assigned by the sportscasters to men and to women, a finding that has been supported in analyses of other, non-Olympic sports telecasts (e.g. Billings *et al.*, 2005). These divergent dialogues can partially be explained because most Olympic sports have gender-specific competitions that require different forms and fashions of athletic skill (see Billings, in press). For instance, gymnastics is a classic example in which men and women both compete, but do so in different events and on different apparatus requiring specifically gendered skills (e.g. women compete on the balance beam and the uneven parallel bars; men compete on the rings and high bar). The data in Chapter 5 showed that sportscasters employed different adjectives and storylines for men and women when they were describing the competitions and during the general discourse as well. There were also numerous gendered language differences in relation to perceived experience, composure, and general athletic skills. There was an awareness among the NBC professionals of the gendered use of language alluded to by Tom Hammond in Chapter 3 when he conceded that sometimes the words utilized to depict an athletic performance differ by gender.

The largely untested variable relating to these gender differences is the gender of the sportscaster, but paucity of women sportscasters as a whole (roughly an 8:1

split in terms of descriptors employed by men and women sportscasters) makes comparisons in this regard virtually impossible to report, let alone to allow for generalizability. Donna deVarona implied that more women sportscasters would result in better coverage of women's events when she said:

> DdV: Our young women and men need role models. Women athletes are still marginalized, just pick up the sports section of any newspaper or count the minutes devoted to women's sports on any television network or radio station.

Others, such as Ann Meyers Drysdale, felt that inroads for women sportscasters and athletes have been made within the Olympic telecast specifically since NBC has taken over the contract and particularly since the 1996 Atlanta Summer Games. She noted that:

> AMD: I give kudos to Dick Ebersol because it's all about the attitude of the person in charge. If we've got somebody who could not care less about women, you're not going to see it. But who's going to be next in the evolution in sports? Will they spread the wealth the way Dick has?

As illustrated in this comment, the role of gender in the Olympic telecast is viewed as one in which traditional hegemonic distinctions are gradually being deconstructed by NBC but they still remain ensconced within the megasporting telecast to some extent.

The negotiation of ethnicity

The question of ethnicity was seldom addressed by the NBC producers or sportscasters. The fact that Dick Ebersol indicated in Chapter 2 that he could not remember ever being asked about ethnicity within the Olympic telecast speaks volumes about the muted nature of any discussion of ethnicity. This is not an indictment of Ebersol, as he claims colorblindness to be the most appropriate way to convey the Olympic experience. However, it opens a discussion about the lack of discussion—a politics of omission, so to speak. Bryant Gumbel argued for the illegitimacy of the Games because of a lack of ethnic diversity (see Chapter 3, p. 77). Such a lack is starkly evident in the Winter Games, which is dominated by White athletes from the West, and, although at the Summer Games there are athletes from countries across the world with a great variety of ethnic backgrounds, some events such as diving, track and field, and basketball separate athletes according to ethnicity to a large extent. The lack of ethnic discussion or knowledge resulted in wildly disparate notions among US viewers about who were competing and winning medals in the 2006 Torino Games. There was an assumption among viewers that, given their global character, the Olympic Games were substantially ethnically diverse. But the viewers reported a much more ethnically colorful picture of Olympic achievement than the Winter Games actually offered. The nagging query remains about what is the best remedy for this problem. NBC sportscasters largely indicated that their strategy was to let the camera document ethnicity and then to supplement that visual with a comment only if a "valid first" or other notable "ethnic achievement" was attained. Such a strategy could be regarded as minimalist, but if the sportscaster were to highlight ethnic differences and comment on ethnically related athletic achievements, he or she would risk being caught in a determinist and racist trap. John Naber argued as follows against emphasizing the ethnic and social background of speed skater Shani Davis:

> JN: Shani Davis deserves a mention, but I don't think it needs editorializing by saying, "Gee, isn't speed skating doing a wonderful job reaching out to the inner city communities because now they have an African-American speed skater".

But the issue of ethnicity need not permeate the telecast in such a transparent manner. For example, Bob Costas spoke of the potential to have a "miniature *Nightline*" about substantial, hard-news-oriented topics that inevitably arise within Olympic competition—which would include issues such as the paucity of ethnic diversity at Winter Olympic Games. Profiler Jimmy Roberts highlights an "Olympic Moment" each night that features a story that likely would have been bypassed otherwise; such a strategy could be used for identity-oriented controversies as well. The commonality in which all seem to agree is that issues of ethnicity in sport deserve more discussion, even if sportscasters, producers, critics, and academics disagree on the venue in which this discussion should occur. Ironically, it was again Bryant Gumbel who harmonized some of these thoughts most succinctly in his January 2007 commentary on the television program, *Real Sports*. Gumbel referenced the fact that no Black NFL football coach had ever won a Super Bowl before 2007, but that now one would as two Black coaches, Indianapolis's Tony Dungy and Chicago's Lovie Smith, were about to clash in the final. In 2007, Gumbel broadened this discussion of ethnicity beyond the Super Bowl:

BG: Year in and year out, the world's writers and broadcasters routinely take hype and excess to foolish new levels in the run-up to the Super Bowl. Watching them now have to wrestle with race should prove fascinating and instructive. It might produce a YouTube moment or two, but ultimately, I hope, it will also prove helpful. For too long and too often in sports, race has been viewed as the "third rail" of polite discourse, a subject sure to burn those who try to deal with it honestly or speak of it truthfully. It's left most ignoring the topic altogether, as if the elephant in the room would just disappear by itself. Well it hasn't. And it won't.

Black/White distinctions relegating ethnicity to the perception of skin color and relating different ethnicities to different abilities were referred to by several of the research participants for this book in Chapter 6. For instance, the notion that White athletes were those most likely to be depicted as succeeding because of their aptitude for concentration, but the most likely to fail because they lacked the highest level of athletic skill characteristic of Black athletes, is an example of biological determinism that feeds the myth of racially defined athletic aptitude (Edwards, 1969; Entine, 2000; Hoberman, 2007; Murrell and Curtis, 1994). The perpetuation of the Black/White distinction in the language of the Olympics maintains the notion of "essential" differences between two distinct ethnic groups and masks the huge variety of differences within and between those groups.

Aspiring for the "complete picture"

Hardt (1993) states that the "question of authenticity remains one of the major issues underlying the critique of contemporary social thought" (p. 49). This is an issue that is intrinsic to television sport in general (see Moragas Spa *et al.*, 1995; Whannel, 1992) and one that is augmented in the Olympic telecast, in large part as a result of its sheer immensity. The question of authenticity has been addressed in previous chapters specifically in relation to the negotiation of nationality, gender, and ethnicity. Jim Lampley claims that "authenticity" of the Olympic telecast is simply unattainable:

JL: At the Games, a complete picture is never possible. The nature of media is to be selective: there isn't time for everything. In television specifically, our experience of the athletes is mostly limited to their competitive crucible. We see them winning or losing. But what gets lost in the moment is the journey that was years in the making.

Also lost in the process of negotiating identity is a discussion of patriarchal relations, racial ideologies, ideas of nationhood, and the entrenchment of standards and expectations assigned to an athlete based on nationality, gender, and ethnicity. It is folly to claim that there could be one Olympic "reality"; rather, there are many different versions of each Olympic Games. Visker (1995) argues that the "subject" of any story should be dropped from any argument pertaining to authenticity and that the only important aspect of the story is the author/storyteller's ability to recall or retell the story to the best of his or her collective memory. Peter Vidmar noted the problems that a sportscaster—even one who is a former Olympian such as himself—has with trying to convey a "complete" notion of the Olympic experience:

> PV: I wish that there could be a better way to explain just how difficult and challenging many of these sports are. When you watch a sport once every four years, we all sit as armchair quarterbacks and say, "Well, if he had just done that better, he'd have won the gold medal". It's a lot more complicated than that and we struggle to convey it.

It is clear from the discussions with NBC producers and sportscasters that traditional notions of agenda-setting (McCombs and Shaw, 1972) and framing (Goffman, 1974) are cemented during the production processes of an Olympic telecast. But in recent times, the shaping of the stories of the athletes and even their performances has become influenced as a result of massive sports news mechanisms. Ann Meyers Drysdale refers to the ubiquitous sports conglomerate ESPN—whose slogan is "The Worldwide Leader in Sports"—as the exemplar:

> AMD: ESPN has changed the face of how sports are perceived today in the US and the rest of the world. Who doesn't want to be on *SportsCenter?* Everyone wants on there, so they are performing for the camera, trying to think of something outside the box.

By being the "biggest show on television", NBC's Olympic telecast is also the biggest sports journalistic target, with critics frequently arguing that the megasporting telecasts are important but can overstep boundaries. For example, Starr (2006) contended that "Sports remains our most compelling reality show—more thrilling and unpredictable than any island or idol contrivance. The Olympics demonstrated that truth again and again until, at last, the 'up close and personal' conceit began to border on parody" (p. 53). Although NBC would likely take exception to such a claim (and David Neal specifically does so in Chapter 2), Donna deVarona declared that the overall style of the Olympic telecast must change to match more appropriately the ways in which people consume televised sport.

> DdV: Sports bring people together in arenas, cities, in their living rooms, in bars, in restaurants and clubs. Watching the games in an informal group setting should be mirrored in the coverage where anchors talk to each other and their guests. In this way the viewer feels like he or she is participating in the conversation. The day of the serious, wooden anchor, staring out at the camera in a tie and suit and pontificating should be over!

Bob Costas spoke frequently about the criticism the telecast receives every two years when the Summer and Winter Olympics are alternately staged. He agrees that the telecasts should always strive for an ideal, with as much live programming as time zones allow and with the "fairest" coverage of all modern sportscasts being a necessary aim of every program. He finds much of the criticism of the telecast to be short-sighted:

> BC: If a lot of people who are critical of some of the decisions made sat in the producer's chair, they would find themselves moving in the direction of the same decisions. If you spent hundreds of millions of dollars for the rights plus production costs, you wouldn't say, well gee, we should show this skating live, so that someone in the *Seattle Post Intelligencer* will write something nice about us, even though it will diminish our primetime ratings significantly, and we're in a dogfight with *American Idol*. That's just crazy! The person who has the luxury of writing that would not have the luxury of doing that if they were in Dick Ebersol or David Neal's chair.

Still, Costas maintains that more could be done to widen the scope and discussion of contemporary issues beyond the immediately observable sport.

> BC: I think there are times when controversies—legitimate controversies—could be tapped into more. It has got to be done in a way that's

> compelling and entertaining as well as journalistic. But the definition
> of entertainment is broad. It isn't just emotional moments and stir-
> ring competition that's entertaining. Legitimate topics, controversial
> topics—when well-told—are entertaining in a different way.

The focus of the Games has now shifted from Italy to China, the site of the 2008 Summer Olympic Games in Beijing. Given the controversy apropos of even awarding the Games to a Communist country, perpetual questions will abound specifically regarding national identities and global politics. There will be inevitable discussions about whether the Olympic telecast should serve an escapist function for sports and entertainment fans or whether political, social, and cultural stories should emanate from within the production and dialogue of NBC's sportscast. When queried in this regard, Dick Ebersol responded that:

> DE: We're just now finalizing plans to shoot in China and it will be expan-
> sively shot throughout China, not just regionally in Beijing. We'll have
> short 20–30 second pieces that will give people a real sense of all of
> China throughout the Games. How much of that is culture as
> opposed to just getting to know the people? I can't really tell you
> right now. As for the politics, the *Today* show and the nightly news
> through the course of the Games ... that's their sort of area. I'm not
> really thinking that someone's going to tune in to watch the Olympics
> at eight o'clock in primetime and really want to get into the politics
> unless somehow or another they have intruded on the field of play.

Ebersol maintains that the primary viewers consuming the Games wish to watch unadulterated sport with just a flash of cultural backdrop, which the focus-group data repeatedly affirms. It will be interesting to scrutinize the ways in which US viewers respond to China as the host and as potential competitor for the overall medal crown. Nonetheless, all the NBC professionals believe that the biggest challenge is likely to be the time difference, which they directly link to problems with ratings in Sydney 2000. This book has repeatedly returned to the notion of NBC's Olympic telecast as chronicling history, but, with major time zones to cross (12 hours to the East Coast of America from Beijing), the aim will be to maintain a sense of authenticity that was so difficult to attain in Sydney. Even though some of the major events, particularly gymnastics and swimming, have been shifted to early morning Beijing time to allow for live US primetime view-ing, the time-zone challenge remains for the majority of the sports offered in 2008. Bob Costas recalls the problems encountered in Sydney in 2000:

BC: Sydney was like one ongoing party. The whole mood of the city was very upbeat and fun and it was very difficult to capture that with this tape delay. We weren't trying to kid them. We said up front several times that we were presenting all of this on tape, but the essence of sports is spontaneity. Anticipation and immediate reaction. In this particular case, there were times I felt like I was on the History Channel. We did the best we could, but given the circumstances, there couldn't be an appropriate tone.

Comments such as these will inform NBC about how to tackle the time delay issue again in 2008—along with the much more highly politically charged environment that China hosting the Games will inevitably enact. Despite the criticism that is sometimes levied at them, NBC interviewees repeatedly stated that working an Olympic telecast is a career highlight. As Jim Lampley iterated: "It would be fatuous to say there was anything difficult about it. It is a joy and a privilege. An incredible adventure". When asked whether they agreed with my assertion that the Olympics are the biggest show on American television, they were unanimous in support of the seemingly bold statement. David Neal stated that:

DN: Without a doubt the Olympic Games are the biggest show on television. If you aggregate the different numbers, the different hours, the different venues, you've got broadcast excellence, over 17 nights of primetime. You've got sports television at a level of quality that is rarely seen anywhere else. The prestige of working on an Olympics is something that is recognized and acknowledged throughout the industry.

Indeed, the talent assembled for the NBC Olympic telecast is unmatched by any other worldwide telecast of any sports event and the production quality and epic magnitude of athletic achievement is unsurpassed. Members of the NBC production team are undoubtedly cognizant of the additional power that the Olympic rights bring to the network and have a sense of responsibility and pride in their work. They continually reiterated their understanding of the gravity of the Olympic influence. An emotional anecdote from Jim Lampley reveals his feelings of reverence and inspiration resulting from his experiences of the Olympic Games over time:

JL: I was a huge fan starting in 1960 when I was 11 years old, and watched the Rome Olympics. I'll never forget my mother explaining to me that there was a huge significance in an Ethiopian palace guard [Abebe Bikila], not just winning the marathon in Rome, but finishing under the Arch [de Constantine] that Mussolini had structured for soldiers who had plundered his country 21 years before [in World War II]. That was the first moment. My mother was indicating to me that there's a big world into which sports fit, and this is where it all comes together. From that moment on, I've always been told these stories illuminate a path to a better world. When athletes at closing ceremonies hold hands and begin to spontaneously hug, they share meaning that's not like anything else. When they trade the national jerseys and jackets that they've worn for three weeks as their identity to someone from another country who they've never met and they're never going to see again, there's nothing else on the planet that beats that. So, anybody who wants to denigrate it, all they demonstrate is that their cynicism is irretrievable and that they don't realize where their hope lies.

The emotive pull of the Olympic Games is explained in a different way by Dick Ebersol, who claims that they unite American families in a unique and effective way, and, by implication, the American family symbolizes the American nation as a whole—what was mentioned in Chapter 4 by Benedict Anderson (1983) as an "imagined community", suggesting an arguably spurious cohesiveness that transcends gendered and ethnic differences within the nation state of America:

DE: The Olympics are the absolute last thing that brings the whole American family together in front of the television set. There has been certain growth in the phenomenon of *American Idol*, but television as it was in the sixties and seventies where father, mother, children would sit in front of the television set [is largely over]. Now, with the usual television fare, dad is in one room watching the NBA playoff game, mom is somewhere watching *ER*, one of the kids is off somewhere watching MTV; there's very little that's a unifying force that puts everybody together. The Olympics have proven through the nineties—and well into this millennium—that they are the one thing that still does put everybody together in front of the television set.

This book has examined the processes behind the production and delivery of the NBC Olympic telecast. focusing on the experiences and philosophies of the tele-cast professionals—the very people who construct the story of every Olympic Games for millions of American viewers. I have given the final words to them because they reflect so graphically the powerful idea that sport is a unifying force and that the Olympics, par excellence, are hugely significant in their effect on people's emotions and sense of belonging. Through the investigations of nation-ality, gender, and ethnicity it was confirmed that Americans, men, and Whites continue to receive inordinate prominence in both Summer and Winter Olympic telecasts. But it is also clear that there is a sensitivity among the media professionals to differences between American athletes and between athletes from different nations across the world, and to the need to increase the visibility of athletes from different nation states, both genders, and all ethnicities. Ways of producing Olympic telecasts are not set in stone and fixed for all time, and new approaches and ideas are negotiated as part of a constantly moving process. Although highly commercialized and technologized developments have become major determinants of NBC's Olympic telecasts in recent years, nevertheless, the telecasts retain their unpredictability and huge public appeal and perceptions of them remain both diverse and divisive. These complexities are part and parcel of airing the biggest show on television.

References

Abdel-Shehid, G. (2007) Welcome to the "sportocracy": race and sport after innocence. In J.A. Hargreaves and P. Vertinsky (eds), *Physical Culture, Power, and the Body*. London: Routledge.

Adams, T. and Tuggle, C.A. (2004) ESPN's *SportsCenter* and coverage of women's athletics: it's a boy's club. *Mass Communication and Society*, 7, 237–248.

Aday, S. (2007) The framesetting effects of news: an experimental test of advocacy versus objectivist frames. *Journalism and Mass Communication Quarterly*, 83(4), 767–784.

Allison, L. (ed.) (1986) *The Politics of Sport*. Manchester: Manchester University Press.

Allison, L. (2000) Sport and nationalism. In J. Coakley and E. Dunning (eds), *Handbook of Sports Studies* (pp. 344–355). London: Sage.

Anderson, B. (1983) *Imagined Communities* (2nd edn). New York: Verso.

Anderson, C. (2006) *The Longtail: Why the Future of Business is Selling Less of More*. New York: Hyperion.

Anderson, E. (2005) *In the Game: Gay Athletes and the Cult of Masculinity*. Albany, NY: SUNY.

Antcliff, V. (2005) Broadcasting in the 1990s: competition, choice, and inequality? *Media, Culture and Society*, 27(6), 841–859.

Ashforth, B.E. and Mael, F. (1989) Socialization tactics: longitudinal effects of network adjustment. *Academy of Management Review*, 14, 20–39.

Ayres, C. (2006, Apr. 16) While all America switches on the TV, Hollywood turns to its basest instincts. *The London Times*, p. 17.

Bairner, A. (2001) *Sport, Nationalization, and Globalization: European and North American Perspectives*. Albany, NY: SUNY.

Bandura, A. (1986) *Social Foundations of Thought and Action: A Social Cognitive Theory*. Upper Saddle River, NJ: Prentice Hall.

Banning, S. (2007) Third-person effects on political participation. *Journalism and Mass Communication Quarterly*, 83(4), 785–800.

Bass, A. (2002) *Not the Triumph but the Struggle: The 1968 Olympics and the Making of the Black Athlete*. Minneapolis, MN: University of Minnesota Press.

Beamish, R. and Ritchie, I. (2006) *Fastest, Highest, Strongest: A Critique of High Performance Sport*. New York and London: Routledge.

Bellamy, R. (2006) Sports media: a modern institution. In A. Raney and J. Bryant (eds), *Handbook of Sport and Media* (pp. 63–76). Mahwah, NJ: LEA.

Bernstein, A. and Blain, N. (eds), (2003) *Sport, Media, Culture: Global and Local Dimensions*. Portland, OR: Frank Cass.

Berry, S. (2006, Feb. 15) Sportscaster's comments take a Turin for the worse. *The Columbus Dispatch*, p. 8C.

Bianco, R. (2006a, Feb. 13) Prime-time Olympics: a variety show. *USA Today*, p. 1D.

Bianco, R. (2006b, Feb. 26) NBC should go for the gold in Beijing. *USA Today*, p. 1D.

Billings, A.C. (2000) In search of women athletes: ESPN's list of the top 100 athletes of the century. *Journal of Sport and Social Issues*, 24(4), 415–421.

Billings, A.C. (2003a) Dueling genders: announcer bias in the 1999 US Open tennis tournament. In R.S. Brown and D. O'Roarke (eds), *Topics in Sports Communication* (pp. 51–62). Westport, CT: Praeger.

Billings, A.C. (2003b) Portraying Tiger Woods: characterizations of a "Black" athlete in a "White" sport. *The Howard Journal of Communications*, 14(1), 29–38.

Billings, A.C. (2004) Depicting the quarterback in Black and White: a content analysis of college and professional football broadcast commentary. *Howard Journal of Communications*, 15(4), 201–210.

Billings, A.C. (2007) From diving boards to pole vaults: gendered athlete portrayals in the "big four" sports at the 2004 Athens Summer Olympics. *Southern Communication Journal*, 72 (4), 329–344.

Billings, A.C. and Eastman, S.T. (2002) Nationality, gender, and ethnicity: formation of identity in NBC's 2000 Olympic coverage. *International Review for the Sociology of Sport*, 37(3), 349–368.

Billings, A.C. and Eastman, S.T. (2003) Framing identities: gender, ethnic, and national parity in network announcing of the 2002 Winter Olympics. *Journal of Communication*, 53(4), 369–386.

Billings, A.C. and Tambosi, F. (2004) Portraying the United States vs. portraying a champion: US network bias in the 2002 World Cup. *International Review for the Sociology of Sport*, 39(2), 157–165.

Billings, A.C. and Angelini, J.R. (2007) Packaging the games for viewer consumption: Nationality, gender, and ethnicity in NBC's coverage of the 2004 Summer Olympics. *Communication Quarterly*, 55(1), 95–111.

Billings, A.C., Eastman, S.T. and Newton, G.D. (1998) Atlanta revisited: primetime promotion in the 1996 Olympic Games. *Journal of Sport and Social Issues*, 22(1), 65–78.

Billings, A.C., Halone, K.K. and Denham, B.E. (2002) "Man" that was a "pretty" shot: an analysis of gendered broadcast commentary of the 2000 men's and women's NCAA Final Four basketball tournaments. *Mass Communication and Society*, 5(3), 295–315.

Billings, A.C., Angelini, J.R. and Eastman, S.T. (2005) The hidden gender biases in televised golf announcing. *Mass Communication and Society*, 8(2), 155–171.

Billings, A.C., Angelini, J.R. and Eastman, S.T. (2007) Wie shock: television commentary about playing on the PGA and LPGA tours. *The Howard Journal of Communications*, 18(3).

Billings, A.C., Craig, C.C., Croce, R., Cross, K.M., Moore, K.M., Vigodsky, W. and Watson, V.G. (2006) Just one of "the guys": an analysis of Annika Sorenstam at the 2003 PGA Colonial golf tournament. *Journal of Sport and Social Issues*, 30(1), 137–143.

Billings, A.C., Brown, C.L., Crout, J.H., McKenna, K.E., Rice, B.A., Timanus, M.E. and Zeigler, J. (in press, 2008) The Games through the NBC lens: gender, ethnic and national equity in the 2006 Torino Winter Olympics. *Journal of Broadcasting and Electronic Media*, 52(2).

Birrell, S. (1989) Racial relations theories and sport: suggestions for a more critical analysis. *Sociology of Sport Journal*, 6(3), 212–227.

Bishop, R. (2003) Missing in action: feature coverage of women's sports in *Sports Illustrated*. *Journal of Sport and Social Issues*, 27(2), 184–194.

Blinde, M.E., Greendorfer, S.L. and Sankner, R.J. (1991) Differential media coverage of men's and women's intercollegiate basketball: reflection of gender ideology. *Journal of Sport and Social Issues*, 15, 98–114.

Boyd, T. (1997) Anatomy of a murder: O.J. Simpson and the imperative of sports in cultural studies. In A. Baker and T. Boyd (eds), *Out of Bounds: Sports, Media, and the Politics of Identity*. Bloomington, IN: Indiana University Press.

Bryant, J. and Raney, A.A. (2000) Sports on the screen. In D. Zillman and P. Vorderer (eds), *Media Entertainment: The Psychology of its Appeal* (pp. 153–174). Mahwah, NJ: LEA.

Bryant, J. and Miron, D. (2002) Entertainment as media effect. In J. Bryant and D. Zillman (eds) *Media Effects: Advances in Theory and Research* (pp. 43–67). Mahwah, NJ: LEA.

Bryant, J., Comisky, P. and Zillman, D. (1977) Drama in sports commentary. *Journal of Communication*, 27(3), 140–149.

Bryson, L. (1987) Sport and the maintenance of masculine hegemony. *Women's Studies International Forum*, 10(4), 349–360.

Buffington, D. (2005) Contesting race on Sundays: making meaning out of the rise in the number of black quarterbacks. *Sociology of Sport Journal*, 21, 19–37.

Buscombe, E. (ed.) (1974) *Football on Television*. London: BFI.

Byrd, J. and Utsler, M. (2007) Is stereotypical coverage of African–American athletes as "dead as disco"? An analysis of NFL quarterbacks in the pages of *Sports Illustrated*. *Journal of Sports Media*, 2(1), 1–28.

Capranica, L. and Aversa, F. (2002) Italian television sport coverage during the 2000 Sydney Olympic Games: a gender perspective. *International Review for the Sociology of Sport*, 37, 337–349.

Carey, J.W. (1989) *Communication as Culture: Essays on Media and Society*. Winchester, MA: Unwin Hyman.

Carrington, B. (2007) Sport and race. In G. Ritzer (ed.), *The Blackwell Encyclopedia of Sociology* (pp. 4686–4690). Oxford: Blackwell.

Cashmore, E. (2000) *Making Sense of Sport* (3rd edn). London: Routledge.

Caudwell, J. (1999) Women's football in the United Kingdom: theorizing gender and unpacking the butch lesbian image. *Journal of Sport and Social Issues*, 23(4), 390–402.

Christie, J. (2006, Nov. 10) NBC catching onto the Net. *Globe and Mail* (online). Retrieved from http://www.globeandmail.com/breakingnews.

Christopherson, N., Janning, M. and McConnell, E.D. (2002) Two kicks forward, one kick back: a content analysis of media discourses on the 1999 Women's World Cup Soccer Championship. *Sociology of Sport Journal*, 19(2), 170–188.

Chyi, H.I. and McCombs, M. (2004) Media salience and the process of framing: Coverage of the Columbine school shootings. *Journalism and Mass Communication Quarterly*, 81(1), 22–35.

Claringbould, I., Knoppers, A. and Elling, A. (2004) Exclusionary practices in sport journalism. *Sex Roles*, 51(11–12), 709–718.

Clarke, A. and Clarke, J. (1982) Highlights and action replays: ideology, sport, and the media. In J. Hargreaves (ed.), *Sport, Culture, and Ideology* (pp. 62–87). London: Routledge.

Coakley, J. (2004) *Sports in Society: Issues and Controversies*. Boston: McGraw-Hill.

Collette, L. (1998) *The World on a Screen: US Network TV Coverage of the 1984, 1988, 1992, and 1996 Summer Olympic Games' Opening Ceremonies*. Paper presented at the meeting of the Broadcast Education Association, Las Vegas, NV.

Connell, R. (1987) *Gender and Power*. Cambridge: Polity Press.

Costas, B. (2006, May 12) Personal telephone interview.

Cox, T. (2006, Feb. 10) Fasten your seat belts, fans ... two more hours of coverage. *Chicago Daily Herald*, p. 9.

Crawford, M. and Kaufman, M.R. (2006) Sex differences versus social processes in the construction of gender. In K. Dindia and D.J. Canary (eds), *Sex Differences and Similarities in Communication* (pp. 179–194). Mahwah, NJ: LEA.

Crepeau, R. (1996, Aug. 16) Sport and society broadcast.

Critcher, C. (1986) Radical theorists of sport: the state of play. *Sociology of Sport Journal*, 3(4), 333–343.

Cuneen, J. and Sidwell, M.J. (1998) Gender portrayals in *Sports Illustrated for Kids* advertisements: a content analysis of prominent and supporting models. *Journal of Sport Management*, 12(1), 39–50.

Daddario, G. (1992) Swimming against the tide: *Sports Illustrated*'s imagery of female athletes in a swimsuit world. *Women's Studies in Communication*, 15(1), 49–64.

Daddario, G. (1994) Chilly scenes of the 1992 Winter Games: the mass media and the marginalization of female athletes. *Sociology of Sport Journal*, 11(3), 275–288.

Daddario, G. (1998) *Women's Sport and Spectacle*. Westport, CT: Praeger.

Daddario, G. and Wigley, B.J. (2007) Gender marking and racial stereotyping at the 2004 Athens Games. *Journal of Sports Media*, 2(1), 29–52.

Davis, L.R. (1997) *The Swimsuit Issue and Sport: Hegemonic Masculinity and Sports Illustrated*. Albany, NY: SUNY.

Davis, L.R. and Harris, O. (1998) Race and ethnicity in US sports media. In L.A. Wenner (1st edn), *MediaSport* (pp. 154–169). New York: Routledge.

Dayan, D. and Katz, E. (1992) *Media Events: The Live Broadcasting of History*. Cambridge, MA: Harvard.

Denham, B.E., Billings, A.C. and Halone, K.K. (2002) Differential accounts of race in broadcast commentary of the 2000 Men's and Women's NCAA Final Four Basketball Tournaments. *Sociology of Sport Journal*, 19(3), 315–332.

Dewar, A. (1993) Sexual oppression in sport: past, present and future alternatives. In A.G. Ingram and J.W. Loy (eds), *Sport in Social Development* (pp. 147–165). Champaign, IL: Human Kinetics Books.

Dietz-Uhler, B. and Murrell, A. (1999) Examining fan reactions to game outcomes: a longitudinal study of social identity. *Journal of Sport Behavior*, 22, 15–27.

Drzewiecka, J.A. (2003) Collective memory, media representations, and barriers to intercultural dialogue. In M.J. Collier (ed.), *Intercultural Alliances: Critical Transformation* (pp. 189–219). Thousand Oaks, CA: Sage.

Duncan, M.C. (1986) A hermeneutic of spectator sport: the 1976 and 1984 Olympic Games. *Quest*, 38(1), 50–77.

Duncan, M.C. (2006) Gender warriors in sport: women and the media. In A. Raney and J. Bryant (eds), *Handbook of Sports and Media* (pp. 231–252). Mahwah, NJ: LEA.

Duncan, M.C. and Brummett, B. (1987) The mediation of spectator sport. *Research Quarterly for Exercise and Sport*, 58, 168–177.

Duncan, M. and Hasbrook, C. (1988) Denial of power in televised women's sport. *Sociology of Sport Journal*, 5(1), 1–21.

Duncan, M., Messner, M., Williams, L., Jensen, K. and Wilson, W. (eds) (1990) *Gender Stereotyping in Television Sports*. Los Angeles, CA: the Amateur Athletic Foundation of Los Angeles.

Dyer, K. (ed.) (1989) *Sportswomen Towards 2000: A Celebration*. South Australia: Hyde Park.

Eagan, M. (2001, July 1) Pro golf remains over par on race. *The Hartford Courant*, p. A-1.

Eastman, S.T. and Billings, A.C. (1999) Gender parity in the Olympics: hyping women athletes, favoring men athletes. *Journal of Sport and Social Issues*, 23(2), 140–170.

Eastman, S.T. and Billings, A.C. (2000) Sportscasting and sports reporting: the power of gender bias, *Journal of Sport and Social Issues*, 24(1), 192–212.

Eastman, S.T. and Billings, A.C. (2001) Biased voices of sports: racial and gender stereotyping in college basketball announcing. *Howard Journal of Communications*, 12(4), 183–202.

Eastman, S.T. and Billings, A.C. (2004) Promotion's limited impact in the 2000 Sydney Olympics. *Television and New Media*, 5(1), 339–358.

Eastman, S.T., Brown, R.S. and Kovatch, K.J. (1996) The Olympics that got real? Television's story of Sarajevo. *Journal of Sport and Social Issues*, 20(4), 366–391.

Eastman, S.T., Newton, G.D. and Pack, L. (1996) Promoting primetime programs in megasporting events. *Journal of Broadcasting and Electronic Media*, 40, 366–388.

Edwards, H. (1969) *Revolt of the Black Athlete*. New York: Free Press.

Edwards, H. (1973) *The Sociology of Sport*. Homewood, IL: Dorsey.

Entine, J. (2000) *Taboo: Why Black Athletes Dominate Sports and Why We're Afraid to Talk About It*. New York, NY: Public Affairs.

Entman, R. (1993) Framing: toward clarification of a fractured paradigm. *Journal of Communication*, 43, 51–58.

Espy, R. (1979) *The Politics of the Olympic Games*. Berkeley, CA: University of California Press.

Farrell, T. (1989) Media rhetoric as social drama: the Winter Olympics of 1984. *Critical Studies in Mass Communication*, 6(2), 158–182.

Fink, J.S. and Kensicki, L.J. (2002) An imperceptible difference: visual and textual constructions of femininity in *Sports Illustrated* and *Sports Illustrated for Women*. *Mass Communication and Society*, 5(3), 317–340.

Fitzgerald, T. (2005, Dec. 16) Philadephia NAACP head rebuked for McNabb remarks. *Philadelphia Inquirer*, p. 1A.

Foley, D. E. (1990) The great American football ritual: reproducing race, class, and gender inequality. *Sociology of Sport Journal*, 7, 111–135.

Ford, B. (2004, Dec. 27) Complex legacy left by White: one of NFL's greatest linemen died yesterday. *The Philadelphia Inquirer*, p. S6.

Fuller, L.K. (2006) *Sport, Rhetoric, and Gender*. New York: Palgrave Macmillan.

Gantz, W. and Wenner, L. (1991) Men, women, and sports: audience experiences and effects. *Journal of Broadcasting and Electronic Media*, 35, 233–243.

Garland, J. and Rowe, D. (1999) War minus the shooting? Jingoism, the English press, and Euro '96. *Journal of Sport and Social Issues*, 23, 80–95.

Gerbner, G. (1998) Cultivation analysis: an overview. *Mass Communication and Society*, 1(3/4), 175–194.

Gerbner, G., Gross, L., Morgan, M. and Signorelli, N. (1986) Living with television: the dynamics of the cultivation process. In J. Bryant and D. Zillman (eds), *Perspectives on Media Effects* (pp. 17–40). Hillsdale, NJ: Erlbaum.

Gerbner, G., Gross, L., Morgan, M., Signorielli, N. and Shanahan, J. (2002) Growing up with television: cultivation processes. In J. Bryant and D. Zillman (eds) *Media Effects: Advances in Theory and Research*. Mahwah, NJ: LEA.

Gitlin, T. (1980) *The Whole World is Watching: Mass Media in the Making and Unmaking of the New Left*. Berkeley: University of California.

Goffman, E. (1963) *Stigma: Notes on the Management of Spoiled Identity*. Englewood Cliffs, NJ: Prentice Hall.

Goffman, E. (1974) *Frame Analysis: An Essay on the Organization of Experience*. New York: Harper and Row.

Gordon, S. and Sibson, R. (1998) Global television: the Atlanta Olympics opening ceremony. In D. Rowe and G. Lawrence (eds) *Tourism, Leisure, Sport: Critical Perspectives*. Melbourne, VIC: Cambridge University Press.

Gorrell, M. (2006, Feb. 6) Games conjure up memories of 1956; Utah recalls Cold War Olympics. *The Salt Lake Tribune*, p. 1.

Gramsci, A. (1971) *Selections from the Prison Notebooks*. London: Lawrence and Wishart.

Gratton, C. and Solberg, H.A. (2007) *The Economics of Sports Broadcasting*. London: Routledge.

Gruneau, R. (1983) *Class, Sports, and Social Development*. Amherst, MA: University of Massachusetts Press.

Gruneau, R. (1989) Making spectacle: a case study in television sports production. In L. Wenner (ed.), *Media, Sports and Society* (pp. 134–154). Newbury Park, CA: Sage.

Halbert, C. and Latimer, M. (1994) "Battling" gendered language: an analysis of the language used by sports commentators in a televised coed tennis competition. *Sociology of Sport Journal*, 11, 298–308.

Hall, S. (1971) *Innovation and Decline in the Treatment of Culture on British Television*. Paris: UNESCO.

Hall, S. (1972) The determinations of news photographs. *Working Papers in Cultural Studies*, 3, Birmingham: CCCS.

Hall, S. (1975) *TV as a Medium and its Relation to Culture*. CCCS stencilled paper: Birmingham: CCCS.

Hall, S. (1981) Notes on deconstructing "the popular". In R. Samuel (ed.), *People's History and Socialist Theory* (pp. 227–240). London: Routledge and Kegan Paul.

Hall, S. (1984) The state in question. In D. McLennan, D. Held, and S. Hall (eds), *The Idea of the Modern State* (pp. 1–28). Milton Keynes: Open University Press.

Hall, S. (1986) Media power and class power. In J. Curran (ed.), *Bending Reality: The State of the Media*. London: Pluto Press.

Hall, S. (1992) Cultural studies and its theoretical legacies. In D. Morley and K. Chen (eds), *Stuart Hall: Critical Dialogues*. London: Routledge.

Hall, S. (1996) Introduction: Who needs "identity"? In S. Hall and P. du Gay (eds), *Questions of Cultural Identity* (pp. 1–17). London: Sage.

Hallmark, J.R. and Armstrong, R.N. (1999) Gender equity in televised sports: a comparative analysis of Men's and Women's NCAA Division I basketball broadcasts, 1991–1995. *Journal of Broadcasting and Electronic Media*, 43(2), 222–235.

Hansen, C.H. and Hansen, R.D. (1988) How rock music videos can change what is seen when boy meets girl: priming stereotypic appraisal of social interaction. *Sex Roles*, 19, 287–316.

Hardt, H. (1993) Authenticity, communication, and critical theory. *Critical Studies in Mass Communication*, 10, 49–69.

Hargreaves, J.A. (1982) Theorizing sport: an introduction. In J.A. Hargreaves (ed.), *Sport, Culture, and Ideology* (pp. 1–29). Routledge and Kegan Paul: London.

Hargreaves, J.A. (1994) *Sporting Females: Critical Issues in the History and Sociology of Women's Sports*. London: Routledge.

Hargreaves, J.A. (2000) *Heroines of Sport*. London: Routledge.

Hargreaves, J.A. and McDonald, I. (2000) Cultural studies and the sociology of sport. In J. Coakley and E. Dunning (eds), *Handbook of Sport Studies* (pp. 48–60). London: Sage.

Harris, O. (1993) African-American predominance in collegiate sport. In D.D. Brooks and R.C. Althouse (eds), *Racism in College Athletics: The African-American Athlete's Experience* (pp. 51–74). Morgantown, WV: Fitness Information Technology.

Harrison, K. and Cantor, J. (1997) The relationship between media consumption and eating disorders. *Journal of Communication*, 47(1), 40–67.

Harry, J. (1995) Sports ideology, attitudes toward women, and anti-homosexual attitudes. *Sex Roles*, 31(1–2), 109–117.

Hartmann, D. (1996) The politics of race and sport: resistance and domination in the 1968 African American Olympic protest movement. *Ethnic and Racial Studies*, 19(3), 548–566.

Hartmann, D. (2003) *Race, Culture and the Revolt of the Black Athlete: The 1968 Olympic Protests and their Aftermath*. Chicago: University of Chicago Press.

Herrett-Skjellum, J. and Allen, M. (1996) Television programming and sex stereotyping: a meta-analysis. *Communication Yearbook*, 157–185.

Hiestand, M. (2006a, Jan. 18) Ebersol expects Olympics ratings will be solid. *USA Today*, p. 1C.

Hiestand, M. (2006b, Jan. 18) NBC aiming for Olympic viewers to stay tuned. *USA Today*, p. 2C.

Hiestand, M. (2006c, Feb. 23) Unlike NBC, world feed keeps nations' smaller Olympic coverage afloat. *USA Today*, p. 8D.

Higgs, C.T, and Weiller, K.H. (1994) Gender bias and the 1992 Summer Olympic Games: an analysis of television coverage. *Journal of Sport and Social Issues*, 18(3), 234–246.

Higgs, C., Weiller, K. and Martin, S. (2003) Gender bias in the 1996 Olympic Games: a comparative analysis. *Journal of Sport and Social Issues*, 27(1), 52–64.

Hilliard, D. (1984) Media images of male and female professional athletes: an interpretive analysis of magazine articles. *Sociology of Sport Journal*, 1, 251–262.

Hiskey, M. (2006, Feb. 10) Turin 2006: women of winter; advertisers, broadcasters know who will be glued to their screens this Olympic season. *Atlanta Journal Constitution*, p. 1A.

Hoberman, J. (2007) Race and athletics in the twenty-first century. In J.A. Hargreaves and P. Vertinsky (eds), *Physical Culture, Power, and the Body* (pp. 208–231) London: Routledge.

Hogg, M.A. and Tindale, R.S. (2005) Social identity, influence, and communication in small groups. In J. Harwood and H. Giles (eds), *Intergroup Communication: Multiple Perspectives* (pp. 141–164). New York: Peter Lang.

Hogg, M.A. and Reid, S. A. (2006) Social identity, self-categorization, and the communication of group norms. *Communication Theory*, 16(1), 7–30.

Houlihan, B. (1994) *Sport and International Politics*. Hemel Hempstead: Harvester Wheatsheaf.

Howard, T. (2006, Jan. 6) Ad sales boom for Super Bowl, Olympics. *USA Today*, p. 1B.

Hult, J.S. (1989) Women's struggles for governance in U.S. amateur athletics. *International Review for the Sociology of Sport*, 24(3), 249–263.

Human Rights News (2007) Retrieved from http://hrw.org/english/docs/2007/05/31/china16029.htm.

Human Rights Overview (2006) Retrieved from http://hrw.org/english/docs/2006/01/18/china12270.htm.

Hutchby, I. (2005) Conversation analysis and the study of broadcast talk. In K.L. Fitch and R.E. Sanders (eds), *Handbook of Language and Social Interaction* (pp. 437–460) Mahwah, NJ: LEA.

Ingham, A.G. and Donnelly, P. (1990) Whose knowledge counts? The production of knowledge and issues of application in the sociology of sport. *Sociology of Sport Journal*, 7, 58–65.

Ingham, A.G., Blissmer, B.J. and Davidson, K.W. (1999) The expendable prolympic self: going beyond the boundaries of sociology and psychology of sport. *Sociology of Sport Journal*, 16, 236–268.

IOC Marketing Fact File (2006) Retrieved from http://multimedia.olympic.org/pdf/en_report_344.pdf.

Jackson, D.Z. (1989, Jan. 22) Calling the plays in Black and White. *Boston Globe*, pp. A30, 33.

Jarvie, G. (1993) Sport, nationalism, and cultural identity. In L. Allison (ed.), *The Changing Politics of Sport* (pp. 58–83). Manchester: Manchester University Press.

Jones, R., Murrell, A.J. and Jackson, J. (1999) Pretty versus powerful in the sports pages: print media coverage of US Women's Olympic gold medal winning teams. *Journal of Sport and Social Issues*, 23(2), 183–192.

Jutel, A. (2002) Olympic road cycling and national identity: where is Germany? *Journal of Sport and Social Issues*, 26(2), 195–208.

Kane, M.J. (1988) Media coverage of the female athlete before, during, and after Title IX: *Sports Illustrated* revisited. *Journal of Sports Management*, 2, 87–99.

Kane, M. J. (1989) The post-Title IX female athlete in the media: things are changing, but how much? *Journal of Physical Education, Recreation, and Dance*, 60, 58–62.

Kane, M. J. (1995) Resistance/transformation of the oppositional binary: exposing sport as a continuum. *Journal of Sport and Social Issues*, 19, 191–218.

Kane, M.J. and Parks, J. B. (1992) The social construction of gender difference and hierarchy in sport journalism—a few twists on very old themes. *Women in Sport and Physical Activity Journal*, 1, 49–83.

Kane, M.J. and Greendorfer, S.L. (1994) The media's role in accommodating and resisting stereotyped images of women in sport. In P.J. Creedon (ed.), *Women, Media and Sport: Challenging Gender Values*. Thousand Oaks, CA: Sage.

Kassing, J.W., Billings, A.C., Brown, R.S., Halone, K.K., Harrison, K., Krizek, B., Meân, L. and Turman, P.D. (2004) Communication in the community of sport: the process of enacting, (re)producing, consuming, and organizing sport. *Communication Yearbook*, 28, 373–410.

King, C.R. (2007) Staging the Winter Olympics, or why sport matters to White power. *Journal of Sport and Social Issues*, 31, 89–94.

King, C.R., Leonard, D.J. and Kusz, K.K. (2007) White power and sport: an introduction. *Journal of Sport and Social Issues*, 31, 3–10.

Kinsley, M. (1996) Rock solid: no. 1 ranked NBC Sports president Dick Ebersol: the *Sporting News* most powerful. Retrieved from http://findarticles.com/p/articles/mi_m1208/is_n53_v220/ai_18992577?lstpn=article_results&lstpc=search&lstpr=external&lstprs=other&lstwid=1&lstwn=search_results&lstwp=body_middle

Kuper, S. (1994) *Football Against the Enemy*. London: Phoenix.

Lang, K. and Lang, G.E. (1983) *The Battle for Public Opinion: The President, the Press, and the Polls during Watergate*. New York: Columbia University Press.

Langer, J. (1981) Television's personality system. *Media, Culture, and Society*, 3(4), London: Academic Press.

Larson, J.F. and Rivenburgh, N.K. (1991) A comparative analysis of Australian, US, and British telecasts of the Seoul Olympic ceremony. *Journal of Broadcasting and Electronic Media*, 35(1), 75–94.

Larson, J.F. and Park, H.S. (1993) *Global Television and the Politics of the Seoul Olympics*. Boulder, CO: Westview.

Lee, J. (1992) Media portrayals of male and female Olympic athletes: analysis of newspaper accounts of the 1984 and 1988 Summer Games. *International Review for the Sociology of Sport*, 27, 197–219.

Lenskyj, H.J. (1994) Sexuality and femininity in sport contexts: issues and alternatives. *Journal of Sport and Social Issues*, 18, 356–376.

Lenskyj, H.J. (2000) *Inside the Olympic industry: Power, Politics, and Activism*. Albany, NY: SUNY.

Lenskyj, H.J. (2002) *The Best Olympics Ever?: Social Impacts of Sydney 2000*. Albany, NY: SUNY.

Long, J.A., and McNamee, M.J. (2004) On the moral economy of racism and racist rationalizations in sport. *International Review for the Sociology of Sport*, 39(4), 405–420.

Lorber, J. (1993) Believing is seeing: biology as ideology. *Gender and Society*, 17(1), 569–581.

Lumpkin, A. and Williams, L. (1991) An analysis of *Sport Illustrated* feature articles, 1954–1987. *Sociology of Sport Journal*, 8, 16–32.

Lupica, M. (2006, Feb. 12) Parting shots. ESPN's *SportsReporters*.

McCarthy, D. and Jones, R.L. (1997) Speed, aggression, strength, and tactical naiveté. *Journal of Sport and Social Issues*, 21(4), 348–362.

McCarthy, M. (2006, Feb. 15) NBC chooses to keep the faith out of Olympics—for now. *USA Today*, p. 3D.

McCombs, M.E. (1992) Explorers and surveyors: expanding strategies for agenda setting research. *Journalism Quarterly*, 69, 813–824.

McCombs, M.E., and Shaw, D. L. (1972) The agenda-setting function of mass media. *Public Opinion Quarterly*, 36(2), 176–187.

McCombs, M.E. and Ghanem, S. (2001) Convergence of agenda–setting and framing. In S.D. Reese, O.H. Gandy, and A.E. Grant (eds), *Framing Public Life* (pp. 67–82) Mahwah, NJ: LEA.

McDonald, M.G. (2005) Mapping whiteness in sport: an introduction. *Sociology of Sport Journal*, 22, 245–255.

McDonald, M.G. (2006) Thinking through power in sport and sport media scholarship. In A. Raney and J. Bryant (eds), *Handbook of Sport and Media* (pp. 501–522). Mahwah, NJ: Erlbaum.

McKay, J. (1997) *Managing Gender: Affirmative Action and Organizational Power in Australian, Canadian, and New Zealand Sport*. Albany, NY: SUNY.

MacNeill, M. (1996) Networks: producing Olympic ice hockey for a national television audience. *Sociology of Sport Journal*, 13, 103–124.

McQuail, D. and Windahl, S. (1993) *Communication Models for the Study of Mass Communication*. London: Longman.

Madan, M. (2000) It's not just cricket: World Series Cricket: race, nation, and diasporic Indian identity. *Journal of Sport and Social Issues*, 24(1), 24–35.

Maltz, D.N. and Borker, R. (1982) A cultural approach to male–female miscommunication. In J.J. Gumpertz (ed.), *Language and Social Identity* (pp. 196–216). Cambridge: Cambridge University Press.

Martin, R. and Miller, T. (1999) *SportCult*. Minneapolis, MN: University of Minnesota Press.

Martzke, R. (2004, Aug. 20) Ratings bonanza will pay off for NBC. *USA Today*, p. 7F.

Mason, D.S. (2002) Get the puck outta here! Media transnationalism and Canadian identity. *Journal of Sport and Social Issues*, 26(2), 140–167.

Matteo, S. (1986) The effect of sex and gender–schematic processing on sport participation. *Sex Roles*, 15(7–8), 417–432.

Mehus, I. (2005) Distinction through sport consumption: spectators of soccer, basketball, and ski-jumping. *International Review for the Sociology of Sport*, 40(3), 321–333.

Messner, M. (1988) Sports and male domination: the female athlete as contested ideological terrain. *Sociology of Sport Journal*, 5(3), 197–211.

Messner, M. (1993) *Power at Play*. Boston: Beacon.

Messner, M. (2002) *Taking the Field: Women, Men and Sports*. Minneapolis, MN: University of Minnesota Press.

Messner, M.A., Duncan, M.C. and Jensen, K. (1993) Separating the men from the girls: the gendered language of televised sports. In D.S. Eitzen (ed.), *Sport in Contemporary Society* (pp. 219–233) New York: St. Martin's Press.

Messner, M.A., Duncan, M.C. and Wachs, F.L. (1996) The gender of audience building: televised coverage of women's and men's NCAA basketball. *Sociological Inquiry*, 66(4), 422–440.

Michaels, V. (2006, Feb. 27) USA can no longer rest easy in Olympics. *USA Today*, p. 3D.

Miller, T., Lawrence, G., McKay, J. and Rowe, D. (2001) *Globalization and Sport: Playing the World*. London: Sage.

Moragas Spa, M., Rivenburgh, N.K. and Larson, J.F. (1995) *Television in the Olympics*. London: J. Libbey.

Moreland, J. (2006) Olympics and television. The Museum of Broadcast Communications (online). Retrieved from http://www.museum.tv/archives/etv/O/htmlO/olympicsand/olympicsand.htm.

Morris, B. and Nydahl, J. (1985) Sports spectacle as drama: image, language, and technology. *Journal of Popular Culture*, 18(4), 101–110.

Morris, M. (2006) *Identity Anecdotes: Translation and Media Culture*. London: Sage.

Morse, M. (1990) An ontology of everyday distraction: the freeway, the mall, and television. In P. Mellacamp (ed.), *The Logics of Television*. Bloomington, IN: Indiana University Press.

Murrell, A.J. and Curtis, E.M. (1994) Causal attributions of performance for black and white quarterbacks in the NFL: a look at the sports pages. *Journal of Sport and Social Issues*, 18(3), 224–233.

Muschert, G.W. and Carr, D. (2007) Media salience and frame changing across events: coverage of nine school shootings, 1997–2001. *Journalism and Mass Communication Quarterly*, 83(4), 747–766.

Mushnick, P. (2006, Oct. 16) Lyon-ized: Steve joins long list of personalities fired for what they were hired to do. *New York Post*, p. 81.

Nakayama, T.K. and Martin, J.N. (eds) (1999) *Whiteness: The Communication of Social Identity*. Thousand Oaks, CA: Sage.

NBC Sports (2007) Retrieved from http://www.nbcsports.com/olympics/index.html (accessed on June 17).

Nelson, M.B. (1994) *The Stronger Women Get, The More Men Love Football: Sexism and the American Culture of Sports*. New York: Harcourt Brace.

Newton, G.D., Williams, G.C., Billings, A.C. and Eastman, S.T. (in press) Primetime promotion pays off: the Athens exemplar. *Journal of Promotion Management*.

Neuman, W.R., Just, M.R. and Crigler, A.N. (1992) *Communication Knowledge: News and the Construction of Political Meaning*. Chicago, IL: Chicago University Press.

Nordlinger, J. (2001, Apr. 30) Tiger time: the wonder of an American hero. *National Review*, p. 8.

O'Donnell, H. (1994) Mapping the mythical: a geopolitics of national sporting stereotypes. *Discourse and Society*, 4(3), 345–380.

O'Reilly, J. and Cahn, S.K. (2007) *Women and Sports in the United States*. Boston: Northeastern University Press.

O'Riordan, K. (2007) Technologized bodies: virtual women and transformations of the body as natural. In J.A. Hargreaves and P. Vertinsky (eds), *Physical Culture, Power, and the Body* (pp. 232–252). London: Routledge.

Orwell, G. (1992 [1945]) The sporting spirit. In I. Hamilton (ed.), *The Faber Book of Soccer*. London: Faber & Faber.

O'Sullivan, P. (1999) Bridging the mass-interpersonal divide: synthesis scholarship in HCR. *Human Communication Research*, 25(4), 569–588.

Pearce, J.Q. (2007, June 14) Retrieved from http://www.moconews.net/entry/419-mobile-tv-roundup-nbc-sports-tvi-turner/

Pelak, C. F. (2002) Women's collective identity formation in sports: a case study of women's ice hockey. *Gender and Society*, 16, 93–114.

Pinel, E.C. (1999) Stigma consciousness: the psychological legacy of social stereotypes. *Journal of Personality and Social Psychology*, 76, 114–128.

Potter, W. (1986) Perceived reality and the cultivation hypothesis. *Journal of Broadcasting and Electronic Media*, 30, 159–174.

Pound, D. (2004) *Inside the Olympics*. Canada: Wiley and Sons.

Power, J.G., Murphy, S.T. and Coover, G. (1996) Priming prejudice: how stereotypes and counter-stereotypes influence attribution of responsibility and credibility among ingroups and outgroups. *Human Communication Research*, 23, 36–58.

Puijk, R. (1997) *Global Spotlights on Lillehammer: How the World Viewed Norway During the 1994 Winter Olympics*. Luton: University of Luton.

Racism needs a penalty flag in Germany (2006, June 8) *The Pittsburgh Post-Gazette*, p. B6.

Rada, J. (1996) Color blind-sided: racial bias in network television's coverage of professional football games. *The Howard Journal of Communications*, 7(3), 231–240.

Rada, J. and Wulfemeyer, K.T. (2005) Color coded: racial descriptors in television coverage of intercollegiate sports. *Journal of Broadcasting and Electronic Media*, 49(1), 65–85.

Radar, B.G. (1984) *In its Own Image: How Television has Transformed Sports*. New York: Free Press.

Rainville, R.E. and McCormick, E. (1977) Extent of covert racial prejudice in pro football announcers' speech. *Journalism Quarterly*, 54(1), 20–26.

Rawlins, W.K. (1993) Communication in cross-sex friendships. In L.P. Arliss and D.J. Borisoff (eds), *Women and Men Communicating: Challenges and Changes* (pp. 51–70). Fort Worth, TX: Harcourt Brace-Jovanovich.

Real, M.R. (1996) The post-modern Olympics: technology and the commodification of the Olympic movement. *Quest*, 48(1), 9–24.

Real, M.R. (1975) Super Bowl: mythic spectacle. *Journal of Communication*, 25(1), 31–43.

Real, M.R. and Mechikoff, R. (1992) Deep fan: mythic identification, technology, and advertising in spectator sports. *Sociology of Sport Journal*, 9, 323–339.

Rhoden, W.C. (2006) *Forty Million Dollar Slaves*. New York: Crown.

Roche, M. (2004) Mega-events and media culture: sport and the Olympics. In D. Rowe (ed.), *Critical Readings: Sport Culture and the Media* (pp. 165–181). Maidenhead, Berkshire: Open University Press.

Rose, A. and Friedman, J. (1997) Television sports as mas(s)culine cult of distraction. In A. Baker and T. Boyd (eds), *Out of Bounds: Sports, Media, and the Politics of Identity*. Bloomington, IN: Indiana University Press.

Rowe, D. (2003) *Sport, Culture, and the Media* (2nd edn). Buckingham: Open University Press.

Ryan, J. (2006, Mar. 1) How bad were the Olympics? *E! Online*. Retrieved from Yahoo! News, http://www.yahoo.com/s/eo.

Sabo, D., Jansen, S.C., Tate, D., Duncan, M.C. and Leggett, S. (1996) Televising international sport: race, ethnicity, and nationalistic bias. *Journal of Sport and Social Issues*, 20(1), 7–21.

Sagas, M. and Cunningham, G.B. (2004) Does having "the right stuff" matter? Gender differences in the determinants of career success among intercollegiate athletic administrators. *Sex Roles*, 50(5–6), 411–421.

Sandomir, R. (1992, Feb. 26) Winter Games broadcast wasn't a loser, CBS says. *New York Times*, p. B13.

Schaffer, K. and Smith, S. (eds) (2000) *The Olympics at the Millennium: Power Politics and the Games*. Piscataway, NJ: Rutgers University Press.

Schultz, B. (2005) *Sports Media: Reporting, Producing, and Planning*. Burlington, MA: Focal Press.

Senn, A.E. (1999) *Power, Politics, and the Olympic Games*. Champaign, IL: Human Kinetics.

Shanahan, J., Scheufele, D., Yang, F. and Hizi, S. (2004) Cultivation and spiral of silence effects: the case of smoking. *Mass Communication and Society*, 7(4), 413–428.

Sherry, J.L. (2004) Media effects theory and the nature/nurture debate: a historical overview and directions for future research. *Media Psychology*, 6(1), 83–109.

Shih, M., Pittinsky, T.L. and Ambady, N. (1999) Stereotype susceptibility: identity salience and shifts in quantitative performance. *Psychological Science*, 10(1), 80–83.

Simri, U. (1977) *A Historical Analysis of the Role of Women in the modern Olympic Games*. Netanya, Isreal: Wingate Institute for Physical Education and Sport.

Smith, K.K. (1983) Social comparison processes and dynamic conservatism in intergroup relations. In L.L. Cummings and B.M. Shaw (eds), *Research in Organizational Behavior* (pp. 199–233). Greenwitch, CT: JAI.

Sports Illustrated (2000) Retrieved from http:// Sportsillustrated.cnn.com/your_turn/news/2000/10/01/reactions_olympicsontv/.

Staples, R. and Jones, T. (1985) Culture, ideology and Black television images. *The Black Scholar*, 16(3), 10–20.

Starr, M. (2006, Aug. 14) My favorite years. *Newsweek*, pp. 44–56.

Staurowsky, E.J. (1995) Examining the roots of a gendered division of labor in intercollegiate athletics: insights into the gender equity debate. *Journal of Sport and Social Issues*, 19(1), 28–44.

Staurowsky, E.J. (2007) "You know, we are all Indian": exploring White power and privilege in reactions to the NCAA Native American mascot policy. *Journal of Sport and Social Issues*, 31(1), 61–76.

Stempel, C. (2006) Televised sports, masculinist moral capital, and support for the US invasion in Iraq. *Journal of Sport and Social Issues*, 30(1), 79–106.

Stephenson, D. (2002) Women, sport, and globalization. *Journal of Sport and Social Issues*, 26(2), 209–225.

Stewart, L. (2004, Aug. 31) Olympic notes: Athens is most-watched non-US Summer Games. *Los Angeles Times*, p. D3.

Stewart, L. (2006, Feb. 7) Millions more tuned in. *Los Angeles Times*, p. 8D.

Sugden, J. (1995) Sport and nationalism in the modern world. *Working Papers in Sport and Society*, 3, University of Warwick.

Sullivan, D.L. (2002) Coming to terms with cultural studies. *Journal of Sport and Social Issues*, 26(1), 110–117.

Surowiecki, J. (2005) *The Wisdom of Crowds*. New York: Anchor.

Sutherland, M. and Galloway, J. (1981) Role of advertising: persuasion or agenda setting? *Journal of Advertising Research*, 21(5), 25–29.

Suzuki, S. (1998) In-group and out-group communication patterns in international organizations: implications for social identity theory. *Communication Research*, 25(2), 154–183.

Sweeney, B. and Associates (1992) *The Olympic Reality: A Survey into Australians' Views on the Barcelona Olympics*. Oxford: Oxford University Press.

Tajfel, H. (1972) Experiments in a vacuum. In J. Israel and H. Tajfel (eds), *The Context of Social Psychology: A Critical Assessment*. London: Academic Press.

Tajfel, H. and Turner, J.C. (1986) The social identity theory of inter-group behavior. In S. Worchel and L.W. Austin (eds), *Psychology of Intergroup Relations*. Chicago: Nelson-Hall.

Tankard, J.W. (2001) The empirical approach to the study of media framing. In S.D. Reese, O.H. Gandy, and A.E. Grant (eds), *Framing Public Life* (pp. 95–106). Mahwah, NJ: LEA.

Theberge, N. (1991) A content analysis of print media coverage of gender, women, and physical activity. *Journal of Applied Sport Psychology*, 3, 36–48.

Theberge, N. and Cronk, A. (1986) Work routines in newspaper sports departments and the coverage of women's sports. *Sociology of Sport Journal*, 3(3), 195–203.

Thompson, A. (2007, June 15) Event shift gives US primetime. *Wall Street Journal*, p. B1.

Toohey, K. (1997) Australian television, gender and the Olympic Games. *International Review for the Sociology of Sport*, 31(1), 19–29.

Toohey, K. and Veal, A.J. (2000) *The Olympic Games: A Social Science Perspective*. Oxon: Cabi.

Trujillo, N. (1991) Hegemonic masculinity on the mound: media representations of Nolan Ryan and American sports culture. *Critical Studies in Mass Communication*, 9, 290–308.

Tuggle, C.A. and Owen, A. (1999) A descriptive analysis of NBC's coverage of the centennial Olympics. *Journal of Sport and Social Issues*, 23 (2), 171–183.

Tuggle, C.A., Huffman, S. and Rosengard, D.S. (2002) A descriptive analysis of NBC's coverage of the 2000 Summer Olympics. *Mass Communication and Society*, 5, 361–375.

Tuggle, C.A., Huffman, S. and Rosengard, D.S. (2007) A descriptive analysis of NBC's coverage of the 2004 Summer Olympics. *Journal of Sports Media*, 2(1), 53–76.

Turley, J. (2006, Sept. 14) Why race-based "Survivor" makes us squirm. *USA Today*, p. 13A.

Turner, J.C., Hogg, M.A., Oakes, P.J., Reicher, S.D. and Wetherell, M.S. (1987) *Rediscovering the Social Group: A Self-categorization Theory*. Oxford: Blackwell.

Turow, J. (1990) Media industries, media consequences: rethinking mass communication. In J.A. Anderson (ed.), *Communication Yearbook*, 13 (pp. 478 501). Thousand Oaks, CA: Sage.

United Press International (UPI) Report (2006, Feb. 28) Fewer viewers tune in to Olympics on NBC.

Urquhart, J. and Crossman, J. (1999) The *Globe and Mail* coverage of the Winter Olympic Games: a cold place for women athletes. *Journal of Sport and Social Issues*, 23(2), 193–202.

USA Today (2007) Weekly Nielsen ratings (online). Retrieved from http://www.usatoday.com/life/television/nielsen.htm.

Van de Berg, L. and Trujillo, N. (1989) The rhetoric of winning and losing: the American dream and America's team. In L. Wenner (ed.), *Media, Sports, and Society* (pp. 204–224). Newbury Park, CA: Sage.

van Sterkenburg, J. and Knoppers, A. (2004) Dominant discourses about race/ethnicity and gender in sport practice and performance. *International Review for the Sociology of Sport*, 39, 301–321.

Vincent, J. (2004) Game, sex, match: the construction of gender in British newspaper coverage of the 2000 Wimbledon Championships. *Sociology of Sport Journal*, 21(4), 435–456.

Visker, R. (1995) Dropping the "subject" of authenticity. Being in Time on disappearing existentials and true friendship with being. *Research in Phenomenology*, 24, 133.

Wang, X. (2005, Dec. 25) Gold is not sole goal for Chinese sports. *Xinhua General News Service*.

Wanta, W. and Ghanem, S.I. (2006) Effects of agenda setting. In R. Preiss, B. Gayle, N. Burrell, M. Allen, and J. Bryant (eds), *Mass Media Theories and Processes: Advances Through Meta-analysis*. Mahwah, NJ: LEA.

Ward, R.E. Jr. (2004) Are the doors being opened for the "ladies" of college sports? A covariance analysis. *Sex Roles*, 51(11–12), 697–708.

Wearden, S. and Creedon, P. (2003) "We got next": images of women in television commercials during the inaugural WNBA season. In A. Bernstein and N. Blain (eds), *Sport, Media, Culture: Global and Local Dimensions*. Portland, OR: Frank Cass.

Weber, S. (1996) Television: set and screen. In A. Chodolenko (ed.), *Mass Mediauras: Form, Technics, Media*. Sydney, NSW: Power Publications.

Weiller, K.H. and Higgs, C.T. (1999) Television coverage of professional golf: a focus on gender. *Women in Sport and Physical Activity Journal*, 8(1), 83–100.

Weiner, E. (2006, Mar. 1) NBC's multimedia success bodes well for sports on TV. *The New York Sun*, p. 21.

Wenner, L.A. (1989) Media, sports, and society: the research agenda. In L.A. Wenner (ed.), *Media, Sports, and Society* (pp. 13–48). Newbury Park, CA: Sage.

Wenner, L. (2006) Sports and media through the super glass mirror: placing blame, breast-beating, and a gaze to the future. In A. Raney and J. Bryant (eds), *Handbook of Sport and Media* (pp. 45–62). Mahwah, NJ: LEA.

Wenner, L. and Gantz, W. (1989) *Media, Sport and Society*. New York: Anchor.

Whannel, G. (1984) The television spectacular. In A.Tomlinson and G. Whannel (eds), *Five Ring Circus: Money, Power, and Politics at the Olympic Games* (pp. 30–43). London: Pluto Press.

Whannel, G. (1992) *Fields in Vision: Television Sport and Cultural Transformation*. London: Routledge.

Wigboldus, D.H., Semin, G. and Spears, R. (2000) How do we communicate stereotypes? Linguistic bases and inferential consequences. *Journal of Personality and Social Psychology*, 78(1), 5–18.

Williams, J. (1994) Sport, postmodernism and global TV. In S. Earnsham (ed.), *Postmodern Surroundings*. Amsterdam: Rodopi.

Williams, C., Lawrence, G. and Rowe, D. (1985) Women and sport: a lost ideal. *Women's Studies International Forum*, 8(6), 639–645.

Wolfe, R.A., Weick, K.E., Usher, J.M., Terborg, J.R., Poppo, L., Murrell, A.J., Dukerich, J.M., Core, D.C., Dickson, K.E. and Jourdan, J.S. (2005) Sport and organizational studies: exploring synergy. *Journal of Management Inquiry*, 14, 182–210.

Wonsek, P.L. (1992) College basketball on television: a study of racism in the media. *Media, Culture & Society*, 14(3), 449–461.

Yang, J. and Stone, G. (2003) The powerful role of interpersonal communication in agenda setting. *Mass Communication and Society*, 6(1), 57–74.

Index